The Art of Bristle
a memoir

Judy Kowalsky

Legacy Book Press LLC
Camanche, Iowa

My research included books and songs for inspiration and information. These are the most important of those resources.

Aldrich, Marta W. The Seattle Times, $83 Million Later Unfinished Dam Being Dismantled. October 10, 1999
Ackerman, Robert J. Ph. D. *Perfect Daughters, Adult Daughters of Alcoholics* (Health Communications, ©1989 - 2002) p. 46.
Baker, Lynn S. *You and Leukemia: A Day at a time.* (Saunders; 2nd edition (September 10, 2001)
Brault, Robert. *Round Up the Usual Subjects: Thoughts on just about everything* (CreateSpace, 2014) p.42.
Carpenter, Richard. Bettis, John. "Top of the World" Performed by Carpenters (1972)
Diamond, Neil. "Sweet Caroline" (1969)
Godinez, Kristine. *What's Wrong With Your Dad* (CreateSpace Independent Publishing Platform, 2017)
Kloss, Jethro. *Back to Eden* (Lotus Press, 2004)
Lewis, C. S. *The Lion, the Witch, and the Wardrobe* (Harper Collins, 2009)
Peters, Gretchen. "Independence Day." Performed by Martina McBride (1994)
South, Joe. "Rose Garden" Performed by Tammy Wynette (1967)

The stories in this book reflect the author's recollection of events. Some names, locations, and identifying characteristics have been changed to protect the privacy of those depicted. Dialogue has been recreated from memory.

ISBN: 979-8-9874823-6-0
Library of Congress Case No: 1-13158989105

In childhood, we press our nose to the pane, looking out.
In memories of childhood, we press our nose to the pane, looking in.

ROBERT BRAULT

Acknowledgements

I especially dedicate this book to those who have had great loss, not just the loss of self but of a child. To lose my son Nicholas was the most devastating grief I have ever experienced. I have no words to describe this pain.

Before my grandma Gina died, she told me she had been praying for me. Her prayer is what helped me through some of the most challenging times in my adult life.

If I could talk to my grandmother, I'd say, "Grandma Gina, through all the crazy, I want you to know I have a good life. I'm safe. Your precious prayer was answered."

Thank you to my very dear and close friend Barb Smith for all the hours you spent talking and going over my manuscript with me. Always encouraging. I won't ever forget what you said to me, "Be the voice for those who can't speak or those who are not ready to."

Yvonne Sandomir, thank you for cheering me on. You encouraged me to dig deeper and that's what I did. *The Invisible Girl,* your story is one of strength. No child should ever have to endure what you have. Your book will go on to help many.

Kathy Rhodes, you were right; there are many drafts for writing and editing a book. Thank you for your help and for your time.

Thank you, Carole Webb Slater, for all the great resources, and help you offered in your informative memoir writing classes.

A special thank you to those who called or messaged sharing with me your own personal stories. We are all much stronger than we realize, and we're not alone.

Table of Contents

Introduction

I am an adult daughter of an alcoholic. I have learned that this is a thing. In fact, there is an entire organization dedicated to people like me referred to as Adult Children of Alcoholics. ACoA or ACA.

I have been angry for a long time, but the thought of writing a book about my life never occurred until I began writing down my memories.

I had legitimate reasons for my anger, the greatest being the death of my son Nicholas. I have journaled through the years, writing about my feelings, life events, and placing my thoughts on paper rather than outwardly voicing my pain and fear to the outside world. Keeping my thoughts to myself and non-confrontation were easier for me. Although, I have learned I could only keep the hurt locked away inside of me for so long. Looking back, I wish I would have addressed my feelings at every crossroad I'd ever encountered; the frustration, hurt, sadness, all my crazy, and whatever emotion I had at the time and as it occurred.

We all have ways of dealing with our pain. Twice I'd thought of suicide. I wanted to destroy myself, just like my dad did to himself.

Once when my husband Ray and I were building our home. Everything was overwhelming to me. We'd been uprooted from our cute modest home in Michigan to a state I'd never imagined living in. At the time, the chaos of building a home together made me feel crazy. Ray and I argued a lot. I felt the builder had not lived up to his contract and he sued us, we counter-sued, and we lost.

Then almost two years before moving into our new home, a drunk driver killed my mother. My father was also deceased. Everything felt out of control. I felt defeated, stuck, overwhelmed, tired, and very sad. Worse, I hated everything about myself. At the time, I didn't quite understand why because it wasn't only about what was happening to me in the present, but it had been what had happened to me in the past as well.

I walked out of my house one afternoon, leaving my twin ten-year-old sons with Ray. I remember standing nearby watching my boys playing happily with their Legos. They were oblivious to how I was feeling and the stupid thing I was on my way to do. I'm glad they didn't know what their mama was about to do that day.

I spoke a silent goodbye to each of my sons before I walked out of the house and got into my blue 1994 Camaro Z28. I tore out of the driveway, looking up to the sky. I was angry.

"I'll see you in a few minutes!" I cried out.

I drove on Highway 50, the main back road that goes north and south. I was headed for the I-65 exit. I remember that the road was clear of traffic that afternoon. The speed limit is 50 M.P.H. but I stepped down on the accelerator. I watched the speedometer needle race higher, 60, 85, and then ninety miles an hour.

Out of the corner of my eye, a wooden telephone pole came into my view on the right side of the road. But before I turned the wheel toward the pole, I saw stars. The flashing lights were crashing into each other. I could feel my head and heart pounding hard before a peaceful calm came over me, and inside my head, I heard myself say, "Slow down, Judy. Slow down." It seemed strange to me at the time, but I immediately calmed down. I pulled my car over to the side of the road and I cried hard. My mood had changed fast. It was as if someone had flipped a light switch on and off. I hung my head down over the steering wheel, sobbing. My entire body was shaking.

After I had settled down and stopped crying, I drove home, only this time, much slower and way under the speed limit.

What I saw when I walked through the door of my home were my precious boys standing at the door with wide grins across their faces. They had been waiting for me to return. They were happy to see me. I melted. The thought of what I'd almost done has haunted me for years.

The second time, years later, was when my son Nicholas relapsed from Leukemia. Ray had taken him to the hospital for a procedure. Nick was on his way into the operating room to have a Medi port implanted in his chest for the second time when he called me.

Now he would be getting even more chemo treatments since his relapse. My son was in his twenties, and he was crying out to me. "I don't want to do this, Mom. I'm tired," he said while hospital staff continued to wheel him into surgery. I fell to my knees hanging on to the phone, trying hard to sound calm. I was trying to be brave for him. But I wasn't even close to brave. I was upstairs in my bedroom, wrenched over dark blue carpeting, breathing fast. A heavy feeling of morbid gloom overwhelmed me. I felt horrible unworthiness; I was evil and couldn't stop the bad from happening to my son. I couldn't take the pain from him. I felt like I had failed him and caused him to get sick.

I was sobbing while I crawled into my bed. "Help my son, God! Please, help my son!"

I hated me. My entire life, I felt like I had caused only pain to others. I wanted to end my life.

Seconds later my phone rang again, this time it was my sister Rita. I cried out to her.

"Judy, do you have something to help you sleep? You need to sleep."

"No." I said.

"Do you have Benadryl?" Rita's voice was calm.

"Yes. I have Benadryl" I said.

"Take two so you can rest. Please don't do anything."

I can't believe I'd ever contemplated suicide, especially after my dad's devastating death and how it had affected me, my siblings, and my mother so horribly.

After a parent dies by suicide, statistics are high for their children to do the same thing. Had I gone through with killing myself, I would have hurt my children and my husband terribly, but at the time, I wasn't thinking about anyone other than myself. I hated me.

Memories

I remember getting on my knees and asking God so many times, pleading with him for answers, especially since my son Nicholas died ten years ago, "Why am I so angry?" I mean, anger was a normal emotion for me, or any parent for that matter, after their child dies. It's part of the mourning process. I know that, but I have been angry at times to the point of depression. I don't want to be this angry.

So, while I waited for answers, I started to write, and while I wrote, I could see my prayers being answered. I felt like God was showing me why I had been so angry through memories starting to emerge—memories that I had not forgotten but had hidden away.

My memories can be triggered by a song, a scent, or a chance thought; the recollections can happen anywhere at any time.

The fragments of my life that I am about to share with you are not in chronological order. They are random memories that come to mind as I write. I share humorous yet vulnerable, embarrassing, raw, and poignant moments portraying how traits of an ACoA and adult survivor of child abuse can be acquired due to environment. I believe it's time for all of us to tell our stories. This is mine.

The loss of self and the loss of a child are traumatic journeys no one ever wants to experience. I am one of many who knows all too well the suffering these horrific events can bring to our lives. Because not only physical and mental chaos can result from the trauma, but autoimmune disorders can also develop in our bodies. I've heard *the body doesn't forget.*

Through the years, I have tried to be positive. I had hope. There is always hope, but there were times I found myself diving, surging crazy into deep valleys of grief, anger, and depression while at the same time portraying a fake smile across my face for the world to see.

To be honest, I didn't start to acknowledge the anger I had until a few years ago. Throughout my life I pushed my emotions aside. I didn't have time for them, because it hurt too much to go back and revisit those painful places.

Through the years, I had been busy stuffing my past away, desperately hoping that at some point, the horrible memories I had would just leave. But they never went away; instead, they remained on a random shelf, gathering dust somewhere in my brain where I had placed them long ago. I felt a lot of resentment, and my distressing, messed-up experiences only seemed to multiply for me rather than go away.

I remember standing hunched over peering into the water. My hands gripped tight, holding onto the railing, a segment of an old rickety, wooden pier. I was somewhere in Michigan overlooking Lake Huron that day. I was twelve, and my parents had just separated. . . Again.

The brisk, northern wind blew harsh against my skin while white caps formed and built as far out as my eyes could see. On that overcast day, the horizontal waves stood one behind the other but in staggered rows.

I swear I watched every wave set take its turn crashing onto the shoreline that afternoon. My red tear-filled eyes zeroed in on a swell that scattered, dissolved, then started its build all over again. The surges seemed strong, determined like soldiers going off to battle, colliding, slowing down, diminishing then repeating. These breaking waves were something I could identify with because, for me, the surges represented times in my life where I had felt so defeated.

Unloved

I grew up sensing other people's emotions. With no words spoken, I could feel whether they wanted me around or not. I'd had lots of practice sensing the moods and emotions of my parents. I was good at observing and reading my surroundings. The atmosphere in our home changed like the weather. I had to be able to read the room well if I wanted to stay safe. I felt like I was on constant high alert.

I felt unloved, but I didn't have words to describe my feelings. I didn't like myself for being different. I lacked confidence, and I idolized people that seemed so much better. I blamed myself for everything. From the age of eleven, when I was in the fifth grade on into adulthood, I'd considered everyone to be better than me. Now the thought of this makes me cringe. I didn't look at my circle of peers or myself as equals, each of us having our own good qualities yet different from one another. I couldn't see that we were all beautifully unique or that our individuality is what compliments all of us as a whole. I only saw that everyone else was good, I was bad.

I was shy, naïve, and a people pleaser. In my mind, I was beneath everyone. I was "bad and no good," a phrase I often used to describe myself while growing up. My parent's words and actions told me who and what I was. When you're told things over and over again, you come to believe them. It is a form of mind control. (Brainwashing.)

I felt people would like me more if I did what I thought they wanted me to do or if I acted how I thought they wanted me to behave. But it was all a lie because I was not being true to myself. It seems I was always trying to be like the person I was with at the time. If they liked a particular book, I liked that book. If they didn't like a style of clothing, I said I didn't like that style either, even if I did like it, because I wanted them to accept me. I wanted to feel like I was a part of something. I just wanted in. I wanted to be loved.

I was also perceptive of other people's feelings because I was sensitive to my own. I didn't want anyone to hurt.

Therapy

We all experience some degree of pain and suffering in this life. Believe me; I understand this as much as anyone. Some people have more tragedy to conquer in their lives than others. Some have less, but cruelty is wrong on every level so how can it be compared? The horrific stories of abuse that have happened to children and is still happening is at times unimaginable for me to comprehend.

My parents were my parents. They were supposed to be my nurturers; they were my first loves. They were responsible for taking care of me and attending to my needs. While growing up in our home, to me, they were the most intelligent people in the entire world. I know different now. I had an unhealthy attachment to my parents known as Trauma Bonding. My bond with them started with my basic human needs. Needs we all have, especially as children. Only my attachment to my parents became a means of survival for me long after it needed to be. I made excuses for them, I lied about my abuse, I had self-esteem issues, and I blamed myself for everything.

After childhood I continued to meet personalities that in many ways reminded me of my parents, and my unrelenting behavior hadn't changed.

Through the years I'd become increasingly angrier at myself for building people up and in a sense putting others on a pedestal. I'd made them idols. I just wanted to please so that I would be accepted; however, some acted mean and arrogant toward me as if they knew how I felt about myself and, in some strange way, got off on making me feel worse. This was difficult for me to comprehend. Sadly, my mother was good at building me up then tearing me down with her words and actions as well.

My husband and I had just moved into our first home. A small three-bedroom brick ranch in a middle-class neighborhood. I was proud of my new home and the money we'd saved to buy it. We'd both worked really hard. My mother didn't say anything, but she acted out of sorts.

"Jennifer and her husband just bought a new house in Bloomfield Hills with four fireplaces," she said. Bloomfield Hills, Michigan is considered one of the wealthiest cities in the United States.

"And Lisa just bought a baby grand piano." Jennifer and Lisa were my age, and at the time, it had been years since I'd seen them. We were all busy with our own lives, working on our careers, buying houses, getting married, and having babies.

Instead of being happy for me my mother turned her focus in on my friends and their good fortune. While I was happy for my friends, my mom's snub hurt my feelings. As usual, I didn't know how to stop being who I was, so I didn't say anything. Not standing up for myself was what I did.

Healing the inner child was my therapy session today. I asked, "Why am I angrier at myself than I am with my abusers?"

My counselor suggested I go back to the first time I remember being mistreated. During my childhood years, I didn't know I was being physically and emotionally harmed. The things that happened were just the way life was for me. This was the world I was born into and knew.

Part One:
Remembering

After church, and at a time when seat belt and car seat laws did not exist, I sat in between my parents in the front seat of our car while my two younger brothers sat in the back. I might have been four. I sang "Jesus Loves Me" and "This Little Light of Mine" with everything my lungs could give. These were my favorite songs, and I sang them really loud in and outside of church, even though I didn't know all of the words so well.

This was also in a time before cars had air conditioning, so the windows were rolled down while my dad drove the two-lane back country roads.

While I was singing happily, a bee flew through the window, down inside my blouse, and stung me. We were on our way to visit Mr. Trump, a family friend who lived in the woods.

After the bee stung me, my ear-splitting singing was replaced with piercing wails of woe and pain. I have always wondered if this incident wasn't a sign of things to come for me. I mean, I was happy; I was singing and having an enjoyable time. I loved Jesus, and then a bee flew in the window and stung me.

When we got to Mr. Trump's place, there were lots of people outside, sitting on old rustic benches and chairs that surrounded a long, homemade wooden table.

When I said I was thirsty, I watched Mr. Trump, who had dark hair and wore a tatty brown jacket, lower a wooden bucket attached to a thick rope into a well. The well was surrounded by a stone wall.

After he pulled the bucket back up with the rope, he used an oversized scoop with a long handle to retrieve the water, and that is what I drank from.

Everyone was eating corn on the cob with butter. I remember the corn tasted sweet, so I ate nothing but corn until I got sick from eating so much. I ended up spending most of our family visit in Mr. Trump's outhouse, which was scary because I was terrified of falling into the stinky hole.

MY PARENTS

When I was a little girl, I loved looking at family pictures as well as my dad's army photos. I especially liked a snapshot of him posing in front of his temporary barracks while serving as a medic in the Korean War.

A big buoyant grin showed across his face. He seemed strong in his uniform, so sure of himself. I was proud of him. I felt like he was the most handsome daddy in the entire world.

Throughout my childhood, I tried to do nice things for my dad, like baking cookies for him. He loved homemade cookies, and sometimes I'd do yard work like mowing and edging the front lawn. He liked it when I cleaned the house too because it made my mother happy. I liked it when he was in a good mood. I loved him. He was my daddy, but for some reason, he didn't like me.

My mom was petite. She had dark hair, hazel eyes, a pretty complexion, and a beautiful singing voice. I loved listening to her play the piano and sing. There were many times when without being asked, I would do laundry, watch my younger siblings, and run errands for my mom because then she'd be in a cheerful mood. I wanted to be a good daughter. Life seemed much easier for me if my parents were happy and not fighting.

My mother was a substitute teacher in the local elementary schools. She had a special way of communicating with children, and adults alike. People loved her... I loved her.

MY SIBLINGS & ME

I am the oldest of six children. Even though we all lived in the same home together with the same biological parents, we had our own experiences growing up. In a sense, we had different parents because of how they related with us individually, and it was like they had two sets of children. The older three and the younger three. Each of us have our own recollections of what went on inside our home. Some of my siblings don't want to talk about their past; others say they had a good childhood with happy memories. I wish I could say the same. Regardless, I believe we have all been affected by the dysfunction. The stories I share are my memories and not my siblings'.

I believe I was my parents' experiment because I was their firstborn. I have heard that the oldest in dysfunctional families can be the golden child. Trace was the oldest boy, a straight A student, never missing a day of classes all through high school. My dad was proud of Trace. Garrett was the middle child, a little boy with a big, loving heart. I felt that Garrett was sometimes overlooked and ignored——the "middle child syndrome." Garrett was abused, too. There were complications at his birth; he didn't get enough oxygen. My mother told me if she'd had a C-section, he would have been all right. Although my brother was behind in his grade level, he was and is still able to live on his own and take care of himself.

There were times that Garrett did not get up fast enough, at least in my dad's opinion, to manually change one of the four black and white television channels we had back then. The TV looked like a wooden box sitting on four wooden furniture legs with a hanger on top for an antenna. This was a time way before there were remotes.

My dad would kick or punch Garrett. He was a little boy. One incident took place when he was about nine years old, and he was physically abused because of my dad's impatience. I found this so heartbreaking. I was terribly upset because I couldn't stand to watch my brother being hurt. I would cry, but I wouldn't speak up because if I did, I might get belted too. My mother as usual was somewhere in the house, but she didn't do or say anything either.

My parents provided private lessons, piano for me, accordion for Trace and my brother John, and clarinet lessons for my sister Josie. Garrett wanted to take guitar lessons. He talked about wanting to play the guitar often. However, he still wasn't allowed to take music lessons or any other extracurricular activity other than one year when he played on a Little League Baseball team. I remember that made him happy.

The neglect he endured always made me feel sad for him. I wish my parents would've given him a chance. I remember asking my mom why she and my dad wouldn't let him play the guitar. She didn't give me an answer; she just skirted over the issue.

My sister Josie was a light in my parents' eyes, especially my dad's. She was cheerful and loving. My little brother John stood up for himself and strived to be good at whatever he did. My dad respected those qualities he saw in John. I could tell my dad was proud of him. Rita was the family's baby; she was cute, clever, and stood up for herself. She was more like a grandbaby to my parents.

If my siblings ever did anything wrong, people would report the incidents to me. For example, John was playing with our neighbor's car antenna, breaking it off. Another time, one of my siblings accidentally broke a basement window.

Then there was the time Josie walked alone through a desolate park, a park we were not allowed to go to without permission.

Instead of the neighborhood adults going to my parents, they came to me. It seemed the adults felt more comfortable talking to me about my younger sibling's activities than they did with my parents.

When my brothers were old enough to drive cars, neighbors would let me know my brothers had been doing burnouts in the subdivision. Never mind the fact that I'd seen their sons do the very same thing, but I wouldn't tell them that.

There are distinct roles given within dysfunctional families. I believe one of my roles was the scapegoat.

I didn't come to fully realize that I was a serious, scared, and humorless child until my eyes began to open while delving into my past.

As a child I was never skinny for my age. I tended to be more on the plump side. I remember my mom saying "pleasingly plump" on occasion, but I don't think she directed the phrase at me in any derogatory way. I remember grinning inside when she said this. I took her words to be a nice compliment, probably because the phrase started with "pleasingly."

I was blonde; my hair looked more like baby white until I was five. After that, my hair grew darker. I was light-complected except for all the freckles on my face, especially in the summer months when I played outside in the sun.

I have green eyes. Throughout my life, my eyes were always the first thing people would notice about me—until my preteen years. It was then that my peers observed the big hips I was developing. I remember overhearing the neighbor kids discussing and agreeing together one summer afternoon that I would be good at having babies. We were all out in front of my house, huddled together in a small group talking. I stood with a couple of girlfriends while two of the boys sat on their red and blue stingray bicycles. The kind of bikes that had what we called banana seats and stingray handlebars also known as ape hangers. I honestly didn't know what to think of the boys' comments that day other than they were telling me I would be good at having babies. I guess it was their way of saying I had big hips. Inside my head, I disagreed with the "good at having babies" part. At the time, with all the responsibility I carried minding my younger siblings, there was absolutely no way I ever wanted to have babies. I was thirteen and I was already tired.

I was, and I still am, very independent. I still remember racing my mother to the top of the stairs of our two-story duplex with my brother Trace's bottle in hand. I was three. Trace is a year younger than I am. My mom thought it was funny, but even at an incredibly early age, I felt as if my parents didn't take care of my younger siblings like I thought they should have. My brother wanted his bottle. My mom was taking her sweet time getting it to him; at least, that was my opinion. My mother used to say, "God comes first, my husband next, and then you, the children."

BRISTLE

I will admit I am particularly good at pretending, especially during times of shame. I would have never gotten through my life without the art of being fake, and I was good at what I did.

When something terrible happened to me, something that was hurtful, embarrassing, and humiliating—an experience that would make most people want to run and hide—I BRISTLED. My mom told me this is what she did. I guess I learned to bristle from her.

The dictionary says BRISTLE means "to rise and stand stiffly" or "to have an aggressively defensive attitude in response" to a criticism or slight.

My definition of BRISTLE is "pretending." Bristle became my pretense because, after any awkward or shameful experiences, I would throw my shoulders back—stand tall and erect—and make believe the event never happened, that this dreadful thing that had materialized really was just a crazy dream. I repeated this confirmation in my head over and over to myself until I eventually believed my own lie. This is how I got through the tragic experiences in my life.

Throughout my childhood and up through my early adult years, I played a game. It was a game I played often. I would say to myself, in a week, people will be thinking less about the shameful event.

In a month, they will not be talking about the incident as much, even though I know it will be in conversation with them from time to time. In six months or even a year, people will be talking about another person's dilemma or tragedy, and they will have forgotten about mine. Then I would think, in five to fifty years, they will have forgotten the incident entirely or be dead.

In my past, I took insults, beatings, and emotional abuse from others. I didn't ask them why they treated me this way. Instead, I kept quiet. I bristled.

As we have all heard, everything gets better with practice, and I admit I have had a lot of practice at pretending. And bristling.

When I was a baby, my dad lost his eye while working in a factory. "Your dad got mean after he lost his eye," my mom said. I was twelve at the time of this revelation. I was not given specific examples of what my mother meant by her statement, and I didn't ask. As I look back, I didn't question things; I did question inside my head, but I wouldn't confront anyone because as my dad used to say, "Children are to be seen and not heard." I took that to heart.

I am assuming my dad *being mean* was due to his unexpected, abrupt outbursts of anger, his excessive drinking, and the physical fights my parents had. I never saw my dad lash out at relatives other than my Grandma Gina when I was four. The crazy around me seemed to happen only in our home.

A woman told me my dad lost his eye because he was working on the Sabbath. What a cruel thing for her to say, and sad that she actually believed this.

I found out later she'd shot and killed a man accidentally, thinking he was a bear. There was so much talk in the small town afterward that she sent her children to a parochial school in another part of the state.

I was told this is how our family came to attend the rigid church I was raised in.

CHRISTMAS PAST

Along with the usual family laissez-faire there was little calm in our home while growing up. There was drama—yelling, drinking, physical fighting. We couldn't decorate a Christmas tree together without an argument.

Holidays were even more reason for my dad to drink, although I'm quite sure he drank all year round. My parents seemed to argue more at Christmas, and our tree was usually set up three to four days before.

My dad made sure to get a tree with at least one good side. We would place the bad sides in a corner. Those were the cheaper trees to buy. Although I always wanted to have a Christmas tree in the window like my friends' families, we never did.

Every year as Christmas Day grew closer, I could feel the excitement of the holiday season in the air, even though it upset me to see my dad sneak a drink from a bottle of whiskey, but I liked that he was content. The small bottle was usually inside a brown paper bag hidden away in the side pocket of his long, gray dress coat. I knew his cheerfulness would only last for a short while, but I was happy for that short while because he was in a good mood. I loved seeing my daddy happy.

However, the drunker my dad got, the more his euphoria wore off, and then he would get angry. And our restrained but happy excitement of Christmas could shatter into a million pieces in an instant if tempers flared. . . and tempers usually did. And as I have mentioned before, my parents' fights were not just verbal, but they were physical.

I felt anxiety and worry in my body when my dad drank because I feared the unknown. I would panic because I didn't know what disastrous thing would happen next.

Like a beautiful gleaming glass ornament, suddenly and for no reason, falling, smashing on the hardwood floor… exploding.

One minute we were all okay, and the next, everything came crashing down.

So much chaos, so much anger, so many hurt feelings.

Embarrassment, humiliation, sadness, and mortifying moments that were painful. These feelings, this sensitivity, is something that I was used to. I grew up in an uncertain and sometimes repulsive atmosphere where drinking and emotional and physical abuse happened often. I was good at reading a room, sensing moods, detecting vocal tones, and predicting potential chaos in my surroundings.

My dad wasn't born bad, he was a victim of child abuse (at the hands of his father). Generational trauma and the harmful effects of his alcohol addiction were a big part of what fueled the crazy in our home. Drinking combined with an unaddressed personality disorder made way for turmoil, and that's what was bad. My dad knew right from wrong. He had choices. We all do.

Most years our Christmas presents consisted of an orange and a one-dollar bill in our stockings. The stockings were either knee socks or my dad's white socks. I remember getting a two-dollar bill and a bottle of perfume from the dime store when I was in the seventh grade.

One year before Christmas, my dad sent my brother Trace and me to get a four-dollar tree from the grocery store a city block away. He didn't have one-dollar bills, so he gave us a ten.

My brother and I didn't see a nice tree for four dollars that night, but we found a good one for ten, and we bought it. My parents weren't too happy, but we were.

My best Christmas was when I was in the second grade. It was the only one I can remember that we had what seemed to me tons of presents under the tree.

On Christmas Eve, when we were supposed to be in bed sleeping, I peeked out to see my dad busily setting up a race car track for my brothers on our maple wood dining table. We called it the maple table. It was late; after working all day my dad was tired, yet he stood over the table trying out the red, blue, green, and yellow cars with a remote. He looked happy and excited, making sure the toy worked while still wearing his white work uniform. When he was through setting the track up, I watched him put more toys out under the tree, some of them wrapped in pretty red and green Christmas paper, and some gifts were unwrapped. My mom made date nut pinwheel cookies that year, one of my favorites, and I don't remember my parents fighting.

On Christmas Eve, when I was eleven, I tagged along to the grocery store with my mother. I recall feeling happy because it was Christmas, school was out, and she was buying a canned ham and a bottle of Squirt, one of my favorite sodas. For a while, it seemed as though everyone around me was happy, but I soon noticed that mixed in the crowd of blissful holiday faces were people that looked and acted angry. I told my mom I couldn't understand how people could be so unhappy at Christmas. She told me that

Christmas for a lot of people was a sad time. I never understood her explanation that night, but I understand now.

INTUITION

Having intuition is natural. We all have intuition. Animals survive on theirs. Victims of abuse come to rely more on their intuition than those who haven't been abused.

Learning to read people and my surroundings kept me safe. I knew to stay out of my mother's way when she was angry. I didn't want to be yelled at. I stayed out of my dad's way when he was drinking. He'd get mean. I didn't feel safe. I learned to rely on reading my surroundings, unlike other children who feel safe in their environment. Children who feel safe count on their parents to provide for and take care of them because they trust them. They don't have to worry or be on guard, they feel secure, so they can concentrate on being who they are. This is their right; it should be every child's right.

There were times when I had difficulty believing my intuition. I knew what I was feeling, but a lot of times I didn't listen to my instincts because my parents and others told me who I was, and what was wrong with me. I believed them. Sometimes what was said and what my intuition told me was confusing.

I never felt good enough, pretty enough, lovable enough, or smart enough. I felt my parents and people in general would love me if I could just do everything right. In a way, this was magical thinking on my part. Who and what I'd been told I was spoke louder to me than what my intuition had said.

As an adult, I am still good at sensing the moods and emotions of people around me, but I am much better at deciphering whether it is my instinct or the confusing old tapes in my head just spewing off. I have good intuition. I have included several examples of how perceptive I have been in my life, such as recognizing a field-trip predator.

When I was in the fifth grade, our teacher took us on a field trip to the Ford Rouge Plant in Dearborn, Michigan. I noticed that a man working on the line seemed to have the advantage of leaving his workstation often. He would go back and forth on the line to talk to our class. I also noticed that when he talked, he looked at me a lot while showing my class how something on the assembly line worked.

A perpetrator knows by looking at his victim that she is vulnerable and has been abused.

At first, I felt like I was important because this man's attention seemed focused on me and not my other classmates. However, I got a creepy feeling when this man got so close to me that I could feel his body brush up against mine. I felt vulnerable; I felt claustrophobic. I was suffocating. I couldn't breathe. I didn't feel safe even with my teacher and classmates standing around me. I just stood there holding my breath, hyperventilating, feeling scared and helpless.

One chilly winter morning, I had an early English class. I was in my first year of college at the time. Claire, my roommate, was sleeping. I didn't want to disturb her, so I didn't turn the light switch on in our dorm room. Instead, I dressed in the dark. I had good intentions of being quiet.

Claire's half of our room was painted orange. The other side was white. I didn't have enough money to go in with her on the orange paint. The painted areas divided our room down the middle. There was a heavy framed bed on one side of the room and another bed on the other side. Two wooden desks stood side by side on the back wall. Wooden built-in shelves hung above the desks. The shelves covered most of the wall. Our closets were built in on top of a set of drawers. The wooden closet drawer ensembles stood close to the entrance door. We shared a bathroom with two other girls. The bathroom is what separated our adjoining rooms.

I reached into my closet for a green top with layered wispy shoulder sleeves; it was one of my favorite blouses. I wore it with a pair of flared jeans, a trendy style in the mid-seventies. While I started to pull my top on, I had an overwhelming feeling that there was a spider on it. It was only a thought in my brain. Whether my feelings were right or not I had to make sure there wasn't a bug crawling around on me, especially not a spider. I hurried to take it off, flipped the light switch on, turned the blouse around to look at it, and sure enough, there was a yellow house spider on the back collar. I'm pretty sure I screamed. My good intentions of not disturbing Claire that morning were foiled.

My mom bought apple pie for our dessert one night from the day-old bread stand. I was fifteen.

Having dessert after dinner almost never occurred, it pretty much only happened when we had company, but we weren't having visitors, so to me this was a really special occasion.

My mother had placed a pie in front of me and another at the other end of the dark pine trestle table while we all sat on sturdy wooden benches my dad had made. He was good at carpentry. All through dinner, I stared at the pie sitting only inches away from me. This sounds crazy, but while eating my dinner, I kept thinking about it. I was getting a strange vibe from the pie like there was something wrong with it.

It was a summer evening in late June. The aluminum screen door was open and close enough to the table that I could feel a warm breeze caressing my arms. I heard voices from neighbor kids playing outside and cars whooshing by. Occasionally, one of the neighbor boys would rev up the engine on his car, squealing the tires.

We were eating salad, huge chunks of iceberg lettuce with diced red tomatoes and cucumbers. Everyone at the table was talking a mile a minute about their day. Excited about the apple pie we were going to eat.

When everyone had finished their dinner, my mom began cutting the pie. The crust was brown and flaky. A thick, gooey brown sugary syrup oozed into the plate while my mother continued to cut and serve the pie.

I picked up my fork with cautious anticipation. While out of the corner of my eye, I watched my brother John practically inhale his entire piece. He gulped it down with a glass of milk. His eyes smiled while he looked around for a chance to score more pie. I looked up from my slice of pie for a minute to watch everyone enjoying their dessert. I wanted to dig in like everyone else at the table, but again, the feeling of something being wrong with the pie seemed to be growing much louder and stronger.

This was dessert; it was apple pie. I ignored my intuition, and I took a bite anyway. That's when a thought flashed into my head that a fly was somewhere in my pie.

I stopped eating immediately. Some of my siblings had already left the table while I was still pulling the pie apart with my fork. I was looking for this supposed insect that for the most part was only a thought inside my head. Honestly, it was just a stupid thought. I continued to search while destroying the brown flaky layers of pie. Sure enough, I found a dead fly in the crust.

Even with my intuition, nothing could have prepared me for my mother's death. Ray and I took our sons to school that morning as we did every day. I had a doctor's appointment in Huntsville, Alabama, an hour away from home, and Ray was going with me. On our way, we saw a car sitting off the side of the road on I-65 south. The front of the burgundy car, especially the driver's side, was crumpled up and smashed in; it looked like it had been a head-on crash. I looked over at Ray and said, "Wow, I think someone was killed in that car today." My husband nodded his head while keeping his eyes on the road ahead. "So sad," I said.

On the way back from Alabama, we stopped at the property we'd just bought where we were planning to build our Queen Anne farmhouse. The eight-acre land parcel was vacant except for my sons' playhouse.

While we lived in Michigan, Ray built the four-foot by four-foot playhouse for the boys. We stained the wooden walls with a dark walnut color. Ray put in windows with plexiglass and a knob to pull them open and shut. Ray also put gray shingles on the roof. The little building was sturdy and so cute that I couldn't leave it behind, so I hired a trucking company to move it down to Tennessee against Ray's better judgment. Well, in my defense, our sons needed something to be positive about. The move to Tennessee was difficult for them too.

When we drove on to the temporary dirt and gravel driveway of our property, the first thing I noticed was a white piece of paper on the door of the playhouse waving in the breeze. "I wonder what that's all about," I said to Ray. I got out of the car and headed straight for the playhouse through tall green grass that needed cutting. The note was attached to the door with a tack. The man we bought our property from had left the note. He was good friends with Josie's husband, Thom.

I yanked the piece of paper off the wooden door without removing the tack. *Call your sister Josie A.S.A.P.* My hands were shaking.

I ran toward Ray, who was approaching me. "We have to get to a phone! We have to get to a phone!"

"Judy, calm down; it's probably nothing at all," Ray said. His arms extended out toward me. He was trying to comfort me.

I wanted to believe my husband, but I knew whatever… this would not be good. We didn't have a cell phone, so we drove to a country store in a town almost five miles away from our property to use the pay phone. The town consisted of only a post office and a combined store, restaurant, and gas station. Ray was doing his best driving to the store, but to me, it seemed like we were moving in slow motion.

I stuck two quarters in the phone slots. "Plunk, Plunk," I heard the quarters drop.

I called my sister collect.

Josie's husband, Thom, accepted the call. "Judy, your mom died." These were the only words I heard Thom say.

My mother, was on her way to work early that morning when she was killed by a 23-year-old man who'd been drinking and driving. I learned he hadn't slept for at least twenty-four hours before the accident. My understanding is that the truck he was driving came to a complete stop when the front of his vehicle ended up on top of the hood of my mother's car, crushing her. It was a head-on crash just like I'd suspected of the burgundy car we'd seen earlier that morning on I-65 on our way to my doctor's appointment.

Two days before she died, my mother called me twice. It was unusual for her to call, especially while she was working. She never called from work, nor were we supposed to call her unless it was an emergency. It was a rule. On her first call, my mother shared with me how healthy berries are.

"Promise me you will eat berries," she said.

"Okay, mom. I will."

"They are healthy and good for you." My mother continued.

"I know. Okay I will."

When the phone rang again, I recognized my mother's cheery voice. Once more, I remember thinking that this was unusual for her to call me twice in one day, especially while she was working.

The second time she called, I was upset. "Are you crying?" My mom asked.

"Yes."

"Judy, why are you crying?"

"The kitchen countertops are covered in ants. I've tried everything to get rid of them and they just won't leave."

To be honest, I think I was upset about everything else since our move to Tennessee, not just the ants. I didn't want to live in Tennessee. I wanted to go home to Michigan to our cute little house that still hadn't sold. For us to build, we had to sell our house first. I didn't like living in an apartment. There was no backyard for the boys to play in. Ray was working long hours. Although we had two storage units filled with furniture, appliances, and personal belongings, our apartment was becoming a storage unit as well. Everything felt out of control to me. We still hadn't found a builder, and there were times when I thought we'd be living in the dreaded apartment forever.

My mom paused, "Judy, someday those ants won't seem so bad to you."

"You're probably right." I said, only half believing her.

"There are worse things than ants." she said.

"I know" I was still crying.

Sadly, two days later, my mother was gone.

A week after returning from the funeral, I went into the kitchen and once again saw a swarm of ants on top of the counter. My mother was right. The ants didn't seem to bother me as much as they had before.

I knew what it was like to lose my dad to suicide and now, my mom to a tragic accident. But I never expected that I would soon face my own narrow escape from tragedy. Back in 2006, I worked for a company that did insurance inspections. I inspected vacant homes that were in foreclosure or had water and fire damage. I had been working all day, driving from one inspection to the next, and was on my last.

The sun was almost ready to go down, so I hurried to unlock the door of a home in a rural area. The house was a brick two-story building, nearly six thousand square feet. I did this inspection once a month, and every time I went into this property, I'd get lost.

As I got closer to the door to unlock it, my intuition told me to leave. The sensations I had were persistent and growing stronger.

I unlocked the door anyway, but as I did, it was as if my intuition began to shout at me. So, I locked the door and left. I decided I would come back the next day to do my inspection. I reasoned that my troubled feelings were because it was getting dark outside.

The following morning, I headed to the house, unlocked the door, and although I was cautious, I did not have the strong feelings I had the evening before. There were no cars on the property or near the home other than my car, a black 2002 Trailblazer. I felt safe that I was the only one on the property at the time. This was how it was supposed to be, only me, the contractor, on the property, and no one else.

I began walking around throughout each room, taking note of any new visible damage that water, storms, or fire could have caused. This home did have water damage, and a big part of my job was to make sure that the damage was not getting worse, although the unavoidable circumstance of black mold was growing more inevitable. I filled out a form on every property, detailing not only previous destruction but new damages as well.

When I entered what I deemed the front sitting room, I thought I heard a noise. The vacant room I stood in was extensive with a substantial front glass window that looked out onto an overgrown field of weeds. Wallpaper and drywall were peeling and falling from the wall due to previous water damage. The front entry door was also in this room.

Suddenly, I thought I heard footsteps. I stopped to listen. Sure enough, someone was tracking through the property. I freaked.

No one was supposed to be in the house—no one but me. I went to the front door and proceeded to unlock it so I could leave, all the while the echo of the heavy footsteps of an intruder were drawing closer to me.

My hands were shaking, and I was starting to hyperventilate. I was terrified. As hard as I tried, I could not calm down enough to unlock and open the door. I felt like I was in a horror movie. As I turned around with the intention of trying another way of escape, a short man approached. Right away, I started talking fast. I didn't know what I was saying. I just remember talking to him.

His hair was jet black with some gray. The crease lines on his forehead and around his eyes were deep but unmoved. He was probably in his late forties, but what I noticed more was that he had no expression on his face.

"Is this your home? Do you live here?" I asked him. "What company do you work for?" I kept talking. And talking faster. My body was still shaking.

While I spewed my words, my eyes followed his hands. I watched him pull a screwdriver and a bungee cord from his back pocket. He held them in his hands while extending his arms straight out in front of him and within almost two feet of where I stood facing him. He held onto the tools, toying with them, observing me and my fear. He didn't answer my questions until he said.

"I work for everyone, and anybody dot com," He continued to have no expression on his face while speaking to me. For a second, I remember thinking maybe he was joking, but his facial features did not reveal this.

Then without thinking about what I would say, I announced, "I have a document in my car stating that I am supposed to be at this house at this time."

I'm so glad I blurted those words out like I had. Suddenly, he quit playing with the bungee cord and screwdriver. His eyes seemed to bulge. But he continued to stand there glaring at me. I was petrified.

"Follow me." He dropped his arms, putting his tools back into his pocket while he walked ahead of me. He turned toward a side door in the garage I had initially unlocked to get into the property.

I felt that I had to follow him to get out because the front door would not budge for me. I wanted to keep an eye on him, too. It wasn't the time to turn my back on him. I followed slowly. I kept a pace of about fifteen feet behind him. Once outside, I headed straight for my car and drove out of there. I was so scared I cried all the way home.

The following day, my husband went with me, and we did the inspection together. Ray easily opened the door I had struggled with the day before.

The property had been winterized, but someone had been using the toilet—probably the same man I saw the day before. I called the police and the insurance company to report this intruder, and I never returned to that property again.

I am repeating myself. *Trust your intuition.*

EMPATHY

There are people in this world who have empathy. We worry about others' feelings, sometimes having little regard for our own. And then some have no empathy at all—narcissists or those with traits of a personality disorder. I believe they don't understand what it is to care about anyone other than themselves, and that is sad. Narcissists have no problem telling others what they believe to be wrong with them. They emulate traits and preferences in others in order to earn their trust and affection. They use other people as mirrors to evaluate themselves and to find fault. When they can't find fault, they attack the mirror.

One of the sad things people with narcissistic traits will do, especially after building a person up with gifts, their words, their time, and money (love bombing), they will start to destroy them. It is a high for them; it is their drug of choice. These disordered personalities are universally the same. They act and react alike. Everything they do seems to revolve around what's in it for them. As I've mentioned earlier, I can walk into a room and know if I'm wanted. I pick up on others' feelings and emotions. I can tell if something is bothering them. I may not know exactly what their problem is, but I know they are upset. I feel it. If I go where there are a lot of people, I pick up even more on the emotions circulating in the room. The feelings from everyone around me can sometimes become overwhelming. I have to leave the crowd; if I don't, I feel extremely uncomfortable. The walls feel like they are closing in on me. I can't breathe. I feel claustrophobic and anxious.

I try to comfort other people when I feel they are hurt or upset. I will ask, "Are you alright? If you'd like to talk, I'm here for you." Sometimes, I think, it's like me trying to help the ants rebuild their anthill when I was a little girl. The ants didn't need my help, but I don't want anyone to hurt like I have.

I don't want to hurt anyone's feelings. I have never wanted to hurt anyone, although I know, sadly, I have. That's why it is so confusing to know that there are people in the world who try to intentionally manipulate and hurt others.

I have always had compassion for others. I believe empathy is a true quality to have. But sometimes, it doesn't feel like a gift. I was born with empathy. But because I didn't stand up for myself, my boundaries were crossed. I was disrespected, talked down to, and told I was bad. I believed the lies and allowed others to manipulate me into feeling shame and guilt over things that were never my fault.

AGE FOUR

I was sitting up straight in church while I swung and dangled my legs over the edge of a wooden pew. My feet were unable to touch the floor. I wore white gloves and held onto a Bible that sat on my lap—a book that was almost as big as me.

I felt grown up, and I felt pretty sitting with the adults in worship service that day, donned in my frilly church dress that my mom also referred to as my party dress.

I was only four years old, yet I remember feeling concerned because while the tin collection plate was passed from one person to the next in the pew in front of ours, I didn't know what to do. (I think about this now. I was a little child amid many adults. Why would I worry about what I should do? But I felt like I had to do something. I guess I felt responsible even back then.)

I stood up on the bench while watching the collection plate draw closer. I still did not know what to do when the plate finally got to me, so I grabbed a handful of coins. The congregation laughed and watched while my mom tried to convince me to release the money back into the offering plate.

I felt scared. I didn't move. I just stood there observing everyone looking at me.

My fist was tight and clenched. I was holding on to as many coins as I could. I felt some slip through my fingers and trickle into the plate, clinking as they hit the tin.

I know my face had to be somber as I looked at all the parishioners around me watching. I didn't know what I had done wrong or what I should do while they were gasping and laughing at me. I just felt afraid.

At the time, we lived in what the townspeople referred to as the projects—a small cluster of duplexes located on the poorer side of town, literally across the railroad tracks. When people asked me where I lived, I would tell them "the projects." I was proud of where I lived.

I can still remember a dismal rainy night when my parents were upstairs fighting. Their violence scared me, and it made me feel sad to see them treating each other so terribly. They were hurting each other. I remember hearing rage in their voices. I could hear crying and shouting, slamming doors, and what sounded at times like running, hitting, and falling noises.

Then my grandma, someone I loved very much, was knocking on our door. Grandma Gina was my mother's mom. She was 4'10" and tiny. Grandma was standing outside on our back porch in the drizzling rain.

"Grandma!" I cried.

Seeing my grandmother brought a moment of relief for me. I remember wanting her to stop the chaos I didn't understand.

My parents continued to fight while my grandmother stood outside. She sustained her stance out in the rain and in the dark, watching me through a small windowpane in the door. The door was locked, and I stood helpless in the kitchen, peering back at her while my bare feet gripped the cold linoleum floor.

I wanted my grandma to come in, but I was too short to reach the doorknob and unlock the door even when I stood on my tiptoes.

Tears streamed down my face while my grandma continued to knock on the door. I was so young, and it was terrifying for me to see and hear what was going on around me. Even though there were adults nearby, I felt alone. I had so many emotions, but my four-year-old brain could not process all that was happening. My eyes darted from outside the door where my grandma stood over to the stairway that led upstairs to my parent's bedroom.

I remember there seemed to be, for a moment, a lull of quiet. My parents had stopped shouting, and the bangs and pounding of fists against flesh had stopped before I heard a loud thump. Whatever it was, the noise sounded heavy, like a piece of furniture being pushed or thrown hard against the wall.

Within minutes, my dad was headed down the stairs, my mother following. Somehow, my mom was able to move ahead of my dad without an altercation, and she unlocked the back door to let her mother inside.

The moment my grandmother entered the room, my dad began shouting orders at her to leave.

We were all in the kitchen except for three-year-old Trace and baby Garrett, both upstairs in bed. My dad's heavy frame charged toward my grandmother while my mom stood off to the side of the room. She was observing, silent, appearing helpless. I stayed out of the way.

"Can Judy come home with me tonight?" I remember Grandma asked while she looked over in my direction.

"No!" My dad shouted at her. He took my grandma's arm at the elbow, led her to the door, and pushed her back outside. I saw my grandma's pain while I watched my dad lock the door behind her. As I tell this story, I am there now, back in time. I am feeling the chaos; it's as if I'm out of my body watching it happen all over again.

I did nothing but stand there and cry while my dad, this time, grabbed my mother's arm, both heading back upstairs. I was scared. I held my breath trying to hold in the loud sobs of frustration. Even then, I could feel that everything in my life was out of control. I was a baby, yet in my fragile young mind, in some way, I remember feeling responsible for my parents' animosity toward each other, maybe because I felt like I always seemed to be in the way.

Even though my parents were back upstairs fighting, my grandma continued to stand on the porch looking in on me through the small window in the door. She was an adult and someone I loved and felt safe with, but she could not help me with the fear and sadness I felt at the time.

I wanted her to tell me everything would be all right, but she was standing on the other side of a locked door. There were only inches between us, but she was a world away from me, and there was nothing she or I could do.

I was alone and afraid, while the war around me raged. Continued shouts of hateful words that I could not understand rang through our home. . . Until moments later when the police arrived.

WHAT'S WRONG WITH ME?

I recall a time when I was outside running. I might have been five. I fell, and I scraped my knee on the concrete sidewalk. I was bleeding, and I cried because it hurt terribly. My dad saw me fall, but instead of trying to help or ask me if I was alright or take me up into his arms to comfort me, he stood there and said, "What the hell's the matter with you?" I felt like I was a bad girl for falling.

No wonder some of us have a tough time accepting the fact that God loves us. Our own fathers have hurt, judged, and rejected us. This happened so often that I thought this was how God must feel about me, too. Even so, I continued talking to him throughout my life.

Not only did I feel like God rejected me, but I have felt people's silent judgments and their rejection of me my entire life as well. Some people feel they are better than others. These are the same people that talk about how wrong it is to bully, yet they do it themselves. While they point their fingers at others, they forget to take a good long look at themselves first.

For years, I have allowed people to mistreat me; I pretended that their unkind words and actions didn't bother me. And it was true that they had hurt me, but at these times, I wasn't about to give them the satisfaction of knowing they had.

I was pretending again. The art of bristle.

AGE SIX

In the early nineteen sixties, we lived in a small two-story home that was about seven hundred square feet. When the furnace went out, I felt bad for my dad who had to crawl under the house on his belly through a narrow opening to fix it. Of course, every year, the furnace tended to go out in the coldest part of the winter.

Because our house was so cold, we went to our neighbors'— Bob and Jane's. They were older than my parents, and they had five children, their youngest, David, my age. They were from the South and had moved to Michigan, like many other families, to work in the car factories.

Bob and my dad would drink, then inch their way in and out of the small crawl space while doing the repairs. Bob was a thin man, but my dad was heavy, and they were both quite drunk by the time they crawled underneath the house.

I worried because I was so sure my dad would get stuck under the house. He was drunk, and I was afraid he wouldn't be able to find his way out. I was scared he would die in the cold, dark, mouse-ridden crawl space.

Jane conversed with my mom while she made cookies and hot chocolate for us. The women were laughing, but I couldn't enjoy any of the refreshments or conversation with the other kids in the room because my mind was on what I thought adults should generally be concerned about.

My parents didn't seem to care about what I deemed a crisis. They never reassured me that everything would be alright or that it was their job to be parents and that my job was to be a child. I didn't trust my parents or their actions. They had let me down too many times. I only trusted me, so I worried and watched over my siblings. I felt like someone had to.

VANILLA PUDDING

One summer evening after supper, my mom made each of my siblings and me an ice cream cone filled with vanilla pudding instead of ice cream.

I recall feeling happy. We were standing outside on the back porch giggling and eating our dessert when our dog got hold of my younger brother's cone. We started to laugh even more because, to us, the dog was being funny.

My dad must have seen what happened because he came out of the house fuming. He kicked the dog hard on the side of its body and then spanked each of us except for my baby brother.

I was crying, not only for my siblings and me, but for our dog, who had shrieked at the first impact of my dad's foot. The dog had run off to hide somewhere. And that is when I noticed our neighbors were looking over the fence at us. They were staring. I was distraught at everything that had happened, so I looked over at them and shouted, "Nosey neighbors!"

I felt so ashamed. I was angry.

MY WOODEN TEETH

I learned in school that George Washington had wooden teeth. Well, I am here to tell you that he wasn't the only one. However, I recently learned that George Washington didn't really have wooden teeth; it was a fable, like the cherry tree story. So maybe I am the only one to have ever had wooden teeth, at least in the nineteen sixties.

My dad worked for a dairy in the Downriver area of Detroit. He delivered ice cream and ice cream products to stores and restaurants in the metro area until I was in the fourth grade; then, he went to work as a janitor for the elementary school my siblings and I attended.

I think, however, that my dad, in some subconscious way, might've wanted to be a dentist. From what I understand, my Grandpa Randall, my dad's father, had acted as a barber and dentist in the small community my dad lived in while growing up.

When any of my baby teeth became even slightly loose, my dad would pull them out. He didn't wait for them to fall out on their own.

While my siblings played nearby, he'd tie one end of a string around my loose tooth and the other end to a doorknob. He'd tell me to stand still; then, he'd slam the door. He'd repeat until the tooth became looser. If the slamming of the door technique did not take my tooth out, he'd get the pliers and yank it.

My aunt gave me some chocolate candy one evening while we were visiting her home. After eating the candy, I felt a lot of pain in one of my teeth. I had a cavity.

My parents took me to see a dentist—a short man with very little hair on his head. He wore wire-rimmed glasses, a long white coat, and he walked with a limp. To be honest, he scared me. He looked like a mad scientist I had seen in a TV cartoon. When he told me to sit still, I did just that. I obeyed him.

My dad's medical insurance did not cover a local anesthetic to numb my gums, and my dad wouldn't pay out of pocket for it, so whenever I had a cavity that needed to be drilled and filled. I felt everything.

Because of my dad's short stint as a temporary dentist "wannabe," I had a mouth full of missing teeth.

Due to all the empty spaces, my permanent teeth were growing in crooked. The dentist told my parents I would need braces.

Okay, so what do you think? If I wasn't getting an anesthetic while my teeth were being drilled, I wasn't going to get braces either. In a way, I was relieved. Growing up, we called kids with braces "zipper teeth" because of all the metal in their mouths.

My dad had a solution to the missing teeth and teeth growing in crooked. Every night after dinner (a time I grew to dread), he'd take his pocketknife from his white work pants and whittle small wooden teeth from a Popsicle stick. I sat very still on an old quarter-sawn oak chair that had a brown leather seat while my dad inserted small pieces of wood into the gaps between the teeth that remained in my mouth.

The wooden teeth wedged in so tightly that the pulsing pain I felt didn't stop or subside until the following night, almost twenty-four hours later. That was right before the old wooden teeth came out, and my dad inserted the newly whittled ones. And my mom, who was nearby, would observe, but she remained silent. As usual, she appeared helpless, later reminding me how much it hurts to be beautiful.

As I grew older, I got compliments on how nice and straight my teeth were. The flattery was kind, but. . . The pain of what I went through and what I must've looked like while wearing brown boy shoes and Popsicle-stick wood in my mouth only added to my insecurity.

It was proof of just how different I was from most kids my age. Relatives, neighbors, teachers, and the outside world didn't say anything.

Recently, I asked my brother Garrett if Dad had pulled his teeth out with a string and doorknob. He said, "No but he did it to you. He did it to you."

I'M NOT PRETTY

The first time I met my dad's old Army buddy, Mr. Fisher, and his family was the day they came to visit us all the way from Illinois. The farthest place I had been was to a small town in Northern Michigan where my parents were born and had grown up.

Mr. and Mrs. Fisher's daughter, Shirley, and I were six, the same age. She was a tiny little thing, much smaller than me, and she had beautiful red hair. I had never met anyone with red hair before. Mine was more of a dark blonde, and I happened to have a frizzy home perm at the time. It seemed I always had frizzy home perms.

Shirley was my new friend. Her younger brother was the same age as my brother Trace.

When we had visitors, my parents got along much better. My mom made tasty food, and we had desserts like cookies and cake to eat.

I cannot remember much of what we did during the visit, other than it was nice to meet my dad's Army friend and his family for the first time, and I remember feeling happy, but my cheerfulness didn't last long.

Shirley and I slept downstairs in the living room that night on two matching forest green kidney-shaped sofas, and the boys slept upstairs on brown metal twin beds.

The next morning when I awoke, my dad and Mr. Fisher were talking.

The men were drinking coffee and standing over us girls while my mom and Mrs. Fisher conversed in the kitchen. I was awake, but I didn't open my eyes. Instead, I listened to their conversation.

"Shirley is such a pretty little girl." Dad proclaimed.

My dad was repeating himself. He was commenting over and over on what a pretty little girl Shirley was. As young as I was, I still remember having a big pang of hurt overwhelm me.

I didn't like myself. I felt ugly, and unworthy. I thought I was generally just bad anyway. My dad's nice comments about another little girl made me feel even worse.

I kept waiting for my dad to say how pretty I was in conversation, but he didn't. I continued to lie there, still pretending to sleep. At one point, there seemed to be a long pause mid-conversation between the two men, and then Mr. Fisher said, "Well, your daughter is pretty, too."

I wasn't the only one who had noticed my dad's repetitive comments toward Shirley.

"Yeah," my dad said, but his "yeah" had a disappointing ring to it.

My eyes were still closed when I heard Shirley get up from the other sofa. I wondered how it must have felt to her that morning, listening to my dad and her dad talk about how pretty she was. I am sure she felt exceptionally good about herself. Her family was leaving to go back to their home in Illinois after breakfast.

I felt sad that morning, knowing how pretty my dad thought Shirley was, and very much broken to know he didn't feel the same way about me. I was his little girl. I was his daughter, but he didn't say, "Judy is pretty." He wouldn't say, "Judy and Shirley are pretty girls." Or "Wow, look at us, Mr. Fisher, we sure do have pretty daughters!"

My mother called everyone to breakfast. Both parents called out to me when I didn't show up right away. I ignored them. I continued to pretend I was asleep. Normally, I would not be allowed to do this, but we had company, so I felt reasonably safe that I wouldn't be spanked for neglecting their calls.

While everyone was in the kitchen eating, I went upstairs and put my prettiest, lacy, aqua-with-white-polka-dots party dress on. I couldn't zip it in the back by myself, but I went downstairs to the table anyway.

As soon as I entered the room, it got awkwardly quiet.

Mr. and Mrs. Fisher broke the silence by commenting on how pretty I looked. Another uncomfortable moment indeed, for everyone, especially me. Even at six, I knew they were only being nice. I felt like they didn't really mean it. Throughout my childhood, it was what my parents said or didn't say that told me who I was and what was wrong with me.

After I was grown and married, my Grandma Randall, Dad's mother, told me that my dad had dated Mrs. Fisher at one time and that he had introduced her to his Army friend.

Maybe my dad still thought Mrs. Fisher was pretty. I did overhear my parents say that Shirley looked a lot like her mother. Who knows what my dad thought or his feelings at the time? I just knew how he felt about me—I wasn't pretty.

I've heard that girls who have a good relationship with their fathers have healthier marriages and relationships. My dad didn't offer a close relationship to me, although I really wish he had.

NOT GOOD ENOUGH

In the nineteen sixties, my brother Trace brought home a colorful picture he drew in kindergarten. My dad grabbed the classic newsprint, red-and-blue-ruled school paper like it was a chest filled with treasure. He was so pleased with my younger brother's artwork that he went on and on about how great my brother was and how amazing his drawing was.

I wanted my dad to tell me how good my schoolwork was, too. I wanted him to praise me like he was praising my brother. I needed him to. But when I showed my father the full page of slanting and straight lines my teacher had assigned in penmanship class earlier that day, he laughed.

His laughter made me feel stupid, and it left me heartbroken that my classwork was so unworthy of his approval.

MY BIRTHDAY PARTY

My mom planned a birthday party for me when I was six years old. I helped her make out a designated number of invitations, and I passed them out to some of my classmates in school and a few friends in our neighborhood, but not all of the children had been invited to my party. Some of the kids in class who did not get an invitation asked me if they could come to my birthday celebration, and I said yes.

I invited my entire class because I didn't want their feelings hurt. There were about twenty-five kids in my classroom, the neighbor kids, and then some others. And I am quite sure that they all showed up for my birthday gala.

Lines of cars pulled up in front of our house that day, doors opened, kids piled out, and their parents drove off. Some kids arrived holding the hand of a younger sibling, too. They asked my mom if their little brother or sister could come. What could my mom say? Their parents had already left the scene.

I remember my mother throwing her hands up, while smiling to a neighbor lady helping with the party. She told her friend that she was afraid there would not be enough cake to go around.

What my mom did for me that morning still stands out in my mind. I was so appreciative. Throughout my life, I have thanked her many times for walking almost two miles one way to get my birthday cake. It was a cake she had ordered from a bakery.

A homemade cake was special but getting a bakery cake was a big thing back then.

My parents, like most families, had one car to share. My dad had the car that day because he was working, so my mom walked all that way for me, and that made me feel special.

ANTS

Another time, I was outside in our front yard watching a long chain of reddish-brown ants rushing around on a sidewalk outside my house. It was summer vacation. I wasn't wearing shoes, so the bottoms of my feet burned from the scorching concrete. I think it was nap time because my mother and younger siblings were inside the house. My dad was working that day, and I was out front alone.

I sat down on the grass alongside the sidewalk, my legs crossed. I wanted to see what these goofy insects were doing. I spent most of my time watching the ants and the anthill. The lawn was cooler than the blistering concrete, and even though the blades of grass made my skin itch, I continued to watch the ants.

I sat still, and I pulled clumps of grass out of the soil on both sides of my body. I was fascinated with this colony of ants—running, following, circling, carrying, and entering the hill above their home underground.

A huge tree that stood in our neighbor's yard began to cast long shadows over me. The ants, unlike me, hadn't seemed bothered by the heat and continued to busy themselves hauling what looked like small crumbs or tiny granules of sand, or maybe their eggs, in and out of their anthill.

Khaki-brown and gold-speckled mounds of sand were growing bigger before my eyes. My mind wandered as I studied them. Sometimes an occasional car would pass by on the street, distracting my attention. The momentary interruption caused me to focus on the people driving by in their colorful cars rather than the ants. I wondered where the people were going. I could hear distant voices and music playing from a radio inside our neighbor's home. As time went by, the ground felt like it was getting harder. My legs and bottom were tired from sitting still for so long, but I didn't move. The insects continued to mesmerize me until I became bored. I noticed that they didn't seem to be moving as fast as they were earlier. Something felt wrong to me, and my six-year-old brain wanted to help them.

I picked up a small stick. Then I gently stirred the top of the mound, but I accidentally caused the hill to collapse. Within seconds, what seemed like millions of ants began to crawl all over the caved-in mound, each ant carrying minuscule pieces of sand clenched in its mandibles.

I had destroyed their hill, their home. I felt terrible and immediately threw the stick down. I began scraping my hands across the rough concrete, trying to grasp more sand, dirt, and tiny pebbles in what any six-year-old girl's best attempt might be at remaking a home for the ants. The more I tried to make amends, the worse it got.

I have always tried to fix things, even if what I was trying to remedy did not need fixing and was none of my business. I just wanted everyone to be happy. If people were sad, if they were angry, I wanted them to smile. I wanted to make it better for them because if they were happy, then I would be happy too. I honestly thought I was doing good by helping the ants. I wasn't being bad. But the anthill was fine before I interfered.

WAXING THE FLOOR

Summer soon ended, and I was heading back to class, but I wasn't the only one.

Whenever my mom would go back to school to take classes, I noticed she seemed to be more upset than usual. Everything would be okay with her, and then with little warning, she would start screaming.

One night when I was about six, Trace was five, and Garrett was four, my mother was trying to study. She came out of her room upset and started yelling at us. I remember crying. I was making my mom unhappy. I felt her emotional outburst was because of me, it was my fault.

When my parents fought or were upset, I felt shame and unworthy. I felt helpless. I saw my mother as being perfect. I thought she was pretty, people seemed to like her, but the environment I lived in told me I was far from perfection. If Mom was angry, I must have caused her anger and sadness.

Maybe she was anxious about her homework, the house being a mess, or whatever else was going on in her life that I didn't understand. I don't know why she was so troubled that night, but within minutes of scolding us, she went back into her bedroom and closed the door behind her.

My dad was not home. He was working or out drinking again. Maybe that's why my mother was so upset that night. I felt I needed to make things happier and better for her, so she wouldn't be angry and wouldn't cry.

I really believed I could make my mom happy by cleaning the floor. Using a tippy kitchen chair, I crawled up onto the kitchen countertop with a bottle of clear floor wax. Remember, I was six years old, and I was crawling up onto a counter that was a little higher than I was when I stood ground level. My legs were crossed, and I sat on the counter pouring wax down on the floor while giving directions to my younger brothers. Trace wore his brown and white cowboy pajamas. Garrett was in a diaper and white t-shirt. They were both sloshing floor wax around with a wax applicator.

The wooden-handled stick was taller than they were. Two little boys, four and five years old, spreading wax across the linoleum floor in no particular direction.

Imagine the pools of wax puddled up over red, beige, cream, and gray square tiles. I'm sure there were sections of the floor we'd missed altogether. I suppose we were trying to emulate what we had seen my mom do when she washed and waxed the linoleum floor. She wore a dress and heels when she cleaned, but I don't remember her ever sitting cross legged on the countertop pouring wax.

Can you imagine an uncoordinated six-year-old pouring and splashing liquid wax on the floor from above? I am sure that wax dripped all over the cabinets and white appliances as well.

Can you envision the wax drying where it fell?

We didn't want our mom to cry. We wanted to make her happy, even though it was a school night, and we should've been in bed. We were trying to help.

I was still sitting on the counter wearing a white cotton full slip, waiting for the wax to dry, when Mom came out of her bedroom. She was calm, she smiled at us, then began to thank us and praise us for what we had done. I am thinking we probably made more work for her. We didn't sweep or wash the floor; we only waxed it.

MY SISTERS

My dad's eyes would light up when my sister, Josie, walked into a room. She was taller than me, slender, and she had long light blonde hair. His eyes would light up for my youngest sister, Rita, too. Rita had short strawberry blonde hair that curled up and hugged her face. She had a cute mischievous innocence about her.

I never saw my dad look at me the way he looked at my sisters.

His face didn't soften when he looked at me. He didn't have that same sparkle in his eyes he had for my sisters.

Every year in October, there was a German festival in the Downriver area of Detroit. One year, I met my parents and some of my dad's cousins at a table they had reserved for the family. I walked toward the table, and I said hello to everyone. I could see that they were all laughing and conversing with each other. Some of them were playing a card game together. This was a happy occasion.

I sat down, but I felt like I was an observer while their conversations with each other continued around me. Even though this was my family, I didn't feel like I fit in. I was just there. I was a stranger taking up an extra seat at the table, listening to them talk about their lives.

Later, Josie arrived, and as soon as she entered the building, I watched my dad's eyes follow her across the room to our table, where everyone stopped talking and greeted her with a warm, "Hello."

The conversations seemed to subside when Josie approached. How my dad's eyes lit up for my sister and how his face relaxed told me and the world that this was his little girl. She was beautiful.

I wish my dad had known that I was watching; I was waiting for him to accept my worth as his daughter. I wanted him to look at me with admiration and love in his eyes too, but he never did. This hurt.

I had been told by my mother, a long time ago, that Josie reminded my dad of his Grandma Josephine, whom he loved dearly. My mother didn't tell me why. As usual, I didn't ask.

THE MEMORY BOX

I have a small cedar box that my dad gave my mother for Christmas when I was four. My parents were renting an old farmhouse in northern Michigan at the time.

The box was filled with chocolate candy. The confection is what caught my attention and secured the memory of the box for me all these years later.

After I was married, my dad brought the box to my house. He came over alone that day. He knocked on my door, handed it to me then left. Normally my parents visited together. I'm still unsure why he gave it to me since it was my mother's. I think it was hers to give away and not my dad's. I am also thinking my mother probably told him she didn't want it. Maybe, she'd said it during an argument they'd had, and that's why he gave it to me. It was unusual for my dad to give me anything. I believe my mom knew about it or she would have said something to get it back. I didn't ask her why I had her box. She never mentioned it either.

Of the many keepsakes that I have in this box, one is an old birthday card my dad wrote. I was fifteen. My dad mailed the card to me one year when he and my mother were separated and our family was not together. We were staying in Northern Michigan with Grandma Gina. Dad was staying in our family home, or sometimes he'd go to his mom's, who lived in the Detroit metropolitan area, and he would stay with her.

My mother never filed for divorce, but she'd threaten Dad and talk about filing. Throughout the separation, we only saw my dad when he came up north to take us all back to Detroit; that's how I knew their break was over.

Every once in a while, I go back to the box, pull out the card, and read it. It is the only card/letter my dad ever sent me. He wrote nice things.

For Daughter, On Her Birthday.

Dear Judy,

I received your nice letter Saturday. Grandma is fine and talks about you a lot.

I'm glad you are all well and happy. I'm fine, just a little lonesome, but we will all have to make the best of it.

Well happy birthday Judy and write to me.

With Love to you all, Dad

I wrote back to my dad once more. My parent's separations usually lasted three months before they would get back together again. This particular time they were apart for two months.

PANIC ATTACK

When I was married and in my early twenties, I got two tickets to be in the audience of a popular local morning talk show in

Detroit. I wore what I thought was a simple but pretty off-white cowl neck sweater and a nice pair of jeans. I invited my sister, Josie, to go with me.

I was so excited to be in a live studio audience. I could barely contain myself. I was happy until I saw the cameras.

What was I thinking of, getting tickets to this show with the horrible chance of being seen on live television?

The staff directed us to our seats. My sister and I ended up sitting close to the front near the stage. I realized that I would be on camera.

My body clenched tight. I started breathing fast because it felt like I couldn't get enough air. I was hyperventilating. I was having a panic attack.

Throughout my life, it was something I did when I felt nervous or when I felt anxious. I didn't know it was an actual condition or that there was a medical term to describe what I was doing.

The cameras panned the audience that day. My mother, who was home watching the show, saw my sister and me, as did thousands of other viewers.

When I took my sister home and went inside to say hello to my mother, she looked at my sister and said, "Josie, you looked so nice." I was standing next to Josie. Our shoulders were practically touching when my mom paid my sister this nice compliment. Nothing was said to me.

All those familiar feelings I had come to know throughout my life washed over me—ugly, gross, no good, the recognizable emotions of self-hatred.

I went home and cried because I really hated myself. No matter how hard I tried, I felt I couldn't measure up. My parents didn't like me.

MY MOTHER'S PAIN

As I grew older, I noticed that whenever my mom got upset, especially with my dad, she would pull out food and eat. She would invite all of us kids around the table to eat with her, and we'd listen to her cry and talk about things that hurt her. Her stories were incredibly sad for us to hear because we wanted our mother to be happy. At times, I have been guilty of eating when upset, too, although I never invited my sons. My anger-eating was done in private.

Grandma Gina taught elementary school and Grandpa worked for the county road commission. Grandpa also raised, sold, and sometimes trained thoroughbred horses for racing.

My grandparents came from a generation of properness. There were set standards especially in the 1930's, '40s, and '50's when my mother was raised. Proper attire and proper etiquette were essential, specifically for young women. In the summer, my grandparents traveled to various farms and racing events throughout the United States. They took my mom's brothers with them, but my mother stayed with an aunt she'd considered to be her second mom and someone she loved dearly. My grandparents felt racing events were no place for a young lady. My mom didn't like that she couldn't go along with her family, and she cried about that.

It bothered her that my dad's parents didn't attend my parent's wedding. She'd complain because Dad wasn't giving her enough attention, or sometimes she would tell us that life and marriage were a "big fat lie."

One time my mother packed our green Ford Econoline van with all her clothes and personal items. The van could be converted for camping, so we had a table set up. Next to the table was a bench, but if needed the table could be made into a bed.

My dad, me, and my siblings were all home feeling bad because my mom was so angry. We watched her take her personal things out to the van, come back inside for another load while yelling or talking loud enough for the neighbors to hear.

It was summer. The van was parked on the street in front of our home that day. Mom sat inside the van alone, writing her thoughts out all over the white Formica tabletop with a short yellow unsharpened pencil. When she got through, the table was covered in what looked like a graffiti wall of descriptive writing but without color. Hand-drawn pictures, squiggles, and alphabet letters were either printed or handwritten in small and large characters. The entire top of the table was covered with my mother's feelings.

An hour or two later she came back inside the house. She was calm, and she didn't yell. That's when my dad sweetly asked us kids to help her bring her things in from the van. It was late afternoon, neighbors were outside, cars were passing by, and we were carrying armfuls of my mother's things back inside the house while she sat in the camper, erasing most of what she'd written on the table. I had a strong feeling she didn't want us to see her expressive creativity that day.

SOMETHING I SAW

In the frigid winter months, two of my brothers and I slept in a double bed downstairs in the dining room because it was warmer than our upstairs bedrooms. There were no doors in this open space. The room was once a bedroom, but the original owners converted it by taking out two walls so that on one side of the room, I could see the front entrance door, and on the other side, I could see the hallway and into the bathroom.

The room was dark except for a light shining in from the bathroom. I had been sleeping, but I woke up to my parents arguing again. My dad's angry voice boomed over my mother's cries.

I remember carefully crawling out from under the covers, trying hard not to crush either brother with my weight. I was careful not to kick them while I tried to move across the bed quietly. I didn't want to wake them up. I was protecting them.

I maneuvered my body toward the foot of the bed, then extended my neck just a little so I could see what was happening.

The bathroom door was wide open. My mother was kneeling on the floor; her body pressed tight against the porcelain bathtub while she cradled her head in her folded arms. She wore only her panties. My dad stood over her. He was whipping her bare back with a wet towel.

The bathtub faucet was running. After hitting my mom with the towel, he would unfold it, place the towel under the water, wring it out, and then hit my mom with it again.

I was seven, too young to see this, too young to hear the crazy goings-on, and too young to understand. I was upset, but my concern was more for my younger brothers, Trace and Garrett. I didn't want them to be afraid or witness what I was seeing. In my mind I was the one that would keep them safe.

My parents' actions terrified me, but I never told them I saw what went on that night. My brothers didn't say anything either, so maybe they slept through the beating.

Even as adults, my brothers and I have not talked about this.

I am starting to realize that a lot of crazy things that happened through the years were not talked about. It's like these incidents never occurred, but I know they most certainly had.

SING ALONG

One night we had company. All the adults and a few of us children were standing around my mother, who sat on a wooden piano stool with glass ball feet. She was playing the piano in the dining room, my winter bedroom.

The piano, an old mahogany upright from the early 1900s, had a wonderful sound. At least, that is what my mother always said about it. Anyway, I was ecstatic that night. I always liked having guests over because my parents seemed happier then. I liked the snacks, desserts, and pop we had for refreshment too.

We were all singing, and the adults seemed to be enjoying themselves. I sensed excitement in the air. I felt important. I was part of something, and we were all having fun together. At least, I thought we were.

At one point, I laughed at a comment my uncle had made. I didn't understand what he meant, but because my parents laughed, I laughed, too. Joining in on the adults' conversation and laughter made me feel important; I felt grown up.

While we sang, I'm quite sure I made up my own words to the songs because I didn't know all the lyrics to the music my mom was playing, but I was having so much fun singing along that to me, it didn't matter, until my mom suddenly stopped playing the piano. She zeroed in on me, and in front of everyone said, "Judy, you're singing too loud. No one else can hear." The room immediately got quiet. No one said a word. My mom reprimanded me in front of everyone. I was so ashamed of myself. I felt selfish, and at the moment, I hated my voice. Then mom looked away from me. Her eyes focused on the crowd standing all around in the room. She smiled at them, resumed playing the piano and began to sing. I remained quiet, listening, while I watched everyone else in the room have fun.

What I was starting to learn was that my feelings didn't matter and that my feelings pretty much had never mattered. I couldn't express how I felt because my parents would say, "Children should be seen and not heard." Or "Quit feeling sorry for yourself," and another phrase they would say, "I'll give you something to cry about."

I used to think I was too critical of my parents because maybe the parenting techniques they used were all they knew, right or wrong. Actually, they didn't have parenting skills; their punishments were usually impulsive. There were no boundaries, and many lines were crossed.

I wondered at times if it was the way they had been raised. I didn't know then, but I know now, abuse and allowing abuse messes people up, especially children. And if allowed to go on, it will mess up not only their children but generations afterward. There is no excuse for it.

BREAKFAST, AND VITAMINS

I hated oatmeal and any soft cereal or food. The consistency made me feel sick, and if I thought too much about it, I'd start to gag. One morning my mom made cream of wheat for breakfast.

"Eat it, Judy." My dad's tone was harsh.

"I can't. It makes me sick." The smell made me feel queasy.

"I said eat it!" he demanded. Meanwhile, I watched my dad pull the end of his belt buckle out from the loops of his work pants. When my dad did this, we all knew he meant business. I knew I was in trouble, so I hurried to take a bite of the cereal and swallowed, but I immediately threw it up into my bowl and onto the table.

My dad was sitting next to me, so I know he got splashed, too. I started to cry. He didn't move or say anything for what seemed like a long time, but it was probably only a few seconds. I think he was in shock. "Go get yourself cleaned up," he said.

I remember doing exactly what my dad told me to do. I was afraid to speak so I got up from the table. I left the room feeling relieved because I wasn't spanked for not eating my cereal.

Years later, when I was eleven, my friends invited me to the store. They were each going to buy a jar of baby food—sweet baby food like apples or bananas.

Aware that any soft food—cereal or fruit—made me nauseous, I bought a jar anyway because I wanted to fit in with the girls.

When we got back to my friend's house, I took a small bite, then felt nauseous. I'm pretty sure I was able to hide my gag reflex, but

I didn't take another bite.

I have been to different therapists throughout my adult life and was told by two individual counselors that they were reasonably sure I had been sexually abused at a young age for me to be unable to eat soft food. I don't know for sure because if it did happen, I can't remember, and I honestly have no idea who would have violated me that way.

I couldn't swallow pills either. My mom gave us chewable vitamins for a while, but then she started giving us the vitamins you swallow whole.

Every night before bed, my mom gave us a multivitamin with iron. I couldn't swallow it, but I would savor it in my mouth because the outer coating tasted good. After the coating was gone, I would spit it out.

One night I think my dad had had enough of it, making me chew it. I can still remember that bitter iron taste.

BITTER BERRIES

I remember visiting my grandparents' house late one July afternoon. They had a chokecherry tree growing in their yard. The berries were red; they looked pretty and appetizing to me. I was seven.

My Grandpa Randall noticed my enticement with them. He told me to go ahead and eat the berries. I did. I trusted him. After all, he was my grandpa. Grandparents are supposed to love and look out for their grandchildren, right?

When I tasted the pretty berries, I began to spit. The harsh, nasty, vehement flavor was glued to my tongue. I started to cry. I was spitting and blubbering, all at the same time. I couldn't get the horrible bitter taste out of my mouth. When I looked toward another shaded tree where my grandpa was standing, I saw that he was watching. . . and laughing at me.

BAD & UGLY

There were very few cartoons I was allowed to watch as a child. As always, the good guys and the bad guys were portrayed in the programs. I wanted to identify with the beautiful fairy princess. I did not want to identify with the wicked witch.

One Halloween, also when I was seven, my parents told me I couldn't go out trick-or-treating. They told me I was getting too old for that activity. They said they would put a witch hat on me and let me pass out apples to the trick-or-treaters that came to our house. Their joke persisted, and I protested until I cried. For one thing, in past years that I had gone trick-or-treating, I wouldn't eat the apples that were handed out to me, so why would I want to hand out apples to the other kids?

I did end up going trick-or-treating with my friends that year, but my parents' suggestion of me dressing up like a witch and handing out apples reinforced my feelings of being bad and ugly even more.

CAMERAS & MIRRORS

After I was born, my dad took quite a few pictures of me, more so than any of my siblings, probably because I was the firstborn. This made me feel bad for my brothers and sisters, especially when we went through old photos together. I wanted my siblings to have just as many pictures of them as there were of me. I could see the disappointment on their faces the nights my parents got the slide projector out. We waited until after dark for my dad to set everything up. All of us were excited for the show to start. We'd pop popcorn in a large stainless-steel pot over the stove and make Kool-Aid, then turn the lights off, and my dad would flick the projector on. A temporary blindness fell over us because of the bright light that was cast from the projector bulb, but that only lasted until my dad inserted the slides.

We looked at slides portraying my dad's tour in the Korean War and pictures of my mother holding babies after their births. Pictures of us at the lake, splashing in the water with my mom, and photos of us on camping trips. After each slide a sibling would ask, "Who is that?"

"Judy." my mom would say. Another slide would go in.

"Who is that?" one of the kids would ask.

"Judy." My mom answered.

It made me feel like my siblings weren't loved like I was, as if love for us depended on how many baby pictures there were.

My dad took photos of me when I was about to graduate high school. Then one day not long after that, I overheard my mom say to him that he knew when he took the pictures, he did not have film in his camera. At the time, the way I felt about myself, you'd

50

think I would have felt relief at this revelation, but I didn't. I don't know if what my mother said was true that day, but I heard her, and her words stung.

I've always hated having my picture taken. I especially hated school picture day.

On those days I didn't want to smile for the camera because I had too many imperfections. My flaws were not only physical, but they were mental ideas I had about myself stuck somewhere inside my head. I had wooden teeth, my shoes were dirty, and I was spanked in front of our neighbors. I was the squeaky wheel. I was passive aggressive. I was too shy, too sensitive, and I sang too loud, to name a few.

While growing up I was afraid to look in the mirror because I hated who I saw looking back. What I looked like made me cringe, and at times it was horrifying for me.

Sometimes, I flip through old photographs of myself as a little girl. Today, I picked out one of me when I was seven—as usual, with a home permanent, but this perm was starting to grow out.

This picture is the one where my top two front teeth are sticking out of my mouth because I thought it would make me look prettier than my plain ordinary smile.

I didn't know how to smile correctly. Every year, before school picture day, I'd get all worked up and obsess on how I should smile or pose. But in the back of my mind, I figured that even if I did get my smile right, the picture probably wouldn't be good enough anyway.

I felt I didn't look pretty like the other little girls with their naturally flowing hair, clean shoes, and beautiful smiles. I felt there was something that always seemed to be wrong with me. I didn't fit in.

The eyes in the picture I'm holding are looking back at me, haunting me, because they are so incredibly sad. I not only know this child, but I can still feel her heartache.

Back then, this little one was trying to do everything right. She was posing for the camera, so innocent, so unaware of her future and the unknown tragedies ahead, let alone the trauma and dysfunction she had already been through.

As I continue to study the picture, I stare into my own eyes once again. I wish I could remember what I was thinking about the very moment I said, "Cheese," when the photographer's bulb flashed and his camera clicked, but I can't.

Several years ago, I was having a difficult day. I'd been crying, but along with self-judgment and negative critique from me, my worst enemy, I looked into the mirror anyway, very much afraid of what I would see. Whatever it was going on inside my head that day, I just remember I didn't want to see it.

For a few seconds, I stared into my own eyes looking back at me. That's when a calm ensued before I saw the pretty green eyes God has blessed me with—the eyes that have caught the attention of strangers ever since I was a little girl.

While I continued to stand staring into the mirror, I searched for that little girl, the one with the wooden teeth and over-processed perm. The one wearing the scuffed-up brown boy shoes and repeating numbers and prayers over and over inside her head.

My eyes were welling up with tears. I was in the present again. Then just for a moment, I'd found her, and she was looking back at me. In that exact instant, I said with so much love and empathy, "I love you, Judy. I love you."

I still loathe photos of myself and looking in the mirror remains uncomfortable for me. At times, I find myself still trying to avoid both the camera and the mirror. But I'm working on that.

So much had changed in those years between having a lot of baby photos to having almost no pictures taken. But then maybe nothing had changed at all. Maybe my parents had always been who they were, and it just took me a really long time to figure it out.

LITTLE BOY'S SHOES

Kathy, a girl in my third-grade class, wore pretty dresses to school. This was a time when little girls were not allowed to wear pants or jeans. The rules were that girls wore dresses, and boys wore nice slacks. Kathy also wore cute, black patent leather baby doll shoes. But me, I wore boys' brown leather shoes.

When I asked my parents if I could have shoes like my friends had in school, they'd say, "Your shoes last longer because they are made better, and they're cheaper." Some of my friends got their shoes from E.J. Korvette, a department store located near where we lived and in an area known to be a nice middle-class suburb of Detroit, Michigan.

I hadn't noticed that I was wearing boys' shoes until I went to school. The girls in my class wore black-and-white saddle shoes or baby dolls like Kathy. Eventually, my parents bought me saddle shoes, which I never seemed to keep clean.

Times were hard for my parents, and money was always tight for them. After all, they had six kids. My dad's side of the family often reminded me of this as more of a slam than a nice comment.

When we needed a new pair of shoes, my parents would take us to a little store called The Shoe Fair, located near Detroit's downtown area. There were steel bars covering the store's windows and front entrance. The buildings along the heavily populated street were squeezed in tight. Traffic buzzed by, horns honked, and people walked busily in and out of neighboring storefronts. The scent of buttered popcorn and roasting nuts fanned from another building nearby. The delicious smells hovered over me, reminding me of the Sears and Roebuck store in Lincoln Park. Sears was where my dad bought his Craftsman tools, and my mom bought clothing and housewares. I don't ever remember getting to sample the snacks. We knew better than to ask. The answer would be, "No."

Seeing bars on windows and doors made me afraid to go downtown, but my parents said the shoes were cheaper there, and that's why we went.

Even if the soles of our shoes had holes—and I am talking literal holes—or my shoes wore out before my brothers and sisters' shoes, we waited until we all needed them. In other words, we all got shoes at the same time.

2X10

It was Parents' Day in fourth grade. Mr. Knox, our teacher, was a short, stout man with strands of thinning, red hair on top that he combed over to cover his mostly bald head. Our teacher had a temper, which my classmates and I had witnessed on occasion. When his face grew bright red, we knew he was angry.

One time he lifted a chair high up over his head with a boy, one of our classmates, still sitting on it. The boy had been acting up, and I believe even he was surprised to find his feet touching the ground one minute and his body flying through the air the next. Our teacher held the chair with his right hand, gripping one out of four chair legs. The room became silent, and our eyes grew wide while we watched our teacher fly the boy out into the hallway. It really was an amazing and scary feat for fourth graders to see.

Our classroom was filled with not only my classmates, but our parents, who sat together in the back of the room on brown, metal folding chairs.

After Mr. Knox introduced himself to the parents, he asked our class to illustrate another way to show two times ten equals twenty.

I was eager, and I was the first to raise my hand. Mr. Knox smiled and asked me to come to the chalkboard so that I could demonstrate my example in front of everyone. I grinned. I was delighted and determined to make my mom and dad proud.

After crossing the room in front of everyone to get to the chalkboard, I froze.

"I can't remember the question," I said sheepishly to my teacher. Mr. Knox smiled. His face turned slightly red.

Mr. Knox reiterated the question, and I proceeded to draw an example of two times ten equals twenty with a small piece of white chalk. I did so by writing twenty single number ones across the board. I could hear muffled laughter from where the parents sat. It was at that moment that I became aware of my mistake.

I felt so dumb. I tried hard, but I couldn't seem to do anything right.

When I finished my example and turned around to head back to my seat, I looked over at my parents. The color on their faces appeared red like Mr. Knox's. They seemed to be masking their laughter, so I avoided looking into their eyes before I slumped down into my chair.

AGE NINE

When I was nine, I was asked to be a flower girl for Pam, a neighbor girl that was also our babysitter. I wouldn't say I liked the dress that Pam had picked out for me to wear because it was scratchy and hurt my skin. It was pretty, but the white dress was starched stiff and seemed a size too small. But I think what felt worse to me was the home perm my mother gave me before the wedding.

Tight, stinky curls glued to my head. I did not look at all like my classmates and neighborhood friends. Their hair was long and straight. Sometimes their moms would set their hair with pink curlers we called Spoolies so that their hair was wavy for a day but not curly and frizzy for months at a time, like mine was.

I felt ugly. I was itchy, uncomfortable, and angry. My little neighborhood friends who were invited to the wedding wore pretty dresses. Their hair was flowing naturally. It wasn't stuck to their heads or matted down with hairspray like mine was.

I was an outcast even then. I never fit in. Every time I was invited to go with one of my friends shopping on a warm summer day, my mom made me wear my party dress, while my friends wore comfortable shorts, sleeveless blouses, and canvas shoes. I still remember how often I felt out of place. I sensed my friend's pity for me, too.

A good part of my childhood fashion statement was frizzy permanents and fancy party dresses. I think that is why I prefer wearing jeans and comfortable clothing versus wearing dresses now as an adult. I was so unlike my mom, who seemed to dress up for every occasion.

My parents stayed late at the wedding reception that night. They should have taken my siblings and me home because it was well past our bedtime. I wish they would have been adult enough to leave a little early and put us to bed. I was overtired.

I suppose their reasoning for why they didn't take us home was that they couldn't find another babysitter since Pam always took care of us.

My dad didn't sit with us at the reception, but I saw him standing at the bar. He liked to drink, although I can't remember whether he was drunk or not that night because I was only thinking about myself—comparing myself to my neighborhood girlfriends, their dresses, and their hair. I was concentrating on how uncomfortable I felt and how different I looked.

So as any normal nine-year-old up past her bedtime would do, I got pouty and sassy, then started to cry. My mom spanked me in front of everyone at the reception.

My mother was good at making scenes in front of other people. I believe she liked the attention. I would not come to recognize her pattern until later in my life.

Example: One time, one of my siblings brought home a note from school stating that there was a case of head lice in their classroom. My mom went outside and began talking to neighbors, telling them we had head lice. We did not have head lice. Why would she say that?

Anyway, on the night of the wedding reception, my mother really could have taken me outside away from the crowd, away from onlookers. She could have dealt with my poor attitude any way but that way, but no, she had to do her nasty deed in front of everyone, right in the middle of the music and festivities.

The scene turned into a sideshow at Pam's wedding. Not only was I embarrassed that my mom was hitting me through the profuse white, over-starched ensemble, but I was humiliated. I can only imagine what it must have looked like to everyone else. I did notice that people had stopped dancing to watch us. I felt conspicuous and even uglier than I had before. I had been spanked by an overreacting parent.

I learned later from several of my mother's close relatives that she was never spanked growing up because her parents did not believe in the concept of spanking and that she had been raised by the book—whatever book that may have been. I never asked.

The following day, while playing outside, I waved and smiled at two little girlfriends walking past my house. I cringed at the memory of the night before while my stinky permanent was wafting in the breeze. My friends were holding hands and eating ice cream. I was oblivious to them, so I bristled. I stood tall. I pulled my shoulders back and pretended that the embarrassing fiasco from the night before had never happened.

But was it pretending, or was it some kind of disconnection? It's been difficult for me to be in the moment my entire life anyway. My mind was always on something other than what I was supposed to be doing at the time.

For instance, if I were at the beach, I couldn't fully enjoy the sunshine or the calm that the sound of the rushing water brought to me. Instead of being in that particular moment in time, I was thinking of other things. I was mostly worrying—about the future, about someone I loved getting injured or dying. It's almost like I expected the scary scenarios being played out inside my head to actually occur because, from my personal life experiences, that's exactly what happened. People got hurt, they got sick, they were abused, and they died.

RIDLEY'S STORE

One day my mom took us to an old country store while visiting my Grandma Gina and my grandpa in Northern Michigan. The store was a two-story clapboard barn-shaped building in a small village, not even a mile from where my grandparents lived. A large painted sign hung over the door. *RIDLEY'S STORE* and advertising such as "Salada Tea is Sold Here," was hand painted white on the window.

The wooden screen door was rickety. When we opened the door, bells jingled upon our entry, then again when the door slammed behind us.

To my right was a long wooden counter that held the cash register. Behind that was a high wall of wooden shelves filled with canned goods. On the left side of the store was the cooler. I always looked forward to going to Ridley's because of the ice-cold pop we got out of the vintage red-and-white Coca-Cola chest. Inside, there were so many flavors of pop to choose from. Orange, red, and grape, to name a few. The cooler was nostalgic, like nothing I had experienced at home in the city, and the entire store smelled like big chunks of pink bubble gum to me.

The Ridley family had owned the store since 1939. Mrs. Ridley, the daughter-in-law of the original owners, greeted us with a smile. She was short, her face plump, and she wore a dab of orange lipstick that complimented a brown tee shirt she wore under a long white apron. She was about ten years older than my mother and she'd known my mom since she was a young girl.

While I was busy deciding pop flavors and browsing the candy counter, I heard her speak to my mom. "Judy has broad shoulders." That's all she said. My mother didn't reply. There was only a lull of quiet. Then Mrs. Ridley continued. "She's cute, but she will never be a model." My mother remained silent.

I was listening. I heard what Mrs. Ridley said about me while I pretended to look at merchandise in the store. At the time, I dreamed of being a nurse, not a model, but still. There were several minutes of awkward silence before we cashed out and left to return to my grandparents' house.

I rehashed the woman's words over in my head quietly while my mom drove. *Judy has broad shoulders. She will never be a model.* Why would the woman say this to my mom, and why would she say it so I could hear her? My mother and I never talked about this incident.

LODGING & HUNTING TRIP

One of the times my dad went out drinking, he didn't come home until the following day. My mom painted big black letters—LODG-ING—on a piece of corrugated cardboard and placed it on the inside of our front living room window, a window that faced the street.

Outside, she stood in front of the sign. Then she looked into the viewfinder, aimed, and hit the shutter of my dad's German Leica 35-millimeter camera. She took a picture of her sign as if it were a trophy of some kind for her to memorialize later.

I heard the neighbor ladies' hums of gossip and laughter that day while they stood around my mother, talking with her, and while they watched the comical drama unfold.

I think this was my mom's way of telling my dad that if he went out drinking and didn't come home again, she would rent out rooms, even though there were no extra rooms in our home.

My dad didn't seem to be bothered by the sign. There were other nights that he went out and didn't return home until the following day, but I didn't see another lodging sign.

Every November, my dad would go deer hunting with his cousin and uncles in northern Michigan. The hunting camp was a good five hours away from home. One year in the late 1960s, my dad's cousin Bart, a married man with five children of his own, for some reason, wasn't able to go.

A day or so after my dad had left for this trip, I got the feeling that my mother wanted him home because she called a family member that lived close to the hunting camp. The camp was a long way back off the main road, and it was deep in the woods. She asked our relatives if they would go to the camp and tell my dad to call home. There were no cell phones then.

Several hours later, my dad called collect from a pay phone. I heard my mother say, "Bart just called. He said he's bringing dinner over tonight." Bart didn't bring dinner, and my dad was home later that night.

THE KIDS

One of my uncles once told me he couldn't believe how I called my siblings "the kids," or how I had taken on so much responsibility for a child under the age of nine. I remember smiling at him. I took his words as a compliment. There was no conversation between us other than his comment.

Looking back, I like to think that I was an old soul in a child's body. I honestly didn't understand what my uncle meant until later in my life: the responsibility I took on at such an early age was unusual behavior for a nine-year-old.

My youngest sister Rita, who is thirteen years younger than I am, told me she didn't remember my mother until she was five, and before that, she only remembers me. The year Rita turned five was my first year away at college.

Responsibility for my younger siblings, "the kids," was what I did. I loved them, and I felt they needed someone to protect them. What I did not realize back then was that I needed to be loved and protected, too.

I was only a child, but I felt there were no other options than to look out for my brothers and sisters. I was like a mama bird, lifting her wings and wrapping them around her baby birds, covering them with her feathers during the storm.

My parents were not doing the best of jobs—at least not in my opinion. I respected my parents and loved them—because of their honored position as parents—but inside my head, I sometimes questioned their behavior.

JOHN MIGHT DIE

I woke up in the middle of the night to hear a loud discussion between my parents, who were awake in their bedroom. Their room was across the hall from mine. I was eleven.

I could see the lights in their room, but their door was closed and locked. My five-year-old brother John was with them. He'd been sick for a few days, and his body was trying to fight a fever.

I knocked on the door.

My parents were arguing over whether or not they should take him to the hospital. That's how sick he was.

I lost it when I heard my mom tell my dad that my brother might die. I knocked even harder on their door, pleading with them, "Please take him to the hospital." There was urgency in my voice.

My parents had tried giving my brother something for his elevated temperature earlier, and they put him in cool bath water, but his fever wasn't letting up.

They ignored me. I was still standing outside their door in the dim light of the hallway. I continued listening to their conversation while still begging them to take my brother to the hospital.

"John might die. I think we should go to the hospital." My mom sounded breathy and anxious. There was fear in her voice.

"No, he'll be alright," Dad said. He spoke with confidence.

"I can't get his temperature to come down. He's burning up." Mom sounded panicky.

"No, the doctors aren't going to do any more for him than we are." My dad's voice remained convincing but calm, while my mother's voice was filled with uncertainty.

"Besides, we can't afford it. He'll be alright," my dad insisted.

"But what if he dies?" My mother pleaded.

"He's not going to die."

"Please, please take John to the hospital!" I shouted.

My voice was as loud or louder than my parent's while my fists banged against their door. I was still shouting from the other side, experiencing my own bout of anxiety. Panic was taking control of me.

I was terrified that my brother was going to die. But my parents didn't take him to the ER that night. They didn't acknowledge my feelings, and they didn't try to calm my fears either.

Thankfully, John's fever broke the following morning.

OCD

I remember starting fights with kids on the playground. There were some I'd never met before, and they had all been nice to me. As a kid, I was angry and ready to fight. As an adult, I think how strange for a child to want to pick a fight with children she didn't know. This picture is so wrong.

What would make a little girl so angry at the world? Children are inquisitive and friendly at first meeting. They naturally want to be nice to each other and make friends. So, what was my problem? I believe it was the frustration I felt, an internal knowing some behaviors were not quite right in our home. My dad's drinking, at times, my mother's rage, and my parents' physical fights. The stress of mothering and feeling responsible for my siblings may have triggered bouts of OCD. I think choosing to argue with other children was a way for me to release the pent-up anger raging inside of me. I didn't understand my feelings or express them to my parents. When I tried, I was told to quit feeling sorry for myself, among other things.

I learned to scream quietly, to hold back my tears, and to keep the bad thoughts about myself inside my head. I tried hard to live in each day and to focus, but it was challenging for me. I had a tough time concentrating on the tasks at hand. My attention span was short because I was always fighting the thoughts in my brain that kept interrupting. I was afraid of everything, and I seemed to worry about everyone more than myself.

When I was a little girl, I washed my hands a lot, and it took me forever to walk up the flight of stairs that led to my bedroom on the second floor of our home, and it took me forever to go back down the stairs again. My ritual went something like this: I counted one, two, three on my way up the stairs, then went back down two steps, one, two. Then I started back up the steps all over again, only this time it was one, two, three, four, while praying, counting, and repeating the entire process again.

I counted numbers, or I prayed the same words inside my head over and over. If I concentrated on counting or praying, my mind was on numbers and prayers—not on all the crazy thoughts that came at me all at once. I believed that if I didn't do this ritual, something terrible would happen.

I can see myself now in my brown jumper, red pilling tights, and dirty black-and-white saddle shoes climbing up the stairs, going backward and forward, counting over and over.

I laugh at the visual of me now, but really it was sad and exhausting, especially for a child.

The only OCD tendency I might have now is when I become overly stressed. The last time this happened was after my son's death. I walked around the house checking doors, making sure they were all locked. I was checking, repeating, and making myself more stressed. Even after I stopped, I had to fight off the urge to continue this behavior.

MITCH MILLER

I received a *Sing Along with Mitch* record album when I asked for a Monkees album for Christmas the year I was twelve. My parents usually got me what I needed: hats, coats, shoes, and clothing. They picked things out for me to wear. I didn't have very much to say about what I wore until I made my own money, either working part-time at the Ben Franklin Store when I was fourteen or babysitting. I felt ashamed asking for things I wanted. Even when I did ask, I wouldn't get what I asked for anyway. The underlying message in my head was "there isn't enough money." My mom would say, "There are five other children in this house besides you, Judy. I'm doing the best I can." That made me feel guilty, and ashamed of myself to ask for anything.

Mitch Miller was my parents' generation's style of music. The Beatles, The Monkees, along with other late 1960s and early 1970s music, was what was popular for me and my siblings' generation at the time. It wasn't Mitch Miller.

I still have the album. I don't know why I have kept it for so long. I guess, in a way, it is kind of symbolic—an example of accepting less for myself than I ever had to. Now, I think it may be time for me to throw it out. I felt uncomfortable playing the music on the record player, but I did it to please my parents. I didn't want their feelings to be hurt because I didn't like my gift. When I hold the album in my hands, I can still remember how disappointed I felt after excitedly tearing the red and green Christmas paper off my package. My sister Josie had asked for an album that same Christmas too. I can't remember who the artist was, but it was the one she'd asked for.

GO-GO BOOTS

Another Christmas, I asked for go-go boots like my friends at school wore. Go-go boots—a trendy fashion that year—were white, low-heeled, and came up mid-calf or higher in height. I did not get them that Christmas. In fact, I didn't get them until they were well out of style, and on sale.

I laugh while writing this. I seemed to be the only one in junior high school wearing go-go boots the year past the trend, but I liked them so much that the snickers and gossip about how out of style I was, not to mention how poor my family was, didn't matter to me. I bristled.

My family was criticized and laughed at many times before. One time a neighbor lady sent her husband to the store for groceries. When he returned, she was angry at him because he didn't get the right brands. She yelled, "Give the Randalls your groceries!"

SHELBY'S CLOTHES

When I was in the fifth grade, I had a pretty pair of aqua blue stretch pants and a white blouse that I repeatedly wore to school. I didn't have many clothes—none of the Randall kids did—but what we did wear, for the most part, was clean and looked nice.

My mother's cousin Shelby, who was in her twenties then, gave my mom clothing she no longer wanted—clothes intended for a twenty-year-old and not an eleven-year-old child. My mom gave the clothes to me anyway. There were pastel jackets with matching skirts and a full sleeveless dress with pleats. The flowery blouses were busty and darted. I didn't have breasts. There was a gray pillbox hat and a forest green hat with netting and a feather. This hat looked like Robin Hood's.

I didn't like the clothes because they weren't like what the other girls my age in school wore, but it was something different than my stretch pants.

I wore a tight beige pencil skirt to school one day. It was so tight around my legs that I could barely walk. The skirt was wide at my hips but was still snug, and the material gradually narrowed to below my knees. I tried to keep up with my neighborhood friends on the way to school that morning, but when they started to run, I fell.

"Hey, wait up." I called out to them. They might've looked back to see where I was, but they didn't slow down; they kept running. Although they didn't say anything to me, I'm sure they all found it amusing like I do now.

I laugh, thinking about what it must have looked like. I never wore that skirt again, and come to think of it, I never wore another pencil skirt either.

SQUEAKY WHEEL

Sometimes before school, I would stay in bed a little longer, listening to my mother's high-heeled shoes click over the multi-colored linoleum floor in the kitchen. My mother typically wore dresses and high heels for everything—not only for teaching but at leisure, too. As I have mentioned, I rarely ever saw her wear a pair of jeans or pants.

My mom was frying eggs for my dad's breakfast and making coffee before he left for work. For the most part, my parents seemed cheerful, talking and laughing with each other in the mornings. They were morning people. By dinner time, their moods seemed more subdued. They were quieter, not so talkative.

My mom talked to my dad about a hundred different things all at once, while he slurped his coffee and replied.

The minute my dad left the house, the cheerfulness in my mother's voice went out of the door with him. She seemed angry, and instead of eggs, she made oatmeal for us.

"Why can't we have eggs? Why do we have to have oatmeal every day?" I asked her. Oatmeal made me feel sick, so I wouldn't eat.

"The squeaky wheel gets the grease, doesn't it, Judy?" My mother said, but I still didn't get to have eggs for breakfast. My mom would repeat this phrase to me throughout my childhood and adolescence. It puzzled me every time she said it. I mean, if a wheel is squeaky, it needs grease, right? I guess they ignored the squeaky wheel in our family (me) because I did not get what I asked for or needed.

Other times she told me that I was passive aggressive. The times when I'd disagree with her about something, or I was trying to stand up for myself.

She was my mom. Parents are supposed to love and protect their children, so my mom should know all the things that were wrong with me, right? I believed the things she'd say about me, but if I was a squeaky wheel, I wasn't that squeaky or that loud because I didn't ever seem to get the grease.

In my early teen years, I started apologizing. I was constantly saying "I'm sorry" to people for everything. If I tripped and fell or ran into a wall, I would apologize for it.

I grew up afraid to have a voice. I wouldn't share my feelings or speak my mind for fear of being passive aggressive or the squeaky wheel. If I tried to speak up, I would hear my parents' descriptions of me in my head.

BIKE RIDE & A BIRD

When I was in the fifth grade, two girlfriends, Lisa and Cheryl, invited me to go to a swim meet at the high school. Lisa wore her hair short. It was blonde with pretty streaked layers lightened by the summer sun. Lisa was outgoing; she was the life of the party when she was with us. Cheryl wore her chestnut brown hair shoulder length. She was tall and skinny, and she had a jovial personality. She was mischievous and fun. The girls lived in our neighborhood and were classmates in my local elementary school. The high school was close to a mile away. We were going to walk that day. This was one of the first times my parents allowed me to walk this far. I was excited; happy that friends asked me to go along with them. That had not happened too often for me, especially since my family had moved to a new neighborhood the summer before. That was the summer my mom made me ride my bike with the neighbor kids.

We had just moved into our new home days before; it was summer vacation. (This was where I lived until after junior college.)

My mother and I were sitting in the living room looking out of the huge walled aluminum picture window that faced the street. The metal molding framed nine smaller windows that fit within this extensive frame.

A large group of kids, at least twenty, were riding their bikes out on the street and around the subdivision. The bikes, like the kids, were different ages and sizes. The streets looped in and around the houses. We watched the group pass by our house several times before I heard, "Go ride your bike with them." I didn't want to do what my mom said. I was shy. I didn't know anyone.

"I can't just go out there and ride with them," I said matter of fact. They hadn't invited me. I was new in the neighborhood. I was an outsider. My mom looked at me; she lowered her voice.

"Go ride with them." I wasn't one to defy her, especially hearing the tone in her voice. So, I got on my bike, and I waited for the group to come around again. It was a warm summer evening with the perfect breeze touching my skin and gently blowing through my hair. As the group rode by, a few waved but continued riding, laughing, and talking with each other. I waved back, but they hadn't invited me. After the last of the bike entourage passed by, I started to pedal my bike behind them. I followed them. I felt uncomfortable. Occasionally the kids would look back, giggle, then ride a little faster. I was lagging, so I would pedal faster to keep up. I rode with them, or shall I say behind them, until we came around to my house again. I coasted my bike smoothly to the driveway, got off, put the kickstand down, and went back inside the house. Clearly, the neighbor kids didn't want the newbie joining them. My mother greeted me at the door. Her hands were on her hips.

"Go ride with them, now."

"But..." I tried to defend myself.

"Go ride with them," she said. I obeyed.

The houses we lived in for the most part all looked the same. They were brick ranch-style homes built in the 1950s. Some homes were red brick; others were gray brick. The majority of homes had three bedrooms, one bathroom, and a full basement. Some homeowners refinished the basements and installed an extra bathroom for their growing families.

There were a lot of kids of all different ages who lived in our subdivision. When they weren't in school, they were outside playing. Every one of us had the same curfew. Our cue was to go home when the streetlights came on. The parents were teachers, some worked for insurance companies, or they were employed by the "Big Three" (General Motors, Chrysler, and Ford Motor companies). Detroit is known as the Motor City.

My friends and I planned to meet early the following morning, on a Saturday. I didn't have an alarm clock and was afraid I wouldn't wake up on time, so I prayed. I asked God if he would wake me up. I didn't want to be late to meet up with my friends.

Looking back, my family was always up early. Normally, we were the first ones up in the neighborhood. The Randall kids did not need an alarm clock. Although my parents had one, I didn't want to bother them.

Sometimes, we got complaints from neighbors who wanted to sleep in on the weekend. Seriously, I don't think there was ever a chance of me being late for anything.

The following morning, I woke up to a little bird tapping on my window with his beak. Just as I opened my eyes and looked up to see where the sound was coming from, the bird flew away. I will never forget this. It was one of those significant moments in time that stood out to me. God had answered my prayer by working through a small bird tapping at my window.

He was watching over me in the most innocent of prayer requests. I believe that this was his way of showing me he was there for me and would always be there for me. Through the years, I have treasured the memory of this tiny creature waking me up that morning. I didn't know there was more to the bird story than I realized, but the fifth grade is when my dad started to physically abuse me.

I know now, God is my true father, but I didn't know that in the fifth grade. I think back to all the times in my life I felt alone, not realizing God was with me.

BEER BOTTLE

On a Friday afternoon in early spring, my dad's cousin Bart, his wife Margie, and their children, invited us up to what they called "the farm." It was a weekend getaway for them and my family too. It was like a camping trip, only instead of a tent, we slept in an old farmhouse that felt dark and unstable to me. The house was a wood clapboard structure probably built in the early 1900s and filled with various old pieces of furniture. Most of the walls were plaster and lathe with thin strips of wood nailed between studs, chicken wire, and troweled plaster. One or two walls had been repaired with drywall. The house, in general, was in disrepair, and the old Dutch wood barn leaned.

After my dad left work, we headed to "the farm" in Port Huron, Michigan, almost a two-hour drive from our home in the city.

My sister Rita was two, and the bottle of milk she'd been drinking was gone. At the time, we were driving down a two-lane blacktop highway in a rural area of Michigan. We were a long way from any convenience store, and we had at least another hour of driving to go.

I was holding Rita on my lap in the back seat of the van. It was the late 1960s. There were no seat belt laws and no car seats in those days. My parents hadn't brought food or drink with us other than my dad's beer. They planned to get groceries and refreshments from a nearby party store when we got to our destination. Anyway, my sister started to fuss and cry; she wanted her bottle, and she wanted it now.

My dad pulled the van over to the side of the road and filled her bottle with some of his beer. Yes, my dad was drinking a beer while driving.

I protested; it made me angry watching him pour the beer into her bottle and that my mother let him do this.

"No, it's not right to give Rita beer. She's a baby!" I said, but as usual, my parents ignored me.

Once Rita had the bottle back in her hands, she'd stopped crying and drank the beer, but minutes later she'd thrown it all up.

UNPLANNED

"Judy wasn't planned." I overheard my mother tell a friend while they were having tea together. It was as if I was some misfortune that had happened to her in life. "Judy was an accident," my mom said.

My mother and her friend Mrs. Daughtery from church sat at the kitchen table sipping their hot tea while my mom continued to tell her friend that my brother Trace, however, was a planned pregnancy.

I was in the next room eavesdropping. In my preteen years, I did that a lot—spying and listening in on personal conversations while trying to make myself both invisible and as elusive as possible.

I know many of us were unplanned pregnancies but hearing that I was not intended at such an early age made me feel sad and unwanted.

LEAVING MY DAD

My mom left my dad quite a few times—when I was four, twelve, and fourteen for starters—but she always went back to him.

We would wake up, have our breakfast, and go to school—a typical day for my siblings and me—and then my mom would pull us out of school in the middle of the day without notice.

One of the times my mother left my dad, she checked me out of school first. I was in junior high. I didn't understand why she was leaving him that day or why the van was packed with our clothing jammed in trash bags and cardboard boxes. When I left for school that morning, things had seemed fine between my parents.

On our way to the elementary school to get my siblings, I was so upset I started to cry. My mother turned to look at me, lowered her voice, and told me to stop crying because I would upset my brother, Trace.

After my brother got into the van and my mom explained what she was doing, he got upset, too. She let him express his feelings. She didn't tell him to stop. I felt bad for him, but I was hurt that I couldn't say how I felt. I could've probably said something, but I didn't want my mother to accuse me of being passive aggressive or the squeaky wheel.

We had no clue as to what was going to happen. It didn't matter what plans we had with friends after school that day because we found ourselves on our way to stay with my grandparents instead. My grandparents lived in Northern Michigan, almost five hours away from our home. Every time my mom left my dad, we'd go to Grandma Gina's and Grandpa's house.

We left without going back to the house to pack our personal things. We never said goodbye to my dad. We just left. Dad lived in the house while we were away, but we didn't see our books, toys, or games until my parents got back together and we returned home.

PERSONALITY DISORDERS

My dad was an alcoholic, both of my parents seemed mentally unstable at times, and I didn't start to acknowledge this cracked reality until I was well into my forties, because I'd spent most of life living in denial.

I am learning to recognize a few of the obvious characteristics of not only the alcoholic but those with personality disorders as well. Neither of my parents were diagnosed, I'm not a psychologist, but I believe my dad had traits of BPD. Borderline Personality Disorder is a condition characterized by instability and impulsivity. Terrified of abandonment, people with BPD cling to those close to them, crave reassurance and validation, and are upset by seemingly insignificant changes. Turbulent emotions and sense of self that can involve angry outbursts, severe mood swings, hopelessness, and ten percent of those with the condition die by suicide. They are also prone to addiction such as alcohol.[1]

My dad didn't like to be alone. I think it almost killed him when my mom would leave him. He needed to feel validated. He was susceptible to angry outbursts, he had addiction issues, and sadly, in the end, he took his own life.

I believe my mother had traits of a Covert Narcissist. A covert is good at mirroring other people and playing the victim. This is how they win people over. They will go out of their way to accommodate strangers while ignoring those closest to them. They are sensitive to criticism; they don't like to be told or shown they are wrong. They will blame another person or their partner to avoid responsibility. They show contempt and give the silent treatment to dominate or control. They are good at humiliating others verbally or emotionally in subtle and not-so-subtle ways. At times they appear to be so overly nice that a person might question or berate themselves for feeling negative or hurt by them.

I have found a lot of useful information on the *Psychology Today* website describing personality disorders.

PRAYER WARRIOR

I'm happy I can focus on things today, but while in school, I could never concentrate on schoolwork. It was difficult for me to get into extracurricular activities if and when I did participate in them. I was too busy thinking about my family, and what was going on at home to focus. I prayed the entire time I was away from them. I prayed that

---

[1]Borderline Personality Disorder, Psychology Today. August 30, 2022 https://www.psychologytoday.com/us/basics/borderline-personality-disorder

my parents were not fighting and that my siblings were okay. I was so afraid that terrible things might happen, like my parents hurting each other, one of the kids getting hurt, or someone was going to die. I worried and prayed constantly. I remember praying for strangers I would see out walking or people driving by in their cars. I cared about people; I didn't want anyone to hurt. I felt people and animals that were within my view should be prayed for. I still pray for them.

My mom called me a prayer warrior. That made me feel good. I felt that praying was one good thing I did that my mom approved of. But my prayers seemed to be more than just praying. For all the years that I was praying, I realized that I was chanting words or counting numbers in my head too. I really wanted to believe that counting and praying the same words over and over again in my head would keep not only the bad away but also the awful intrusive thoughts that repeated over in my head, telling me something horrible was going to happen. Thoughts like my dad getting drunk, my mother yelling, my siblings being kidnapped, my parent's abusive fights, siblings getting hit by a car, and dying. Sometimes I worried about someone getting bit by a rabid dog even though there wasn't even a good chance of that happening in the neighborhood I lived in. I was scared that I would be at school and not around to stop the bad from happening. As if I could stop it. My magical thinking again.

CARETAKER

When my parents separated, it seemed to be in February or March. Their separations usually lasted for no more than three months, so we were all together on one of Michigan's cold, gray January days when my family was sick with the flu.

Everyone was sick except for me, so I bundled myself up with a warm coat, and I walked to Wrigley's, a grocery store only a city block away from our house. That's where I purchased four cans of chicken noodle soup and a large bottle of ginger ale.

Other than it being cold outside, the walk was uneventful. The neighbor kids were in school at the time. It was too cold to snow that day, but the wind howled and tried to push my body around while I walked home. The frigid air stung my face, so I was happy to get home and inside where it was warm.

My parents and siblings were literally lying around the house. A few were sprawled out on the couch in front of the television set, and others were lying on the floor, all of them wrapped in blankets or homemade quilts, while empty tissue boxes and nearly depleted toilet paper rolls loomed throughout the area. Bodies, pillows, and dirty dishes, along with used tissues lay scattered and strewn everywhere.

We passed a jar of vapor rub throughout the house. When we were sick, we not only would dab the mentholated ointment under our noses, but my dad believed in applying it to the outside of our throats. We then wrapped a cloth baby diaper or winter scarf around our necks and secured it with a large safety pin. The clasp on the pin was either a yellow plastic duck or some other blue or pink baby motif, since the largest safety pins we had at the time were diaper pins. My dad said the vapor rub and cloth kept the heat in the body, therefore, healing it. The smell of camphor, eucalyptus oil, and menthol filled the house as medicated vapors soothed the sick.

I heated the soup on a gas stove that more times than not didn't light on its own. When I turned the knob, the electronic mechanism that was supposed to light automatically just clicked until I lit a match and threw it into the gas fumes. I watched the pilot light catch flame. I saw my mom light the stove enough times to do it myself. While the soup heated, I poured ginger ale into seven cups and passed them around. A few minutes later, the chicken noodle soup was ready.

After serving the soup, I continued to make sure my family members were all comfortable, warm, and had enough blankets. "Are you warm enough? Would you like a cup of tea?" I would ask. I was eleven at the time, but I learned to make tea in kindergarten. My teacher Mrs. Forjoni gave our entire class the recipe. One hot cup of Red Rose tea, lots of sugar, and milk. Stir well. I personally felt much better after drinking the tea.

Occasionally, I would place my right hand on everyone's foreheads, checking for fevers, including my parents. We didn't have a thermometer, but my hand seemed to do the trick just fine.

I felt like a second mom. I cleaned the house, babysat the younger ones—"the kids"—and sometimes I bought groceries for them with babysitting money I'd earned from neighbors. When I was a child, my mind was on being a caretaker. I felt funny asking my parents for money, especially that day. They were sick, and I didn't want to bother them.

MY MOM & GRANDMA RANDALL

Ever since I can remember, my mother and grandmother, my mom's mother-in-law, did not get along. I never really understood what it was they disliked about each other. I loved them both. I did understand the hurt and pain it caused me when they argued. Their arguments were not always audible. I sensed their unspoken hostility for each other because I am perceptive to such things.

I could read the room and my surroundings; it was how the adults looked at each other, what they said to each other, the tone, and how they spoke their words. It was their body language, the silent treatment used while walking away, ignoring the fact that someone had been speaking to them and they weren't going to reply.

When I was in the seventh grade, my family left on a week-long camping trip to northern Michigan. When we got home, Grandma Randall, was troubled that my parents had not told her they were going on vacation, and my mom got angry at Grandma for being ruffled about it. This, too, was way before cell phones. I think this was probably the first time my parents hadn't told my grandma that they were leaving town.

I was twelve, and even then, I could understand my grandma's feelings of worry and not knowing where her children were. My mom was mad because she felt it was none of her mother-in-law's business.

As I grew older and had my own children, I could understand even more the feeling of my grandmother wanting to know where her kids were. She was concerned; she wanted to know we were safe, especially knowing my parents' history.

WHAT'S IN THIS CAN?

In the 1960's, my mother either sent us to Wrigley's grocery store a city block away from our home or she went herself to purchase food items for our meals every day. Since we lived close to the store, we didn't need a weekly shopping trip. The everyday store runs were routine because we didn't need a car to get there; we could walk. Although, when we had too many things to carry, we would wheel our purchases home in a grocery cart, immediately returning it to the store. It felt like stealing if we didn't return the shopping cart right away, at least it did to me. Once in a great while, I would see abandoned carts on the sidewalk in front of homes or street corners. Sometimes when we experienced high winds, I'd watch the unattended carts racing down the street.

It seemed there was always enough money for alcohol and tobacco products for my dad, but my mom would purchase huge jars of peanut butter, flour, powdered milk, oatmeal, eggs, dried beans and peas for baked beans, bean soup, and pea soup. She'd choose grocery items consisting of day-old and sometimes more-than-day-old bread and cans of food without wrappers because they were cheaper. She'd purchase large five-pound orange and blue boxes of powdered Tide for the laundry. A lot of times we washed our hair with this because shampoo was too expensive. I'd stand on tip toe over a muted green laundry tub in the basement, my head and neck bent down underneath the faucet fighting to get the solid blue and white soap particles that were tangled throughout my hair completely rinsed out. This was a feat all its own.

I am not dissing the aluminum cans that were void of their wrappers or the day-old bread items that my mom purchased. We were hungry. There were eight of us, including my parents, to feed, and there was very little money, or so I was told, until years later when my Aunt Karen, my dad's sister, said she'd borrowed money from my parents and at the time still had not paid them back. This puzzled me. How could my parents loan money if there wasn't enough for us?

Sometimes my mom would color-coordinate our meals. That was where everything to eat was the same color—orange or green or purple. I remember times when we sat down to dinner and had squash and pumpkin. Or beets and purple cabbage. Some nights, we had green spinach, green beans, and green coleslaw. I think she thought it was funny, but she was also a teacher, so maybe she was trying to teach my younger siblings their colors.

I remember my mom laughing about the unwrapped cans from the grocery store. She would say to us, "I wonder if this is canned pumpkin, or maybe it's dog food." It was fun trying to guess what was in the label-free cans, but it was also stressful—at least it was for me—because what if it had been dog food? I doubt we could have taken the label-free cans back to the store to get reimbursed. Wouldn't that be a waste of money, and what would we eat then? We'd have to go back to the store. Then what if we got another can that turned out to be dog food? The statement, "There isn't enough money," that I had so often heard my parents say, played in my head. I worried about everything.

My mom baked and made our meals from scratch. She was frugal, and she was good at keeping her large family fed. She worked hard to make ends meet. For the most part, she was a stay-at-home mom but did substitute teach occasionally. My dad worked a forty-hour week as a custodian in the local school district with little overtime. Most days, my mom seemed to be in the kitchen singing, baking bread, and preparing soups, stews, and casseroles in the fall and winter—healthy food we could eat for several meals during the week.

In the summer months, we ate salad almost every night, but instead of tuna in our salad, which I loved, my mom would serve mackerel because it was cheaper than tuna. I think the mackerel was ten cents a can back then.

Mackerel is oily, and it doesn't taste as good as tuna. There was a lot of skin attached to the fish. It made me feel sick to pull off the skin before eating the fish in my salad.

We had mackerel fish salad more nights than not, and because the fish made me nauseous, I wouldn't eat it. I haven't eaten mackerel since I was seventeen. My dad used to say, "If you don't eat it, you're not hungry," but he was wrong. I was hungry; it was just easier for me to be hungry than eat something that made me feel sick.

I can honestly say I don't remember there not ever being food in the house while I was growing up. There was always food. But most of the time, we had to be creative. I remember we had large ten-pound bags of potatoes in the house. We fried, boiled, and baked them for meals and sometimes for snacking.

My parents would go to the farmer's market in Detroit and get bushels of produce in the summer, and we would sit outside at the picnic table, washing and cutting up vegetables to help prepare for canning.

One year, my parents bought a bushel of concord grapes, and my mother made delicious grape jelly that lasted all winter. She home canned the jelly in huge jars that had once contained peanut butter. The jelly tasted so good on fresh just-out-of-the-oven homemade bread.

In the winter, we had oranges, and there were apples in the fall. As a child, I learned to appreciate whatever we had. Sometimes, however, things were a little odd—like the time my mom made a huge crock of baked beans.

I think my parents were trying to save money. There were two yellow plastic bottles in the refrigerator. The containers were filled with milk (dry powdered milk) we would add water to and shake. This tasted and looked like a thin watery version of skim milk. We had condiments in the fridge and the crock of beans. This is what we ate for three days straight. Three days!

We complained (well, at least I remember protesting), but if we were hungry, this is what we had to eat. And we ate the beans morning, at noon, and dinner until one of my younger brothers got sick. Sick at both ends. He was literally pooping and throwing up baked beans. This is what put an end to eating beans for quite some time afterward. I, for one, was happy about that.

MIDNIGHT VISITOR

My dad's Uncle Herman who had only one arm came to our home sometimes after the bars closed. I overheard my parents talk about the car accidents he'd been involved in while drinking and driving. That's how he lost his arm, in a crash. At least, that is what I was told.

It was nothing for him to stop in unexpectedly, sometimes visiting as late as two a.m. on any given night of the week. I thought this was perfectly normal.

The man was drunk, pounding on our front door, calling for my dad. Sometimes my parents tried to ignore him, but our uncle's voice would only get louder. Voices carried more at night, and our neighbors were trying to sleep. When my parents invited him in, the entire house was suddenly wide awake.

My brothers, sisters, and I were not allowed to get out of bed during these visits. Although, my little brother John would, and he got away with it, probably because he was younger than the rest of us. One night John asked Uncle Herman if he could have his dancing shoes. Regardless, it was party time for our uncle and my parents.

Now, I think of how hard it was for us to get up the following morning and go to school. We never knew when these parties would happen, but we heard them. My dad's uncle was drunk, and he would dance around our living room in the wee hours of the morning. I believed every family in the world had relatives who did the same thing and that this behavior was common. I was wrong about that.

"I went to the bar and danced in my dancing shoes. Do you like my dancing shoes, Barbie?" the inebriated relative would ask my mom while belching out his words, and my mother would laugh.

My parents were laughing, so why wouldn't I think this behavior was normal?

Our home was a three-bedroom brick ranch, approximately 965-square-feet with a basement and one bathroom shared by seven family members, and there was a baby on the way.

I remember peeking out of my bedroom door to watch my dad walk down the hallway that passed by my room and into my parents' bedroom, where I knew he had a pint of whiskey hidden. On his way back to the living room, I watched him take a swig of the liquor, then offer the bottle to his uncle, who was very drunk, crying and carrying on about his life. My mother typically drank wine on occasion; she wasn't a whiskey drinker, and I'm quite sure she didn't participate with my dad or uncle on these nights, especially when she'd been pregnant.

Our uncle danced around our living room, singing lyrics he'd make up on the spot while he sang. "I'm just a German. They call me Herman the German." He'd sing loud. His voice would bellow through our house while he'd stomp his feet on the hardwood floor. The floors vibrated, and I swear the entire house shook.

My three brothers slept in the basement, and at times I'm sure they must've thought the upper floor would fall on top of them. We knew of several families whose kids slept in the basement. It was kind of the cool thing to do back then. My dad put up walls and sectioned-off areas in the basement. There was a playroom with bookshelves that held our encyclopedias, various other books, toys, and whatever else got placed on them. There was also a black cast iron wood-burning stove in this area that heated the basement. We had a large laundry room with an eight-foot table my dad made my mother for sewing and folding clothes on. Next to that was the furnace room. The hot water tank and incinerator were also in this room. Then there was the bedroom with a triple bunk bed my dad made for my three brothers. Although for it to fit into the basement, my dad cut it down to a bunk and a twin sized bed. My parents, sisters, and I slept upstairs.

When Uncle Herman wasn't drinking, he was a totally different person. This man was a salesman for a popular appliance store. He wore expensive clothing and carried himself well. His wife had his shirts tailored to fit his missing arm and he always looked nice. At those times when he was sober, he was quiet and reserved.

The party ended when Uncle Herman left and when the lock on the front door made the familiar clicking sound. Our home was quiet again. Everyone went back to bed and slept. The show was over for the night, but there would be more nights like this to come. As I have mentioned, we never knew when our uncle would come to visit.

"Get up! Get dressed!" My dad alerted the house. Six thirty a.m. on a school day. I remember being especially tired after those party nights, but obviously, it didn't seem to matter to my parents that we hadn't gotten a good night's sleep.

Funny, but I never heard my parents talk about these middle-of-the-night visits. Maybe they wanted us to believe that we were dreaming or that it had never happened, or that it was none of our business.

I guess it was just another crazy, dysfunctional moment in the life of the Randall Family.

LAST DAY OF SCHOOL

It was early June, and junior high had just let out for the summer. Seventh grade was over. I arrived home, papers and notebooks in hand. I was happy to be out and away from the monotony of classes and homework for a while, but when I opened the front door of our red brick ranch to let myself in, I saw my dad's two-hundred-pound frame sitting on top of my mother, who was less than half his size. My parents were down on the floor, sprawled out in the hallway.

My dad was pounding on my mother with one fist and pulling her hair with the other. I screamed, not only from fear but from anger. I didn't plan on screaming. It just came out.

My dad was abusive. My mother was abusive in her own way, but she had taken these fights for too long. Yet she continued to take the abuse.

Why hadn't she ever fought back? I mean really fought back, get-the-hell-out-of-there fought back. Blood was coming from her face. It was difficult for me to see her bleeding wound. It was when I began screaming that I felt a heavy blow to my face.

My books and everything I'd carried home in my arms had scattered on the floor. I was scrunching my body up against the nearest wall. I began to sob while my dad stood over me, ready to belt me again. I am 5'2", and at the time, I might have weighed 90 pounds, a little smaller than my mom.

I held my arms out in front of me to protect myself, but they were only a fragile barrier. We both knew my arms wouldn't protect me from his fist or hard, black leather work shoes. I heard my mother begin to scream at him. "Stop it!"

At that moment, I detested my dad. "I hate you!" I screamed, then I ran outside. I was embarrassed and ashamed, so I crouched in the shrubs behind our pine privacy fence, peering through knot holes in the wood and open spaces in the shrubbery.

I couldn't hear the shouting from inside the house anymore. It was just quiet, but I was looking for neighbors or anyone who might have heard the ruckus. I was hoping there were no witnesses.

We were supposed to keep what went on inside our home to ourselves, and even though I couldn't see anyone nearby, I felt like everyone in the neighborhood had heard.

It was during moments like this that I dreamed of running away. More disconnection.

I'd tell myself I wasn't about to stay around this crazy any longer. I tried to convince myself, but I could not leave my siblings behind.

I felt I had to protect them.

My mother told me that my grandfather had beaten and killed my dad's favorite dog in front of him when he was eight years old. I cannot imagine how horrible that must have been for my father, a child. How traumatic, but then, even though he didn't kill them, I have watched my dad kick and beat up our dogs, too.

I have to wonder if there were other cruel incidents in my dad's life I hadn't heard about that caused him to be so abusive. Sometimes I felt sorry for him, but it was no excuse to hurt animals, his wife, or his children.

HYPOCHONDRIAC

I lay awake in bed, covered up with a crisp, white cotton sheet I shared with my younger sisters; both were sleeping next to me. We shared a room before my brothers moved to the basement.

Our room was plain and painted white. My parents wanted all the walls in the house white. They said it was cleaner looking. Against one wall was a long, wide pine dresser with six drawers that we girls shared. The double bed we slept in sat against another wall. The small closet was maybe four feet wide and eight feet tall. Metal bifold doors were supposed to glide across the track when the door was opened or closed. The doors came off the track a lot. I still don't like bifold doors in closets for that reason.

It was summer, the windows were open, and for a while, I watched the curtains dance in the warm breeze. It was late but I couldn't sleep. I was in pain. My jaw was pulsing, and the first thought I had of why it hurt was terrifying. I had lockjaw. For generations, lockjaw and leprosy were considered to be dreaded diseases. Although I didn't think I had leprosy, I was quite sure I had lockjaw. The memory I share is an example of how I worried about everything. I was afraid, and I never felt safe.

I knew I hadn't stepped on a rusty nail or scraped my skin, but I was sure I had lockjaw.

I walked into my parents' bedroom, tiptoeing to my mother's side of the bed. I stood over her, watching her breathe for a minute before I whispered, "Mom." She didn't budge. She hadn't heard me, so I spoke a little louder. "Mom." But she still didn't move.

I felt tears fall down my face while trying to wake her with my terrifyingly sad news. I was going to die. I was sure of it.

I placed one of my hands on her shoulder, gently shaking her. She stirred in her sleep before waking. "Wah, what, what?" she asked.

"I, I have lockjaw."

My mother didn't move. "You don't have lockjaw," she said. "You're talking. Go back to bed."

Oh, I thought, then smiled to myself. I was relieved. I walked back to my room feeling much better, grateful that I had been wrong. Of course, I didn't have lockjaw. I didn't know what caused my jaw to hurt, but my mother was right. My mouth was moving.

MY DAD DOESN'T LIKE ME

I deeply cared for each member of my family. I loved them more than life. I mean this literally. Normally, in the mornings before school, I went through the house hugging and kissing my sibling's goodbye for the day. That is, those of my brothers and sisters who would allow me to. Sometimes, I would sneak into my parents' room, trying hard not to wake my dad, and I kissed him, too.

My dad worked afternoons at my junior high school when I was in the seventh grade, so my siblings and I were usually in bed when he returned from work.

One night after he got home, I overheard him talking to my mother. There was a thin wall between my bedroom and the kitchen, so I heard everything my parents said.

"I don't like Judy," my dad said.

"Why don't you like her?" My mother asked.

I felt tears roll down my cheeks while I adjusted my pillow to be sure I'd heard right. My dad's words had my attention, so I continued to listen.

"Who do you think gives you a kiss before she goes to school in the morning?" My mom said.

My dad didn't reply; that's when I noticed the conversation subside.

I wondered if he'd felt this way because he thought I didn't care about him.

I found out later that my dad's feelings were hurt because I wouldn't say, "Hi," to him while I was at school. There were times when I did say it, but I didn't do it all the time. I wasn't trying to be mean. I loved him. I contemplate his words now, years later: "I don't like Judy." His words still hurt.

Years earlier, my parents' friend did some substitute teaching at our school. We could call him Rick when he was visiting our home, but out of respect when he was at school, we had to call him Mr. Johnson. There were times at school that I would speak to him and call him mister, but Rick didn't answer. I felt like I was embarrassing him, so eventually, I stopped speaking to him while at school.

Sometimes, my dad subbed for another janitor. On one of those days, he worked the day shift, and as I passed him in the hallway, I didn't acknowledge him. I honestly didn't know what to say. This was my twelve-year-old brain, and it hurt his feelings. I'm sorry I hurt him.

One day, I was looking at myself in a mirror that hung in our hallway. I was startled when my dad came up from behind me, but it is what he said to me that I remember most. "Judy, you are like me; you have holes in your face." I had some acne and big pores, but why would he say that to me? I was in junior high, trying to look pretty and fit in. Why couldn't he have just wrapped his arms lovingly around me and said, "I love you. You're my daughter; you're beautiful."

MY FAULT

My parent's argument was finally over, at least for the time being, and as I knew from past experiences, this abusive ritual between them would happen again. I couldn't tell you what they were fighting about at the time. Their arguments, whether physical or verbal, happened so often that sometimes I tried hard to tune them out.

It wasn't an argument they'd had. Calling it a fight would be more accurate. It was a knockdown, drag-out, literally punch in the face or anywhere else they could reach at the moment, just to beat the hell out of one another scream fest. This was their pattern. I never knew when it would happen or what the altercations were about. I know their abusive physical brawls happened at least twice, if not three times a year. I'm not sure why that was.

Any time my parents hit each other was horrifying. Usually, my siblings and I would scatter throughout the house or run outside during these times.

We lived in a time when people minded their business; they looked the other way. I guess they didn't want to get involved. No one ever called the cops on my parents, but how could the neighbors not hear the shouting, shrieks of pain, breaking glass, and slamming doors? The crying clashes of anger could be heard throughout the house, our front and back yard, and I was quite sure, up and down our quaint city block.

Just as fast as their fifteen-minute brawl had come on, it was silenced—turned off as if someone had hit the light switch. Quiet now. Perfectly quiet. My parents would watch TV, make dinner, and carry on as if nothing had happened between them.

Ever since I was a little girl, I had somehow gotten it into my head that everything wrong that happened in my life was my fault. My parents' arguments were my fault; my younger siblings misbehaving was my fault; my dad getting drunk was my fault.

My Uncle Jerry and Aunt Hazel (dad's sister) and other relatives reinforced this belief. They'd take me aside and start pointing their fingers. "You kids are to blame for your parent's problems," they said.

When people repeatedly tell you what they think is wrong with you, you start to believe them.

A cousin told me that her family swept their house of toys and hid them before my family arrived on visits. I guess they were afraid we'd break them. My cousin also shared with me that my parents had too many kids. She said this a lot. After a while, I got tired of hearing this because the ill comments made me feel as if there was something wrong with my siblings and me in a trashy sense. It made me angry; it made me feel like we didn't belong, but I knew we did. We were typical kids behaving and doing what was age appropriate for each of us.

Sometimes I wonder if my parents having six children was, in their minds, a way to keep them together through their tumultuous relationship. I've heard that some people believe having children will save their marriage, although I don't think this was the case for my parents.

My younger siblings and I seemed to get on our relatives' nerves. My eleven-year-old cousin had no problem telling me what we all did wrong. A lot of the opinions she voiced were, I am sure, what she'd overheard from her parent's conversations because I don't think it's normal for children to think or talk of such things on their own.

On a bright sunny August morning my parents were fighting again, it was a Sunday. I felt pretty that day because I was wearing my favorite pair of shorts. They were orange with a small navy-blue paisley print design on them. I wore a short sleeve navy top that matched the blue in the shorts. My dark blonde hair was straight and cut short. The length of my hair came down to the middle of my ears. I was starting to wear makeup, a little dark brown mascara and a natural light Cover Girl foundation, for the most part.

I was never paid to watch my younger siblings. I was part of the family. My jobs were babysitting and cleaning the house for my parents. Sometimes, but not all the time, my siblings and I got a quarter for our weekly allowance up until I was seventeen.

My parents were going out to have coffee somewhere, or that's what they told me before they left the house. I was, as usual, to watch my five younger siblings while my parents sorted out their problems. In the meantime, my Uncle Jerry called and very sternly told me it was my fault—and my brothers and sisters' fault—that my parents were not getting along. We—the kids—were causing discord between our parents.

After my uncle's telephone conversation that day, I felt terrible. I really believed that my parents' fighting was because of me. I was bad. Somehow, I had to make the situation better. I was thirteen, and I thought I could improve things. I really did.

Garrett and John were playing outside in the dirt with their toys, and my sister Josie was at her girlfriend's house. I'm not sure where Trace was; I just know he wasn't in the house. I locked the doors and began not only to watch my baby sister Rita but clean the house, too, until my six-year-old brother John started pounding at the back door. I asked him what he wanted. He wanted water, and he wanted to come inside. I got him a glass of water, but I wouldn't let him in because I was cleaning. I wanted the house to stay clean for when my parents got home because I hoped a clean house would make them happy and not fight.

My brother didn't like that I had locked him out. He pounded so hard on the door with his fist that the glass in the door broke, cutting his hand. All I could think of was that he had hit an artery and he was going to die.

I was told that I was a horrible daughter for causing my parents to argue and for letting the house and yard go, as Uncle Jerry had suggested. I felt I was a bad sister and cruel because it was my fault that my brother's hand was gushing blood. I should've let him come inside the house. Mrs. Brim, one of our neighbors across the street, was a nurse, so I hurried to get her, realizing I had left my baby sister alone for a few minutes, but it couldn't be helped because my brother might be bleeding to death.

I ran all the way to her house. I was starting to hyperventilate. I pounded on her door, trying to catch my breath.

Mrs. Brim was tall and slender. She wore her light blonde hair relatively short. When she answered the door, I was relieved she was home and not working that day.

"John's bleeding. Please help!" I cried out to her.

"Where is he?" She asked.

"He's in the house." I said, then ran back across the street to John and Rita. Mrs. Brim and another neighbor lady who had heard what was going on followed me into our home. I could smell the scent of bleach I had been cleaning with when we entered the house and while Mrs. Brim looked at my brother's hand. She advised that John should get stitches.

While she continued to observe my brother, my parents arrived back home. My dad grabbed hold of my brother's hand, seriously taking note of his wound, and then he looked over at me and glared.

He was really angry, and I knew I was in serious trouble. My dad charged at me, then started hitting me hard in the face and head with his fist. I was backing away from him, but I was still facing him while he continued knocking me around. I kept backing up until my body hit hard against the kitchen cabinet that held the sink. My dad would not stop hitting me. I pulled my arms up in front of me in an attempt to protect myself from more facial blows. Then I found myself sliding down to the floor, my back aligning with the cabinet, and my body crouching on the way down. My nose was bleeding, and my dad had started to kick me hard from the waist down. His leather work shoes struck me over and over again, and I felt like he wouldn't ever stop hurting me.

Our garbage disposal was broken, so there were carrot and potato peels, along with a small plastic bag stuffed into a colander that sat inside the sink. My dad slammed the colander with the kitchen waste over the top of my head, and I started to bleed even more.

My hair became fused with my blood and vegetable peelings, and water had poured down my face from the refuse that splayed across my head. And then the beating stopped. It was over. At that moment, I hated myself. I was so bad. And in some sick way, I believed I deserved this horrible abuse. The memory of my mother's repeated words through the years, "You've had this coming for quite a while," came to my mind.

While all this crazy was happening, I realized that not only my mother, but the neighbor ladies were still in our house. As I have mentioned, we lived in a time when people minded their own business; they looked away from such abuse. They didn't want to get involved.

If I ever see abuse, I want you to know I won't just stand there and do nothing. I hope you won't either.

My dad shouted at me and told me to clean myself up.

When I passed down the hallway, my body must've stumbled up against the wall because I left a blood streak on it. So, I hurried to clean that up, too.

I never really could understand why the neighbor ladies who witnessed this horrific beating didn't do something about it. If it had been me, I would have called the police.

I asked my sister Josie if my dad had ever beaten her up. She said, "No, but I remember that day."

I have since learned that people who are abusive feel the need to be in control over their victims. They might come off as good, compassionate people to the world, but it is a different story inside the walls of their own homes.

My mother mirrored people. She was outgoing, and she had a way of connecting with them. She also played the victim; this I noticed seemed to be an attribute that pulled people in toward her.

My dad appeared quiet and reserved. He seemed to get along with other people while in their company, but he didn't seem to have much to say to them, especially when he wasn't drinking.

NO BOUNDARIES

I was brought up to believe that I was supposed to be nice to everyone regardless of the way they treated me. From an early age I was caring toward others even when my kindness wasn't reciprocated.

When I was thirteen, my mom asked if she could borrow five dollars. She promised she would pay me back. About a week later, after she returned from the store, she handed me a new, white slip.

"This is the five dollars I owe you," she said.

That's right. I didn't get the five-dollar bill that I had lent her. I got an undergarment and an article of clothing I did not need.

The price tag was still attached to the slip. The original price was five dollars, but it was marked down to ninety-nine cents. The funny thing is when I owed my mom money, even if I was short a penny, she'd let me know about it. I was upset that my mother had cheated me, but even if I had complained and stood up for myself, it wouldn't have done any good.

I felt powerless. I couldn't defend myself because I didn't want to set my mother off. My mom was my mom. She got her way. Besides, I didn't want to hear, "Judy, you're so unappreciative."

She didn't like when I was gifted money.

My Grandma Randall would give us a five-dollar bill in our birthday card every year. But on other rare occasions when it wasn't my birthday, twice that I remember, she gave me more. Once a ten-dollar bill, and another time, she gave me fifteen dollars.

My mother's reaction made me feel ashamed. She got angry at my grandmother for giving me the money, and I felt my mom resented me, too.

"Why did she give only you money?" My mother asked me. I felt selfish.

I shrugged my shoulders, and said, "I don't know." I felt embarrassed.

So, I shared what my grandma had given to me with another sibling.

I learned that when someone gives me a gift, I should feel ashamed and unworthy, because it isn't fair to everyone else. Receiving a gift was a stressful event for me.

I liked buying nice things for my family at Christmas and throughout the year. My mom told me not to do it. She said it makes people feel bad because they can't afford to reciprocate. I was not looking for reciprocation. I only wanted to do something nice for the people I loved. But I quit buying gifts for my family.

One time my dad told me, "You're not smart like your mother, but you have common sense." Then he said, "Your mother doesn't have common sense." Having common sense was a nice thing for my dad to say about me. It made me feel good about myself, and I believed him, but I felt sad that he thought my mom didn't have common sense. And I felt bad that he didn't think I was smart. I never understood why he shared this observation with me that day. Other than I think my mother had probably done something he didn't like. Sometimes, after an argument, he would take me aside and talk to me as if I were an adult, but when my parents got along, he'd tell me, "You're just a kid. What do you know?"

Throughout the years, my parents had no problem telling me who I was, but talk about the confusing dialogue inside my head. You have common sense but you're not smart.

PERMS & HAIRCUTS

My mom gave me home permanents throughout my childhood years. My hair frizzed easily from perms, and to be honest, it never looked good.

Sometimes, my mother would cut my hair, too, but this did not end well for me because my dad, who normally cut our hair, didn't like how my mom was cutting it, so he would take over.

I'd be sitting on a chair in the kitchen facing the wall covered in wallpaper. A repeating pattern of white chickens, brown rakes, and beige gardening hoes plastered against a mustard yellow background.

My permed frizzy curls had grown out. One afternoon after school, my mother began trimming off the over-processed ends. She stood above me, barefoot wearing a beige and red house frock while cheerfully cutting away at my hair. That's when my dad walked in from work.

"What are you doing?" He asked my mom, observing.

"Cutting the split ends from her hair," Mom said.

"It's uneven. Here, let me do it," Dad said, taking the scissors.

"That's too short!" My mother's tone changed to fear. I cringed. I felt anxious. I didn't want my hair to be too short. I couldn't see what was happening to me because there wasn't a mirror in the kitchen.

My parents stood over me, shouting at each other while my dad proceeded to cut my hair even shorter. This was not the first time they'd cut my hair together. Me, I sat very still. At the time, I'm pretty sure I was hyperventilating. The last time this happened, I was in high school. My hair ended up quite short, and my bangs, well, they were one inch down from the top of my forehead. Short bangs were not the style then.

My hair looked terrible. I wore hand-me-downs. I had acne.

My mom told me not to touch my face so that I wouldn't get scars, and I listened to her because I wanted to have a pretty complexion like she had.

Then one day, her friend Ellen came to visit. At the time, I happened to have a huge embarrassing blemish between the bridge of my nose and my right eye. Ellen asked my mother for a needle and some alcohol. Ellen was going to take care of my blemish. My mother told her where to find a needle. She did nothing to stop her friend. My mother didn't protect me. I was afraid to stand up for myself so although I was quite upset, I just let it happen. I bristled. I was constantly told to respect my elders. I regret that more than ever now. I still have the scar, and I never did inherit my mom's beautiful skin.

INCINERATOR

When I was in my early teens, my parents installed an incinerator in our home. Anxious to try it out, my mom started cleaning the basement late one night.

She threw trash and my brother's plastic race car tracks into the incinerator. I am sure the burner was for paper only and not plastic.

Suddenly, my mother called out to me. I could hear the urgency in her voice.

"Call the fire department! Call the fire department!"

I was upstairs in the main part of the house. I called back to my mom, "Are you sure?"

"Yes, call the fire department!"

I will be honest. I was hesitant to call because I didn't want there to be more crazy drama focused on my family. But as usual, I did what I was told, and I called the fire department.

I explained to the dispatcher that "our incinerator might be a little bit on fire." However, I did clarify that I thought everything was fine, but my mom wanted me to call. I asked them if they would come to check it out.

"Please send only one car," I said, repeating this request at least three times during the conversation. It could have been more, but I remember three distinct pleas. I was literally begging the dispatcher. I had more instructions: "Please don't turn the sirens or lights on."

One car, no lights, no sirens. I thought my guidelines were simple enough to follow.

Immediately after I ended my call, my mom yelled back up the stairs to me. "Don't call them; it's all right."

I knew it!

"It's too late," I said. My body tensed. I could feel the familiar pangs of humiliation. Another attention-grabbing scene was going to take place at the Randall house.

"Okay, let them come."

Flashing lights and loud sirens blared down our street. Three fire trucks, two police cars, and a fire dispatch car arrived in front of our home.

One firefighter told us they had a practice drill, and this is why they sent all the emergency vehicles out. It was close to ten o'clock on a school night, and the neighbors were outside standing around our house, watching, conversing with each other, and shaking their heads. Probably saying, "There's always something going on with the Randalls. I wonder what will happen next?" I wanted to crawl under a rock.

The curtains in our front window were wide open. The lights from the rescue vehicles were bright and strobing inside and all around our home. My mother laughed. She thought it was funny.

Talk about embarrassing—none of this was funny to me, but now looking back, I will admit it was comical, although much funnier now than back then. There never really was a dull moment at the Randall house.

SUMMER PARTY

My parents were not invited to adult neighborhood parties, nor were we invited to the neighborhood family get-togethers, trips to Cedar Pointe, or the beach in the summer. However, we were invited to a summer party once. Wanting to be friendly and cordial, my girlfriend Connie's parents invited my family. It was a short walk to Connie's since her family lived only a few houses away. Their house was the same brick ranch style as ours; only their wood siding was white, and our siding was cranberry.

Some of my siblings and I arrived at the party on time. My dad had been out drinking, so he came to the party, not only late but drunk, and that is when my mom came, too.

My mother wore a pretty pink print full-skirted dress and beige heels while my dad wore nice gray slacks and a short sleeve light blue dress shirt. I was happy my parents were at the party since my neighborhood friends' parents were all there too.

I watched my dad make his entrance, my mother at his side. My dad staggered in. He was loud, and immediately turned our hosts' music up, then began to dance to Neil Diamond's "Sweet Caroline."

I like that song, too, so I can understand why he turned the music up, but I felt he was being rude. I was horrified at how he was behaving.

I was especially sad and embarrassed when my friend's mother asked him to leave. At the time, I was standing across from my dad, and within two feet of where he stood. The music had been turned down but was still playing. I could hear my mother's voice, along with other neighbors, chatting in the background. The afternoon was sunny and warm with a gentle breeze that felt perfect.

Connie's mom stood next to me in their driveway, and her dad stood next to her mom. That's when Connie's mom looked at my dad, but spoke quietly when she said, "I'm sorry, but I'm going to have to ask you to leave." Connie's mom had every right to ask my dad to leave, but I felt terrible for my dad, and yet I was ashamed too. Here's an interesting thought: my mom sat chatting with neighbors, while I absorbed the responsibility for my dad's behavior.

I sensed relatives and people, in general, tended to look down on not only my parents but my siblings and me, too.

I felt we were being judged by my parents' actions, like my dad's alcohol abuse, my parent's fighting, and their separations. I suspected what they did in public and how they lived their lives behind what they thought were closed doors played a big part in how our family was perceived.

INDEPENDENCE DAY

If I were to describe with a song what my life was like growing up, I would say "Independence Day," written by Gretchen Peters and performed by Martina McBride. It's a song about domestic abuse and the tragedy that follows. The lyrics brought back memories of times as a little girl when I also felt my parents were out of control and I was in the way. In another sense writing this book has been an Independence Day for me.

When I was sixteen, my parents said we could go to the State Fair, but my dad went out drinking the night before, and he didn't come home until the following day, the day we were planning to go. My mother was upset with my dad for not coming home the night before.

I washed the car, straightened the glove box, threw out old candy wrappers that were on the floor, and I vacuumed. I went into the house to gather sweaters for my siblings and me to wear in case the weather turned cold. I made peanut butter and jelly sandwiches for us to eat. Buying tickets was expensive enough for my parents, so normally we didn't buy food from vendors; we'd take our lunch instead.

I was keeping busy, so I wouldn't have to think about my mother's anger or wonder where my dad was or what would happen when he got home. I would have driven myself that day, but my parents wouldn't let me get my driver's license until I turned eighteen. They didn't want to pay the higher premiums on their insurance policy, and yet they let me drive to run errands.

I was getting ready. I was hoping, and determined we were going to go, even though I knew in the back of my mind, none of us would be going. From past experience, instead of a fun-filled day with family, I was quite sure the minute my dad arrived home, there would be an argument with a high potential of it turning explosive.

"I'm ready to go to the Fair," I said when my dad finally arrived home. I tried to act happy, like everything was fine, but my dad just looked at me and smiled. I followed him into the house, where my eyes met my mom's as she approached my dad. "I'm ready to go," I said again.

"It's too late to go. We're not going," my mom said. My hope had died. Although I was disappointed we weren't going anywhere, I was relieved my parents hadn't engaged in a physical fight.

CADILLACS & FORDS

I was in my teens when my dad shared with me a story about Cadillacs and Fords. We lived in the Motor City. I sat on the front porch next to my dad while he explained that Cadillacs were top-of-the-line cars like there were top-of-the-line men. Then he told me about the Fords. The front porch was a square four-foot concrete area with a cement stoop. A Japanese Yew shrub with red berries grew on either side of us. We sat together shoulder to shoulder on the porch while both of my feet rested on the concrete step. I was wearing blue jean cutoffs and a white sleeveless top. My dad wore his green work clothes, and he held a bottle of beer in his right hand, while he talked to me.

"Fords are mediocre men—not the best, but not the worst either," he said. "Fords are good solid men, and they're hard workers."

"There's nothing wrong with a good Ford," he continued.

In so many words, I got the feeling my dad was telling me he was a Ford, too.

"Judy, your type of guy, is like Chase Connor. I think he'd be good for you," my dad offered.

Chase's dad and my dad were only acquaintances.

Maybe my dad didn't know that this boy was into drugs and not very motivated. Maybe he didn't know the boy was a troublemaker in school or that I wasn't attracted to him, but then maybe he did. Because what I heard that day was that I wasn't good enough for a Cadillac or a Ford. My mom had been listening to the conversation because, later on, she came up to me and said, "Wasn't that a nice story dad shared with you?"

My dad was wrong because my type of guy, the man I chose and married, is so much better than my mother or dad could have ever imagined for me.

CAMPING TRIPS

My parents liked to camp. Wherever we went, my dad took us out deep into the woods where there were no other people around. To him, isolation was camping, and camping within proximity to other campers inside a campground was not camping.

We slept in a blue and white tent big enough for ten to twelve people and a wood stove to sit inside. The stove sat close to the middle of the floor so that it wasn't touching the sides of the tent. My dad cut a hole in the canvas fabric for the exhaust pipe so we would be warm on chilly nights.

I always worried about the tent catching on fire and burning us up while we were sleeping inside. For most of the night, I would lay awake making plans. I wondered how I would get us all out alive if the tent did catch on fire. I didn't sleep well on the nights the wood stove was going.

On another camping trip, where once again my dad was drinking, I watched him head toward a little motorboat on the small inland lakeshore not too far away from our campsite. He held a green tackle box and a fishing rod in his right hand. He was going fishing, and he was taking my little sister with him. Rita was four, and she was holding my dad's left hand. Her little legs were tripping while she ran. She was trying to keep up with my dad's long strides.

I followed them to a sturdy twelve-foot aluminum fishing boat through tall, wet grass. The water and mud was squishing in between my toes. My dad didn't want me to come with them, but I got on the boat anyway. I felt I needed to protect my sister, and in some way, I felt I needed to protect my dad, too, because he was drinking.

I sensed my dad's negative emotions for me, and they were strong. I'm thinking he was not only angry, but embarrassed, because instead of a tent, my family was now camping in an aluminum camper/trailer that my dad pulled with the van. I can't remember what the trailer looked like, I only remember that there were bunk beds and room for several sleeping cots inside.

I was sixteen, and the night before, my parents were being intimate in the trailer while my siblings and I were sleeping, only I woke up. I was appalled. Horrified. I remember shouting at them, "Stop it!"

"Go back, Judy; you can't come," my dad said. He didn't want me there. I felt scared because I was defying him, but I was more afraid for Rita.

After putting a life vest on Rita, I sat on the rigid gray metal boat seat opposite from where my dad sat while my arms were wrapped tightly around my little sister. I can't remember if I wore a life jacket, but I am quite certain that my dad was not wearing one. I don't remember ever seeing him wear a life preserver.

While he started the motor and headed out over the lake, he talked to me, but his words were slurred. I couldn't understand him, and I wasn't really listening to him anyway. My concern was transfixed on my sister, and any horrible event that could possibly happen next.

When my dad stood up to pee, the boat began to rock. I felt my body lean way over to one side of the boat. My eyes were fixed on the water. I was worried. I was afraid we were going to fall into the lake. Then within seconds, while my dad took another step, our small craft felt lopsided as we were all leaning, sloping, toward the opposite side of the boat. I was terrified while I held my sister much closer.

When my dad began to unzip his pants, and when he proceeded to expose himself, I turned to look away from him before he leaned out over the side of the boat to pee. Once again, the boat tilted. I kept quiet.

I know my dad wouldn't have behaved this way if he hadn't been drinking. Now, I wonder if he'd ever remembered his ill behavior that day.

Then there was the unforgettable camping trip to Canada one summer. We went so far up into Canada that if a person wanted to travel further north, they would have to take a plane—at least that's what my parents told us.

My parents had been arguing again. I don't remember what about. I'm guessing that's why my dad stopped at a provincial park; it was right after dark.

My sixteen-year-old brother Trace was upset, probably because of my parent's arguments. As a side note, we never talked about our family camping trips either. Strange I know, but we didn't discuss dysfunctional incidents. We just didn't.

Trace said he was leaving, then got out of our light green Ford Econoline camper van and he headed into the park on his own. Garrett got out of the van to go after Trace. I got scared and went after both of them because I didn't want my brothers to run away. I was feeling anxious, thinking about all the terrible things that could happen to them while out in the vast Canadian wilderness. The thought of hungry bears and wolves attacking frightened me.

That night the dark blue sky was clear, filled with stars, and the air was crisp. I shivered. The tops of trees met the sky while towering and surrounding us. Every once in a while, the wind picked up, and I'd get a whiff of fresh pine. The scent of the trees were sweet and refreshing.

My mom was behind me; she grabbed a space blanket (emergency blanket) on her way out of the van and . . . There we were in the middle of nowhere. Nothing but trees and stars all around us.

John, Josie, and Rita stayed in the van with my dad, and within minutes after my mother and I got out of the vehicle, I watched my dad and my younger siblings drive away from us. I didn't chase after them. Things were evolving fast. I felt like I was in shock. I couldn't believe what was happening. I was in a dream, paralyzed. Hyperventilating. I seemed to be in a fight or flight state not knowing what I should do. Run after my brothers or run after my dad?

It was so cold that night. We didn't have anything to keep us warm other than what we were wearing—a pair of jeans, canvas shoes, and colorful sweatshirts. My mom wore the same. She'd bought each of us a different-colored sweatshirt to wear for camping. Mom wore white, mine was aqua, and my brothers wore red and blue.

We soon learned that evening that summer in northern Canada gets really cold, especially during the second week of August.

My mother and I didn't talk while we tried to catch up to my brothers, other than calling out to them. "Trace! Garrett!" I was frantic. We continued to trudge along rough terrain we couldn't see. Our feet led the way while we called out to my brothers.

My mom walked behind me, quiet. She seemed weak and vulnerable, like she needed someone to take care of her. Ever since I was a little girl, I saw her as fragile, powerless, and a victim. Sometimes it upset me that she didn't stand up for herself or even us. I felt we protected her, but she didn't protect us.

Eventually, my mother and I caught up with Trace and Garrett, and we all headed back to where my dad had initially parked the van. We secretly hoped he'd be there waiting for us, but he wasn't.

We stood around someone else's dying campfire to keep warm. For a while, we took turns searching for small sticks and paper trash to keep the fire going, but we didn't find enough, and the fire soon went out completely.

"Mom, I'm cold." Trace said. He was shivering, hugging himself with his arms.

"Here, take this." My mom said, handing him the space blanket.

We were all freezing, so we took turns wrapping the shiny silver space blanket around ourselves. Whether we liked it or not, we knew we would be spending the night in a Canadian forest without any covering, no flashlight, nothing to drink, and no food.

I kept waiting for my dad to come back and get us. For me, the hours seemed to drag on through the night. There were moments when I thought my dad was never coming back. I worried about what we would do to survive. I worried about my younger siblings. They and my dad were somewhere on the road facing the unknown as well.

"Where's dad? When is he coming back?" I asked, knowing my mother wouldn't have a definitive answer. I felt angry, frightened, and helpless.

"I don't know." My mom shrugged. She remained quiet. We were all feeling helpless.

There was no other person around to help us that night. It was only the four of us, trying to keep warm. Garrett found an empty woodshed just big enough to hold all of us while standing up, but it was dark and as cold on the inside of the building as on the outside.

We didn't sleep; it was exhausting having to stand all night, moving our bodies, trying to keep warm.

The following morning as the sun came out, Garrett said, "Look at that man." That's when I saw an old white-haired man whose skin seemed to sag over his bent-up bones crawl into the water naked. At the time, he was about two hundred and fifty feet away from us. He was the only person we saw in the park the entire time we were there. I don't know if he saw us. But we saw him.

My dad didn't come back until later that day; it was around noon when we saw him drive up. He had headed for Toronto the night before. Toronto was almost seven hours from where we were, one way. We had been alone and out in the cold Canadian forest for quite some time.

AGE FOURTEEN

As a child, I thought that dads everywhere had lots of beer in their refrigerators and that they had whiskey bottles hidden around the house. My dad had a hiding place somewhere in his bedroom, in the basement, and I think he had a place in the garage as well.

I'm quite sure he was self-medicating with alcohol all those years ago, especially after I learned some of the history he had endured as a child, going to war, losing his eye, and his unaddressed mental illness.

I was fourteen when I played a trick on him. I went into the refrigerator. I took a bottle of his beer. I carefully pried the crinkles on the cap with a can opener, poured the beer out, and replaced the contents of the bottle with water. I diligently put the crown cap back on like I had found it, and I put it back in the fridge so it would look as if it were an unopened bottle. When he asked me to get him a beer, I was thrilled.

I watched my dad take a swig of what he thought was beer. I felt excited while waiting for his reaction. I was holding my laughter in. I'm surprised I didn't let a burst of my hilarity out before he caught on to my prank. He immediately spat his mouthful of beer on the living room floor. My amusement quickly changed to fear. I was sure he would take his belt off and hit me with it.

My dad didn't think my joke was as funny as I thought it would be. Although he didn't hit me this time, he was really upset. I never knew when he would go off or what triggered his brutal outbursts, but when he was angry, he would get a certain look on his face, and he would move in closer to me. His stance told me he was ready to attack. His eyes glared. His mouth twisted, and his face turned red. Sometimes he'd bite his tongue. I'd watch him slip his belt through the loops of his green work pants. I couldn't defend myself other than to cry out, "No, please, no, I'm sorry." These moments were critical while my brain flashed fearful thoughts, *I've been here before. He's going to hit me.*

My mind and body were on high alert even during times the environment of our home appeared to be calm.

I knew it was better for me to keep quiet and take a chance of not being hit than to open my mouth (defend myself) and say something that would cause an even more brutal blow to my head and body.

A common phrase my dad repeated throughout the years was, "Children should be seen and not heard." Although, I can't remember him saying it to me that day. The phrase was ingrained in my head.

My dad didn't typically rage or yell. Instead, he hit out. My mother, however, raged. I hate loud noise, loud anything. I hate it when people stand over me watching my every move. My heart starts beating loud, and I become anxious, afraid that someone, anyone around me, can hear this amplified drumbeat that I hear coming from somewhere within me. This heartbeat seems to go crazy, fast, loud, fast, then loud and louder again.

The palms of my hands become hot and moist. Beads of sweat gather in pools on my forehead while garish streaks of my dark brown mascara begin to embellish my cheeks.

When someone stands over me, I drop things, and I fumble. I feel vulnerable, as if I am being judged on every tiny detail of my life—my flaws, thoughts, apprehension, past, future, fears, and the unprecedented turmoil that the thoughts cause me.

This voyeur's intrusion makes me feel crazy, but I try not to let them know what I feel. So, I smile on the outside while crying on the inside.

I always seemed to mess up when my dad stood over me. To this day, I get nervous when anyone stands over me. My poor husband did this, too, until I explained to him why it upset me so much. He had no idea what went on regarding my past, and I had no idea what he had to deal with growing up in his. I don't think Ray had such a great childhood either.

My dad stood over me a lot while I washed the dishes or cooked or whatever household chore I was doing at the time. He towered and glared as if he were waiting for me to mess up so he could swoop down and attack me verbally or physically, then say things to me like, "Is that how your mother taught you?"

I learned to rush through my chores, then get as far away from the work area as possible. That way, I wasn't giving any of my opinionated abusers the opportunity to voice their rejection of me. I don't stand over people and ridicule them because it is rude. It is one thing to teach someone, and it is another to judge them. And really, what gives anyone the right to tell another person their opinion of them?

SITTING WITH MY LEGS CROSSED

I was a Girl Scout. I went from Brownies through to senior scouts. At our meetings and camping trips, we sat on the ground, crossing our legs. We did this in school, too. All the kids sat like this. It was innocent.

One morning before school, wearing jeans and my favorite yellow top, I went into the kitchen for breakfast. My dad was finishing his meal, and he was about ready to leave for work. While my parents chatted, I sat down on a wooden bench in front of the kitchen table and crossed my legs—I was fourteen.

Within seconds after my dad left for work, my mom gave me a disgusted look.

"Don't sit like that," she snarled.

I felt ashamed. I hadn't thought anything of the way I was sitting until my mother made it out to be more. My mother made me feel like I was dirty. After the incident, I became super conscious of the way I sat in front of other people.

MY PARENTS' IN-LAWS

My mom married my dad when she was nineteen. He was twenty-six. My mom's parents didn't like my dad, and my dad's parents didn't like my mom. My siblings and I were looked down on by both families because, compared to seeing how my cousins were treated, well... I felt we didn't fit in.

I remember times when my Aunt Hazel and Aunt Karen, my dad's younger sisters, felt they could share with me what it was they didn't like about my mom. This usually happened after my parents were back together again from one of their separations.

She was my mother. Anything derogatory they said about her, whether I believed it or not, hurt me and made me feel sad. My aunts would tell me in defense of my dad what my mother did to him.

"She didn't call him."

"She shouldn't have left him."

"Why do you think she was so mean to your dad?" Just a few examples of what they'd say to me. The conversations usually left me feeling bad for both my mom and my dad.

My dad stayed away from my mom's parents. The few times that he did visit with my grandparents, the adults were standoffish with each other. Their conversations seemed cold and withdrawn. Few words were spoken between them, and their body language appeared ice cold.

WHO DO I REMIND YOU OF?

I woke up one Sunday morning to the smell of coffee brewing and pancakes on the griddle. There was laughter throughout our home. It was one of the nicer moments that I can remember.

After breakfast, I went to babysit for a neighbor. When I returned and walked through our front door, I was hoping, half expecting the same happiness and laughter I had experienced earlier, but instead, my parents were arguing.

They were shouting at each other. They were fighting about whose mother I reminded them of.

"Judy is like your mom," my dad shouted.

"No, she is like your mother," my mom raged.

I'd walked into a bees' nest, and I didn't know what I had done or what had happened while I was gone those few short hours.

I loved both of my grandmas. I couldn't understand what it was about me that reminded my parents of two people they each personally detested. I felt terrible. I thought there must be something really wrong with me that would cause my parents to argue like this.

I wish I'd asked them what they meant that day, but I just wanted peace in the house, and asking was not the way to peace.

My parents were my caretakers. I believed they knew what was best because my dad would sometimes say, "What do you know? You're just a kid." I internalized more self-hatred. I never understood what bad qualities I may have inherited or why I reminded them of their mothers. It was confusing for me because my grandmothers weren't cruel, they never hit me or hurt my feelings, and they weren't critical of me. I felt they genuinely cared for me.

When I was four, my parents had been upstairs fighting. My Grandma Gina stood outside in the rain looking in on me until the police came. She'd send me cards and letters throughout the years, and she'd talk to me like I was special. I knew she loved me.

Grandma Randall loved me too. When we visited her, she always had something good for us to eat and drink. At times I felt like she talked to me more than she did with my parents, and that made me feel important. I looked forward to the crisp five-dollar bill in my birthday cards every year too.

A CERTAIN SUNDAY

My dad beat me up one Sunday afternoon when I was fourteen. I can't remember why, but really, I never understood why I was getting hit. Most times, he used the belt, but this day he was using his fists to hit me. My parents seemed cold and distant with each other that afternoon because the atmosphere around me felt tense. My dad was sitting in a wooden rocker that had a gold pinstripe design on the back, arms, and legs. When I walked into our living room, he jumped up from the chair and started attacking me. I never ran away from him. I would duck or put my arms out in front of me for protection, but I wouldn't run from him. If I had, well... I just knew I would get a worse beating. This is what I did to survive. This is what I felt I had to do to survive!

Some of my siblings were scattered throughout the house, hiding or doing their own thing. Others were at a friend's house. My mom was there. The house was small, so even though she might've been in another room at the time, she knew what was happening. My mom, as usual, remained silent. Sometimes after the beatings, she would speak up to tell me I deserved them.

"You've had that coming for a long time," she'd say.

When I went to school the following day, one of my teachers took me aside and asked if I was all right. My right hand was discolored and puffy. My nose was enlarged, black, blue, and purple. I looked down at my swollen hand and then back up at him. I smiled; I told the teacher I had walked into a door.

I lied. I was afraid.

I couldn't tell him the truth. It would make my dad, my parents, look bad, especially since they both worked in the same school district where I attended school. They seemed to have a good reputation in the school district, but I knew they were also different people to the world outside our home. I didn't want people to talk about my family. There had been enough drama for me, so I didn't speak up.

Even though nothing else was said, I felt the teacher wasn't buying into my story.

My dad told us repeatedly, "What happens in our home, stays in our home." This phrase was also ingrained in my mind. I felt I couldn't ever ask for help or tell anyone what was going on, not even a friend.

Looking back, I know I should have told the truth because what was happening in my home was wrong. I was in trouble. I needed help. Maybe, if I had said something, my parents would have gotten the help they needed as well.

If abuse is happening to you or you know someone it is happening to, I urge you to get help immediately. Tell someone, call 911, talk to a counselor, a teacher, a neighbor, or a trusted friend. Promise me you will get help and not be afraid like I was. Don't stop talking, you have a voice, and you are entitled to it. No one has the right to hurt you ever!

I have listed crisis hotline phone numbers and websites at the end of this book. You can also find help and resources on the https://www.childwelfare.gov website.[2]

---

[2]https://www.childwelfare.gov website.

CHURCH

My family attended a very authoritarian church. There were times we went to church two and three times a week.

The religion seemed extremely strict to me. We couldn't dance. We couldn't wear jewelry. We couldn't go to the movies. We couldn't go to events like pajama parties or basketball games on a Friday night. I felt scared and horrible if I ever deviated from the rules because it meant I was bad.

Sometimes it felt like the only thing I could do was breathe— and nothing else—to keep from being a sinner and going to hell.

Not everyone at church was judgmental, but more members than not seemed to be, and they would talk. Women shouldn't wear hats or wedding rings because that attracts attention. A person shouldn't draw attention to themselves because when someone is looking at, for example, a woman's diamond ring, their mind is off God. Women and girls wore modest dresses that were below the knee. Men and boys wore nice suits that were freshly cleaned and pressed. If you didn't tithe, if you were divorced, if you danced, wore jewelry, swore, smoked, or consumed alcohol, among other things, this was very bad. Eating meat wasn't healthy. Although eating meat wasn't considered a sin, it was looked down on because your body is the temple of God. I wanted to be good. I didn't want to sin. I was terrified of everything.

Most of the girls my age at church went to a parochial school. Their dads drove fancy cars, and they seemed to have a lot of money, at least more money than my parents had.

The girls wore expensive clothes and were cliquey, probably because they saw each other every day at school. I went to public school, so I was an outsider.

One Sabbath, I was standing outside the sanctuary with some girls in my church class, waiting for the teen service to start. We were chatting when one of the girls mentioned going to a park for a walk after the service. She said her dad would drive us; then, her eyes focused directly on me, and she said, "But there's not enough room for you."

This was at a time when I felt like God didn't really love me. I wanted him to, but I felt that I was too bad. I couldn't keep up with all the rules. I didn't wear nice clothing. My parents told me I deserved to be hit and that my feelings didn't matter. In my eyes, I wasn't good enough for God or anyone. I didn't fit in, and nothing I did was ever right. Even though I tried hard to be good, I wasn't good enough. My parents and the church had confirmed this for me.

My relationship with God has become personal and a reality for me; it is not religious. For me, religion is impersonal and based on fear. I have had enough religion in my life.

OLD BAG

When I was fifteen and in the tenth grade, my mother, a teacher, shared an interesting story. She told me that she had studied and observed children who had abusive parents—parents that verbally and physically mistreated their children and were drunks or on drugs. For these children, it did not matter what their parents did to them or how they were treated. The children, no matter what, defended their parents; they shielded them and stood up for them.

One weekend afternoon we went to visit my Aunt Hazel. I overheard my aunt say that her son, my cousin, came home from school and he'd called her an old bag. My aunt said she slapped him. She was his mother. He was being disrespectful.

The following Monday when I got home from school, my mom started raging at me. I hadn't even had time to say, "Hi Mom, I'm home," before she slapped me across the face and screamed, "I'm not an old bag." All I did was walk in the door. My mother was accusing me of something I didn't do.

I had never called my mother an old bag and honestly, it had never crossed my mind to call her that even after the story I over-heard my Aunt Hazel sharing.

This was not my nature. I respected my parents. My mom had behaved this way before. But drama was what she did, and I always stood up for her.

CYANIDE

I walked into the house one day after school to find my mom eating a peach pit. It was September, the beginning of a new school year. When I walked through the door, I noticed the windows in our house were wide open. It was a warm sunny day, and a warm breeze blew the curtains around. The TV was on in the background, cars zoomed past our house, and the voices of kids walking home from school permeated the air.

My mother was on the sofa, her blue paisley full-skirted dress draped down to the floor, partially covering her bare feet. She had a paring knife in her hand. Curious, I stopped for a moment to watch her shave off tiny fragments of the pit with the knife, and then she began to eat the pieces in front of me.

She had a big smile on her face. Her hazel eyes sparkled. The first thing she said to me was, "Judy, if I die, I want you to know that I've had a good life."

I froze. I'd heard my mother say the word die.

"Why are you going to die?" I asked her.

"I'm going to eat a little piece of the pit every day to build up my immunity against disease like cancer." My mother's voice was cheerful and upbeat.

"Don't eat it if it's going to kill you. I don't want you to die," I said. I was worried about her.

She said, "Well, I might not die. So don't worry. I just want you to know that if I do die, I've had a good life." My mother was eating cyanide. How could I not worry?

I couldn't engage in her euphoria because I felt scared. I was so sure she was going to die. Years later, I learned peach and apricot kernels contain properties that help fight illnesses such as heart disease. They also contain the chemical compound amygdalin or Vitamin B-17, which is converted to cyanide in the body; it is claimed to be an alternative treatment for cancer.

SEWING A DRESS

My mother was good at sewing. She made my dad western-style shirts, tailoring them to fit him just right. He was on the heavy side, but the shirts looked really nice on him. My mother bought beautiful cotton plaid material in grays, browns, and cream colors. She worked extra hard detailing the pockets in front and the yoke in the back with extra stitching. She'd fasten pearlized button snaps on the front of the shirt, the pockets, and the cuffs. When she'd finished, her work looked professional. She sewed western shirts for my brothers too. One year she sewed my sisters and me skirts, dresses, and pants in pretty blue and pastel colors.

When I was in the tenth grade, I sewed a cotton brown-and-white-striped dress all by myself. I picked out the pattern and the material. I paid for everything with my own money. I was excited to get started on my project.

This was the first dress and only dress I have ever sewn. When it came time for me to hem the dress, I started the job, but I didn't finish. I think the monotony of pinning pattern pieces to the material, then cutting them out and sewing them together had tired me.

There have been times throughout my life when I seemed to have had problems with finishing the work I started. This was one of those times. Not completing projects is one of the universal traits children of alcoholics can have.

In my home economics class one year, we decorated panoramic eggs. I decorated the outside of my egg with a pretty pale blue and green frosting. My teacher complimented me on it. I was off to a good start. The inside scene of the egg was the problem. Several classmates had piped frosting to look like a chicken or a bunny. For some reason, I couldn't get mine to look right. So, I attempted a flower. I made a mistake and then scraped the frosting off with a knife. Every once in a while, I would lick the frosting off; everyone else seemed to be doing it too. I tried to make a new flower, but it was just as bad as the first. I had blue, green, and yellow frosting smeared together throughout the bottom of the egg; it was a mess.

A classmate finished her egg scene by showing off cute bright yellow chickens that appeared to be hatching from the pale blue eggs. Another classmate designed a beautiful lavender cross inside her egg. The eggs were all so lovely except for mine. We didn't have much time to finish our work that day, so once again, I piped a flower into the center of my egg. The flower didn't turn out; it looked deformed like the others I had made. I wanted it to be perfect, but I could see that wasn't going to happen for me. I didn't finish the project, but I turned it in any way, and I got a C-minus.

I wanted to wear the dress to school the following day, but I didn't feel like finishing the sewing, so I took a stapler and stapled the rest of the hem. I thought the dress looked nice, and I wore it with brown tights.

No one mentioned the staples or my new dress at school, not that I had expected anyone to, because I don't think anyone ever noticed what I wore or looked like anyway. I mostly faded into the background.

I got a hall pass to get out of class early that day. I noticed a boy a year or so older out in the hall, too. He was a popular boy on the junior varsity football team. He was maybe 5'9", muscular with short dark brown hair. He walked proud, and sure of himself, like he knew who he was. He seemed so opposite from the way I felt about myself.

We had never spoken to each other, ever. I had only noticed him at pep rallies and football games when they announced his name and the position he played.

We passed each other, and I held my breath when he walked by. I became anxious and started fidgeting with the hall pass. I didn't know him. I didn't even have a crush on him. I just knew he was friends with a popular crowd.

We were the only two in the hall when I heard him say, "What a fox!" I almost died. I could feel my face grow hot. I was sure it was turning red, and he would see my embarrassment.

I refused to look at him or in his direction. Instead, I looked straight ahead and pretended I hadn't heard him. I searched for a way out. A boy had just called me a fox, and I didn't know how to react. I wondered if he'd really meant it, or was he making fun of me? No boy at school had ever called me a fox, let alone told me I was pretty. I felt I was quite the opposite. I had short hair, my bangs were cut straight across my face, and I wore very little makeup. My clothes were mostly hand me downs. My parents said I was passive aggressive, a squeaky wheel, and too sensitive. Not the most outstanding qualities for a girl in high school to have.

I wanted to crawl inside one of the blue wall-to-wall lockers that lined the school hallway because all I could think of at the time were my mistakes. I wasn't just thinking about my unfinished hem either. My thoughts turned inward to my flaws. I was shy. I didn't have close friends, I didn't have a boyfriend, I'd gotten a D in Chemistry class, and I wasn't invited to parties. I was so sure this boy had seen all my flaws, and he was making fun of me. I never finished the hem, and I never wore that dress again.

I sit here laughing to myself. I think, back then, when a person called someone a fox, it was meant to be a nice compliment.

BOYFRIENDS

I did not have boyfriends in school. For one thing, I was incredibly shy. I was five-foot-two and weighed maybe one hundred pounds. My dark-blonde hair was still above my ears with short bangs cut straight across my forehead thanks to a haircut my parents had given me while they stood over me fighting.

I wore very little makeup because the church I went to frowned on it. I have to say, facetiously, I was a real beauty.

It wasn't until I was a senior in high school that I grew my hair out long. In the summer, I would use two products, one called Sun-In, a hair lightener, and the other Lemon Up shampoo that came in a yellow plastic bottle with a lemon-shaped screw top cap. I paid for it with my babysitting money. After washing my hair with the lemony scented shampoo, I'd spray Sun-In on strands of my hair, then go out in the sun and wait. My hair, if not all of it, usually turned orange, and it wasn't the subtle, gentle blonde streaks the magazine ads suggested I would get either.

I was in tenth grade when I told my mom I liked a boy. I only liked him. There was no relationship.

Diana was a friend of mine. We weren't in the same classes, but we would walk to school together every morning. I would mostly listen to Diana talk about boys and make-up and what was happening in her life. The high school was close to a mile away from my home, so we had plenty of time to talk.

On the way home from school one afternoon, I went with her to Jake's house. He was Diana's friend and lived only two blocks away from the high school. He was a junior, a year older than us. He had big brown magnetic eyes that drew me in right away. His hair was dark brown but with highlights. He was cute, and he was playing the Beatles on his stereo when we got to his house. I let Diana do all the talking even after she introduced us, but from then on, I would look for Jake at school. Sometimes, we would catch each other's eye in the hallway on the way to our classes and say hi to each other. But I was too shy to start a conversation with him, and he didn't approach me either.

"I like a boy, Mom." I said one day. I told her who he was and how I'd met him. At first, I felt a little uncomfortable talking to her, but she was my mom. I really wanted to trust her.

My mother was standing at the sink washing dishes while I stood next to the back door on what we called the landing while I talked to her. I watched her rinse a plate and then place it in a green plastic dish rack before she stopped what she was doing to look at me. Then with a serious expression on her face. She said, "You will never be with him." I felt the walls closing in on me. I felt worthless.

Standing in front of my mother, I felt as if my body were blowing up bigger and fatter, much larger than in reality. I felt ugly and too pitiful for this boy, or any other boy for that matter to ever want to be with me. I was ashamed of myself for liking him and humiliated for trusting my mom enough to tell her my secret, giving her the opportunity to hit me with her words.

This was one more confirmation of how my mother saw me and how I didn't fit in. If my mother felt this way about me, then in my mind, everyone else had to feel the same way. It was no wonder I seemed to shy away from competition and why I felt beneath everyone. I believed what my mother said was right. I mulled her words over in my head. "You will never be with him." Even my mother thought I wasn't good enough. I didn't ask her why she'd said that. I didn't want to provoke her. I was afraid she might have said something to make me feel worse. I just took her word for it and kept quiet. It was much easier that way.

The following spring, Jake asked a girl in one of my classes to a school dance. I was devastated, but I kept my feelings to myself. I cried alone, determined that I wouldn't share my secrets with anyone ever again.

CPTSD

One of the only times I was invited to a party in high school was when I was fifteen. Bobby, a boy from the neighborhood who was also invited to the party, came up from behind me. Bobby was always nice to me. He was tall and stocky, and his hair was dark brown. He had a lot of freckles, especially during the summer months like I did.

As a teenager, I remember feeling afraid of everything. I'd play what-if games inside my head. What if this happens, or what if that happens? I felt guilty about things that were out of my control. I was ashamed of the way I looked or the way I behaved. I continually found fault with myself for being who I was or rather who I thought I was. I seemed to be frightened of almost anything. I could never relax because my brain was so busy with worry.

I didn't see Bobby coming. I hadn't expected him to be standing behind me. He'd surprised me and it scared me. I screamed. Everyone at the party stopped what they were doing to look at us.

Talking and laughing ended; there was only an eerie stillness. It was the same feeling I had experienced at Pam's wedding when my mom spanked me and the wedding guests stopped to watch.

I felt worse for Bobby than I did for myself. I could see the embarrassment on his face. The situation was awkward, and it was humiliating for both of us.

Back then, I startled easily, and at almost anything—a sudden loud noise or something unexpected. I still frighten easily, but not like before. At the time, this was not a normal, ordinary teenage-girl reaction. Although I was never diagnosed, I believe this was a sign of CPTSD, or Complex Post-Traumatic Stress Disorder, a condition caused by prolonged or chronic trauma. CPTSD can happen when multiple traumatic events occur over time. Causes include multiple incidents of child abuse, in particular child physical abuse and or child sexual abuse, prolonged domestic violence, concentration camp experiences, torture, slavery, and genocide, for example.

CPTSD includes symptoms of Post-Traumatic Stress Disorder which is a mental health condition that's triggered by a terrifying event — either experiencing it or witnessing it. Symptoms may include flashbacks, nightmares, and severe anxiety, as well as uncontrollable thoughts about the event.

Most people who go through traumatic events may have temporary difficulty adjusting and coping, but with time and good self-care, they usually get better.

I have experienced years of trauma in my life. Therapy, feeling safe, writing, setting boundaries, learning to love me, surrounding myself with people I can trust and who are respectful of me is big. We all have our own ways of coping and adjusting. Healing is ongoing for all of us, and I can honestly say that I have come a long way in my recovery.

RANDOM THOUGHTS

As a grown woman, I believe we all have a purpose on this earth. It makes perfect sense that I have more of an understanding of the world as an adult than I ever had as a child, but for many years, I felt I had no purpose.

I grew up not knowing what it was to be loved. You know that old cliché, "Actions speak louder than words"? I have lived the cliché. I am not the only one to have grown up feeling unloved. How sad for those of us that believed what we were told, by people who were supposed to love us. Physical, emotional, and sexual abuse is not love.

My parents provided food and shelter, and I learned in church that Jesus loved me, but I didn't feel love, and I didn't feel accepted.

I needed love and protection as a child. As an adult, I tried hard to keep my own children safe. I did my best, but still, my son Nicholas died. I have learned not everything that happens in life is within my control.

As a parent, I feel as though I've sometimes overcompensated. I was probably irritating at times, only because I wanted my husband and children to feel loved, to feel what I deemed comfortable, and to be happy. I tried to provide for them what I would have liked for myself but never had.

Be careful how you treat a child or what you say to them. They hear you, and when they hear you, they will come to believe and internalize who you say they are. How you label them will not be for only the moment you had your ill-behaved say, but it could very well last an entire lifetime for them.

Without therapy, children who have been abused (those who somehow manage to stay alive and grow into adulthood) will continue to meet people who remind them of their abusers. Statistics are high for adult children to become abusers themselves unless they are willing and determined to end the chaotic cycle, get counseling, and maintain healthy boundaries.

Maybe you will see yourself in my recollections. Maybe you'll recognize someone you know. But what if, when you look into the eyes of an innocent child whose potential for abuse is imminent, will you protect that child? Will you do whatever you can to make the abuse stop for them? I hope so.

No one spoke up to protect me as a child. The lack of therapy caused me to befriend the same type of people in life over and over again. From my childhood to my adult years, every face was different, but the people I encountered had similar traits of either an alcoholic or a narcissistic personality. For some strange reason, I would hang on tightly to their mistreatment, denying it was abuse while ignoring my intuition. I would tell myself that my perception of them was wrong because, in my head, all I heard was, "you are passive aggressive," or "the squeaky wheel gets the grease, doesn't it, Judy?" I heard in my head who my parents told me I was. It was a broken record. "You are good, no, you are bad, your type is less than a Ford guy, you have holes in your face, you will never be with that boy." Oh, and one more—"you are too sensitive."

As if my parents' phrases weren't enough, I would add to the list. I'd tell myself, "I am bad and no good." At times, I would physically hit myself hard in the head, especially if I had said or done something that I thought was wrong or if someone pointed out an imperfection they saw in me.

My caretakers who were supposed to love me told me that I was bad. If they said this, it must be true. In my reality, everyone else was better than me, and they deserved to have better.

I saw the love my parents had in their actions for some of my siblings and other people too, but I didn't feel their love. My parents' repeated negative behavior toward me eventually proved that I didn't matter to them.

In some odd way, I felt I deserved to be hurt. I was hit at home; why not hit myself when no one else was around to do the job for me? In a sick way, there was a momentary reprieve for me after I did this. It was kind of like I would imagine cutting would be for someone. I never did that, but still the pain from my own blows was as real as cutting.

When I did good things, my mom sometimes praised me. When I cleaned the house, or if I said something she liked or did, she would tell me that I was an angel. A real angel. She would tell me how good I was, and the way she spoke her words seemed sincere. This made me feel good about myself, but the next day or days after, if I did something wrong or something she didn't like, she'd say, "You're not an angel; you're bad."

This was one of the times I'd hit myself hard in the head and in front of her. This didn't faze my mom. I wasn't hitting myself for the attention or to see what my mom's reaction would be. I did it because I hated me.

I have been an adult since I was a little girl. I learned to depend on only myself. I could not trust my caretakers or anyone. People always seemed to let me down.

I'm learning there are many of us out there—grown adults living a life where we never feel good enough, and we can't make a decision for fear of making the wrong choice.

As children, we were mistreated by the adults we looked up to. They were authority figures; they were our caretakers who were supposed to love and nurture us, but that didn't happen.

The way they talked to us and treated us became our very own personal derogatory dialogue.

Read the previous sentence again.

This dialogue became the bad thoughts we developed about ourselves inside our heads.

I grew up knowing how to handle dysfunction. Drama and turmoil were what I knew. The fight or flight response was a constant for me. I was good at reading people and my surroundings. I knew when to speak up and when not to, but more than not, I didn't speak up at all.

I knew what could set my parents off in any given situation, and for the most part, I tried hard to avoid their reactive outbursts. I was learning how to survive.

This is what was normal for me. I learned all I had to do was hold my breath and hang on tight to get through the outrageous to survive. As I was growing older, my parents' repetitive behavior was becoming more demeaning and embarrassing for me. My friends' parents didn't beat each other up. Their parents weren't taking them out of school mid-semester. They weren't breaking up and getting back together again. My friends weren't physically abused.

They had healthy normal girlfriend/boyfriend relationships. They wore nice clothes. Their mothers spoke up for them, not with just their words but with their actions as well. Their mothers wanted the best for their daughters, and even me, a spectator, could see that.

As a child, I found that when there was a reprieve, when things seemed to be going well, it was like I was on a roller coaster ride making my way uphill. I felt like I could start breathing again, but once the ride started charging down the track, I was its prisoner. I had no choice but to go along with the gaining speed and twisting turns, always quite sure I would crash because of the outcomes of my past experiences.

When I was on my way to the top of the ride, I was trying to laugh, desperately wanting to be in the moment, but I had this huge stockpile of fear in the back of my mind harassing and haunting me. It was my inner critic, the liar, the one who hated me—the one who cringed at every word I said or every movement I made, telling me not only that I was bad, but something troublesome was going to happen. My biggest fear: someone I loved was going to die.

That's when I'd start the repetitive praying and counting inside my head, anxiously hoping these rituals would keep the bad thoughts away. This was exhausting.

When I was six, my mother's aunt wanted me to sing a song in front of my family and people I didn't know. They were strangers from out of town visiting my grandmother's house. I was missing two front teeth, and my elbows and knees were bruised and scabbing over from a recent fall after I'd been running down a hill. As shy as I was, this woman's request made me feel important, even if the feeling I had didn't last long. My audience applauded. My face grew warm, I was shy, so I scrunched up my mouth, trying hard not to smile in front of them. However, the gigantic grin across my face won out, but when I walked away, I heard them laugh. My six-year-old mind felt hurt at their laughter, but the adult me knows it was because I was a little girl being cute.

Then as an adult, I realized how some family members were nice to my face, but when I turned to walk away, I heard their comments too. "I wish she'd do something with her hair." "What does Ray see in her?" Sometimes they felt brave enough to spew their rhetoric to my face.

"You know if my daughter Dara was older, she'd be with Ray not you." Doris, my father-in-law Ed's ex-wife, said this to me years ago. Again, I was speechless, but I was a married woman. Her daughter was eleven at the time. What? I'm laughing again.

Rude behavior bothered me, but honestly, I have learned a great deal from disrespectful people and the garbage they have inflicted. Their abuse has only made me stronger.

I may have put up with it in the past, but I will not put up with it any longer. I have boundaries now. How brilliant is that? I love boundaries!

I now recognize the signs of certain narcissistic personality traits. This is my cue to not engage. I walk away. I cannot change another person's behavior toward me. I can only change me, and how I react to them. Dysfunctional people want a reaction. I refuse to give them what they want.

I have also learned that these same ill-mannered people are not just mean to me, but they generally treat everyone in the same way because it is who they are, it's how their brain works, but shame on them.

I have learned that there were more times than not when no one really cared about me because they had enough of their own problems without dealing with mine, too. When I was seven, I irritated people. Not only was my singing too loud, but falling and hurting myself seemed too much for my parents to handle. When I was seventeen, I seemed to be even more of a bother. Why else would my parents hit me and then tell me I deserved it? "Quit feeling sorry for yourself," my mom would say.

I have been told that the simple, embarrassing, humiliating, and vulnerable moments are only for a season and that I will someday look back on them and laugh. Did I? I don't think I ever did look back and laugh. I cried. Sometimes, I still cry. Abuse is not funny, and it is not something you forget or get over quickly.

I know that beauty comes from within, and innocence starts at birth. I believe that innocence gradually becomes wisdom, but for some, like me, innocence stayed a little longer than it should have. When children are emotionally, physically, and or sexually abused or when they have observed abuse happening inside their homes as I did, we become broken. My life became hampered, the trauma caused not only blunt force to my body, but mental blows to my brain as well. I became stuck because the abuse I had endured held me back from going forward, but working with counselors on trauma has really helped.

I believe wisdom, at least for me, was established through growth, choice, trial, error, and being physically and emotionally abused.

WHO WILL I SLEEP WITH?

When I was seventeen, my parents were having problems still, and again. At the time, my mom's friend was sleeping with a Black man. I didn't know this until my parents bickered about it at the dinner table one evening. Really, why would I want to know? It wasn't any of my business.

My siblings and I stayed quiet while my parents argued throughout our meal. Maybe my dad was afraid my mom would leave him for another man. I don't remember everything they were saying to each other. I was eating my dinner, and although a little curious, I was probably trying to tune out their heated conversation. They hadn't spoken to my siblings or me, but at one point amid their arguing, my dad looked away from my mom and glared at me. His face was bright red.

"Judy," he said, "you will probably sleep with a Black man." Only he didn't say, Black man. He used the derogatory word. He said this to me in front of my mom and my brothers, and my sisters.

My dad's words stung. I sat at the table amid my siblings, feeling humiliated. I was embarrassed that my dad could say these hate-filled words to me and in front of my younger siblings. I felt numb while fighting back my tears. I was afraid to stand up for myself. So, I didn't do anything other than observe my surroundings, my parents' facial expressions, and their body language while knowing the entire time it would be wise for me to keep my mouth shut.

In the seventies, racism was even more prevalent than it is today. There was a stigma for a white woman to befriend a Black man, let alone sleep with him. A relationship like that was not accepted then, as it thankfully is today.

But why would my dad blurt those words out at me like that? And why didn't my mom do anything to stand up for me? She didn't protect me.

If my husband, or if anyone, had ever said anything like that to any one of my children, I wouldn't have just sat there. I would have said something. If my mom was afraid of my dad, which I know at times she was, she could've said something to me privately afterward, when we were alone, like, "I'm sorry; you didn't deserve that." But she didn't say anything.

She didn't protect me.

PROM

I didn't go to my senior prom. Brandon, a boy in one of my classes, did ask me, but I reminded him that he'd already asked another girl, a friend of mine, and I told him, "No, thank you."

After that, I lost my respect for Brandon, although I was happy to hear that he did take my friend to prom as he'd promised her.

Norma, another one of my classmates, wasn't asked to go to prom either, so we went to the movies together that night. Norma was quiet; she was tall and dark-complected with long black hair. She had a pretty smile. I think she was the oldest in her family too. I know she had a younger sister and a little brother.

We saw *The Poseidon Adventure.* I don't think either one of us really cared about it.

At some point in the movie, I felt my throat tighten. The realization that it was too late to go to my senior prom hit me hard. I'd missed out on shopping for a pretty dress and shoes, getting my hair done, being with a boy, dancing, and feeling like I was a part of something that at the time was quite significant for most girls.

I fought back sobs that I knew, if let out, would be loud and difficult for me to control. But as hard as I tried to fight my tears, they wouldn't stop, so I cried as softly as possible so that I wouldn't disturb anyone. My cheeks were wet with tears that would not stop, and my nose was running, but I didn't want anyone to know that I was filled with so much hurt.

I wasn't crying about how sad the movie was, and it really was a distressing movie—a disaster film about a ship hit by a tidal wave, turning upside down, with some people drowning and some trying to climb out. I was crying because I, too, was hit with a crushing blow. I didn't get to go to my senior prom. For me, this moment in time was lost forever. I would never have this time back again.

When I looked at my friend Norma, I saw that she was crying, too.

COLLEGE

When I was in my senior year of high school, my parents gave me two options. I could stay home and go to a local community college or attend a community college in a small town in northern Michigan where my grandparents lived and where my parents had grown up. I chose to be with my Grandma Gina.

I wanted to leave home, yet I was afraid to go because I felt I was leaving behind younger siblings that I thought could become potential punching bags in my place, but I left anyway. I felt guilty, but something in my heart was pushing me to leave. Feeling guilty was pretty much an everyday emotion for me anyway.

I was happy to be away at school. There are no words to describe how I felt. I was glad not to deal with so much stress and drama in my home life. I looked forward to living every day. My only responsibility was taking care of and looking out for myself and my needs. It was a significant change. I still worried about my siblings, but I liked my new independence. I felt free.

I didn't have nice clothes like the other girls had, and there wasn't any spending money coming in from my parents because they couldn't afford it. But I had school loans and was in the work-study program, which helped. I held my head up high, and I pressed on.

I made close friends, which was so unlike me when I was in elementary school. I lived in the dorm, so friendships seemed to be a little stronger because, in a sense, we all lived under the same roof, a two-story brick building that housed maybe 150 students when it was full.

Most of us lived hours away from our homes; some students came from other states to attend the two-year curriculums the community college offered, like Nursing, Forestry, Concrete, Accounting, Automotive, and Law Enforcement, to name a few. I was enrolled in the Law Enforcement program.

Living in the dorm, my new friends and I watched TV, played tag football and soccer, and ate our meals together. We had parties exclusive to the residents in the dorm and keggers around bonfires late at night. One of those nights, I saw the Northern Lights for the first time. The October night air was crisp and biting. I wore layered clothing underneath an aqua blue sweatshirt to keep warm. I stood close, watching red and blue flames eat up pine logs that some Forestry students were throwing into the fire.

"Look at that," one of the boys said while his eyes seemed glued to the sky. Green wavy dancing lights were moving across the horizon in strange patterns.

I felt like I was on top of the world, so I'd sing the Carpenters song "Top of The World," and I'd sing Tammy Wynette's, "I Never Promised You a Rose Garden." Every morning I'd belt out the lyrics while I walked the field from the dorm to the student center where our meals at the college were served. The student center was another brick building where the main floor consisted of long tables covered in white paper, surrounded with chairs. The distance was only a city block or two away from the dorm.

I know my peers thought I was crazy, and I was, but it didn't matter because I was happy. I had never felt this way before. Seriously, I had never felt so happy, and free.

I received an Associate of Applied Science degree, but I didn't work in law enforcement. It was a time when women were at the forefront of entering a career that was mainly dominated by men. I felt that the men on the police force interviewing me for various job titles offered, were apprehensive about hiring me. I soon gave up submitting resumes and going on interviews. Although I was hired to work for a detective agency that would allow me to travel to Hawaii at least once a month, I declined the offer.

While I did very well in my classes and studying police investigations interested me a lot, I was still quite naive and vulnerable. Two years away from home at a small community college hadn't changed this reality.

TEACUPS

My mom collected pretty china teapots and teacups. She had many of them, and she loved having tea with them, especially when we had company. She was also very protective of the china cups and saucers. "Watch," she'd say while taking a deep breath. "Be careful. I don't want you to break it." Once when I was sixteen, she held on to a cup, not letting go of it even after she'd already handed it to me. I was holding it, but she didn't want to let go.

I had arrived home from college one fall afternoon for a long weekend. Our neighbor from across the street was visiting. My mom, my sister Rita, our neighbor Alice, and her sweet two-year-old daughter Lorie sat at my parent's pine trestle table drinking tea. When I sat down, Lorie smiled at me; her little blue eyes twinkled. I couldn't help but notice a flowery teacup and saucer sitting directly in front of her. They were all drinking from my mom's fragile bone china, made in England teacups; even the little two-year-old had hot chocolate in hers.

Every teacup was different. Purple and pink pansies cascaded across one cup and saucer; another was blue violets weaving around a tiny thin green vine. The detailed cups portrayed yellow daisies, blue forget me nots, and dainty roses.

"Would you like some tea?" my mother asked me.

"Yes," I said. A cup of hot tea sounded good, and I wanted to visit with Alice. Sometimes she'd watch Rita on the days my mom was substitute teaching. Alice was a happy uplifting lady. She made people laugh with her funny stories and jokes. I liked being around her for those reasons.

My mother offered me a cup of tea, but the cup she served me was not a pretty china teacup; it was a brown, unbreakable coffee mug. That was her choice. I took the brown cup from my mother, glancing in Lorie's way. I felt like I'd been slapped in the face. I felt like I didn't belong or deserve to drink from a pretty cup and saucer like everyone else. As much as my mom cherished her china cups and saucers, she'd given one to a toddler and not me. I already knew she was pretty nervous about people handling her china but giving one to a two-year-old? I didn't question my mother or ask for a china cup. That would have been considered rude, and I might have paid for it later with an insult. At the time, I was feeling slighted; that alone was difficult enough for me.

My mom could be kind, but she could be hurtful, too; looking back, I see a pattern. I used to believe I was the problem. Always afraid I would say or do something wrong when all I wanted was for her to be happy because if mom was happy, we were all happy.

My mother knew a lot of people; it seemed everywhere we went, she would stop to talk with someone. I tagged along with my mother one day, and I asked her, "Mom how do you know so many people? Everywhere we go, there's someone you know."

"Everyone has their own story," she said, grinning.

I will confess she did have a way of melting a person's heart, including mine… sometimes.

MOM BEING MOM

All through school, when I'd invited friends over after school, they'd leave me behind to follow my mom around and talk to her. I didn't have friends over that often. Like most kids, I had to get permission from my mom first. My mom often said the house was messy, and she was too tired to have company.

"Let's go outside," I'd say, but the girls didn't want to visit with me. They wanted to talk to my mom; she was more interesting. This made me sad, but as usual, I believed it was about me and who I was, unlikeable, while my mom told my friends everything they wanted to hear about themselves. "You have the prettiest smile." "Did your mother make your dress?" "I love your shoes. Where did you get them?" "Would you like some tea?" Recently, a childhood friend shared that as teenagers, my mom took her aside and told her she could be a model, adding "Judy could never be a model, her feet are too wide." The girls liked the attention my mother was giving them. In a way, I sometimes felt like I was competing with my mom over my girlfriends. I didn't go to the girls' houses to visit with their mothers, and I doubt very much their moms would have wanted to hang out with me.

My mom was friendly to the outside world, wanting to be liked and admired by others like we all do, but inside our home, she was different. I had to be careful about what I said or did because she wasn't afraid to say what she thought about me, and it wasn't "you have the prettiest smile." I never knew what might set her or my dad off.

My mom would sometimes speak so loudly that everyone around us could hear what I believe should have been kept private. "Mom, the neighbors will hear." I'd say in a whisper.

"Let them hear!" my mother would say even louder. It was a

warm summer Saturday, and all the windows in our house were open. Neighbors were outside doing yard work, and neighborhood kids were laughing and playing, but she kept yelling. I remember running around trying to close the open windows. I didn't want anyone to hear. I wanted her to stop yelling, but she wouldn't.

My mother played the victim. She could be very convincing. "Judy called me an old bag." "My husband won't let me paint a wall." "I don't know what I did to make them treat me that way." She knew how to play on people's emotions.

MY TWENTIES

When I was twenty, my Grandma Gina was dying from cancer. She was unable to get out of bed.

While I sat next to her one afternoon, I noticed she was growing more uncomfortable. I could see that she was trying to get into a different position, but she was too weak to move, and she was having a tough time speaking as well.

My grandma had always been strong. She had been my hero, and now she needed me. She didn't ask me to help her, but I knew I had to do something. I began to pray for her, while as gently as possible, I moved her body upward so that her neck and back could rest against several pillows. At one point, I saw her face squint and cringe. I felt terrible that while lifting, I had hurt her, but when she leaned up against the pillows, the features on her face relaxed, and that told me she was all right.

We never said a word to each other, but we had simultaneous tears trickling down our faces. Me, because this woman who had been so strong for me was terribly sick. I felt helpless. She was hurting and in a lot of pain. I believe she was crying because not only did she feel defeated, but she knew she couldn't be strong anymore. We were crying because everything in our lives was changing.

I will never forget what my grandma said to me a week before she died. I was attending junior college in town at the time, and she was in the hospital. I visited her every day after school or between classes because I was determined to see her, even if she slept through my visits and did not know I was there.

As I have mentioned before, my grandma was four-feet-ten-inches tall, and every day I visited her, it seemed to me as though she was smaller than the day before. Seeing her weak and helpless was devastating for me, but I remember one afternoon in particular—a bright, sunny day in June.

She was awake when I entered the hospital room. Her voice was soft like it had always been, but it was weak, too, and she said to me, "Judy, I have been praying for you. I have been praying for you to have a good life."

I had prayed a lot for my grandma, my family, and others throughout the years, but I hadn't thought about someone praying for me.

Her words that day were what helped to comfort and carry me through the tough times in my adult life. I will forever be grateful for my Grandma Gina—for her prayers and her genuine love and kindness toward me while I was growing up.

I have taken her words seriously, especially in my times of feeling unworthy and not good enough. Her words gave me strength. I have repeated them to myself throughout the years.

"Judy, I have been praying for you. I have been praying for you to have a good life."

I was someone important enough for someone else to have prayed for.

EXPLOSIONS OF ONE KIND OR ANOTHER

Watching my parents fight and hit each other was, at one time, what I thought happened in every family, and yet something deep within told me I was wrong.

When I was eleven, my dad began to take his frustrations out on me. I didn't realize or understand at the time that he was out of control. Such drama was what happened in my environment.

Hitting others seemed to be a way for him to release his anger. He needed help. I believe he didn't know how to deal with what was going on inside his head, but still, it was no excuse for his hostile behavior. He had a poor self-image. I believe he felt empty, alone, and out of control, thus his explosive outbursts of physically hitting out. He could be aggressive, irritable, and impulsive.

He was reckless about safety, like when he built a moonshine still in our garage without a permit. The distillation process causes flammable vapors. This terrified me. I worried the garage would explode, and I was so sure if he hadn't blown up in the potential explosion, he would be found out, arrested, and go to prison.

The last time my dad hit me, I was twenty. I had been away at school for a while but moved back home to work. I was trying to save money so I could move out and live on my own. Naïveté on my part, but after being away from home, I hoped that since I was changing, maybe my parents were changing, too. Moving back was the wrong choice. Nothing at home ever seemed to change for the good.

After work one evening, I walked into another of my parent's arguments. Another physical fight. I was so troubled that I screamed. My dad reacted by punching my head into a beige telephone hanging on the kitchen wall. Once again, my mother did nothing; she stood back, silent, and appeared to be the victim. My mother never supported me, and she rarely ever apologized for anything.

I screamed at them because I wanted them to stop. It still bothered me to see them hurt each other just like it had when I was a little girl.

After taking the hard punch from my dad's fist to my head, I felt dazed. I was angry, anxious, and demoralized. I had been disrespected in so many ways. I was crazy with fear and confusion that night, but this is when I left home—and the last time my dad ever hit me.

When I was younger, my dad belting out at me was scary, confusing, and demeaning. Yet I felt I deserved his abuse. Throughout the years, my parents told me I deserved to be punished, not with just their words but with their actions. After my dad would beat me up, my mother would continue to tell me I had it coming. She'd say, "You deserved that." And here's the crazy part: I felt if my dad was hitting me, he wasn't hitting my siblings or my mom. I thought I was protecting them. That's how much I thought of myself. I stood up for my mother, but she wouldn't do it for me. Why? I used to think that there was something terribly wrong with me. I know now it wasn't me. It was my parents. They needed help.

Looking back, I think for my parents to hit me in anger—or anyone for that matter to hit out at anyone when they are out of control, especially a child—is wrong in so many ways.

More times than not, I didn't know what I had done wrong to deserve the physical abuse, and I didn't have a clue when the violence would happen.

Voices would escalate, and my dad would jump up from wherever he was seated and charge. My parents' moods could be abrupt. There was peace and calm one minute, chaos the next, and they were aware of what they were doing. This was difficult to understand because why would anyone purposely hurt another creature, especially a parent abusing their child?

The *Psychology Today* website has several interesting articles explaining why an abuser is aware of what they are doing.

I WANTED TO RUN AWAY

When I was thirteen, and until I graduated high school, I would go to bed at night making plans in my head to run away. I would think of where, how, and when I would leave home, but I always came to the same conclusion. I'd never go through with those plans. I was terrified. The what ifs of running away scared me. I was afraid of staying, too, but the planning inside my head took me away from reality for a while.

I knew I couldn't leave because not only would I get it from my parents once they caught up to me, but our relatives and the neighbors would talk. I was afraid of the horrible things they might say about me. I didn't want to hear how terrible I was.

Others had told me my entire life that I wasn't good enough through their words, actions, and how they treated me. I didn't want to feel more shame than I already had. Besides, there were my siblings to worry about. I felt they needed me.

Mary was my dad's cousin, and she was much younger than he was. While growing up, I was told she was a wild child. My parents' derogatory comments told me she got into trouble a lot. They said she was promiscuous and rebellious.

Throughout my childhood, my parents often told me I was going to grow up to be like her. "You're just like Mary," they'd say. This made me feel bad. Even though I didn't know her, I didn't want to be like Mary. I wanted to be Judy. I wanted to be a good girl.

We were told, "What happens in our home stays in our home." I couldn't ask for help or tell anyone what was going on. So, I stayed home, and I protected.

My runaway plans were a way for me to disconnect from my real world, at least for a while. I was giving myself hope—false hope, but hope.

THE DAY BEFORE

Several months before my dad died, his personality seemed to change. He was quieter and more subdued. He seemed fragile to me. He wasn't interested in TV, working out in his garage, or starting a garden that year like he usually had every other year. He seemed tired all the time, and he was sad. It was as if his fight to live was gone. He was depressed, although I never dreamed he would do what he did.

Occasionally while visiting my parents, I would find my dad on his knees, praying. He'd be kneeling next to his bed or sitting quietly alone reading his Bible. This was when I spoke to him more than I ever had. I hoped I could comfort him, but he barely said a word back to me; he only seemed to listen. I remember talking to him about a lot of things, and I told him not to be sad or depressed. "We all love you," I said.

I wonder, when did it all go so crazy for him? Was it his childhood? Was it the war or when he lost his eye? Was it a combination of life events?

The day before my dad's death, I was outside in my yard, mowing the lawn and pulling weeds. I brought a radio outside to listen to music while I worked, as I often did; it made the work seem a little easier and helped the time go by faster.

I had plans for later that day to plant red Geraniums in an old coal bucket I'd painted black. I planned to set the bucket on my front porch for a pretty decoration.

I breathed in the summer day and continued to work. I remember looking away from pulling weeds for a moment when I saw my dad's green Ford Econoline passing down the neighborhood's main street.

My dad worked close by, so he sometimes went home for lunch. I assumed he was on his way back to work. In my mind, I still see him driving the van out of the subdivision for the last time.

Rita came to my house after school that afternoon. "Daddy didn't come home." She said she'd called the school where he worked, but he'd called in sick, he wasn't there; that's when she left my house and went looking for him on foot.

I didn't know what happened to him other than my brothers had been out searching for him all night. We had all been looking for him; calling relatives, friends, and co-workers; trying to find him because he hadn't come home, and this wasn't like him, at least not anymore. My mother told me that they were arguing before they both left for work that morning, but she didn't tell me why or what the argument was about, and I didn't ask.

When my mom got home from work that afternoon, I followed her around the house. I was talking to her about where she thought my dad might be. When we were in the hallway on our way to the kitchen, she stopped suddenly in front of an empty wall. She cupped her hands over her mouth.

"The gun is gone," she said. I froze.

"I had your brothers hide his guns a few months ago," she continued then paused. "All but this one."

"What do you mean?" I asked her. "He wouldn't kill himself... would he?" My throat tightened, and my heart started pounding.

This was the first time I'd heard my brothers had removed my dad's guns from the house. They'd all been hidden. "All but this one." I repeated my mom's words inside my head. My mother and I stood silent, as still as statues.

"Before your dad was born, a man killed himself with this gun. He had six kids too," my mom said. After she'd said this, I felt dizzy.

"What man?" I asked her, but my mother didn't answer me. She just stood there staring at the wall. I remember thinking why wasn't it destroyed? I had grown up in this house. Why would the gun be allowed to hang on our wall? And why would my mother bring this bit of information up to me now? I thought it was strange, and, in a way, it angered me.

DAD'S SUICIDE

On a June morning, and within minutes of my husband leaving for work at 5 a.m., my phone rang.

"Judy, come home," my mother said. "The police are here, and they want to talk to us."

"Is Dad all right? Did they find him?" I asked.

"Just come to the house," my mother said.

The morning was quiet, still dark outside, although the sun was about to rise. I walked through the neighborhood fast. My parent's home was only about a city block and a half from mine. The air was so calm and dense that it almost felt like I couldn't breathe. I remember hearing birds chirp. Only a few at first, then more birds clucked and whistled, all growing noisier by the minute. As I got closer to my parents' home, I saw a city police car parked out in the street.

I don't remember climbing the steps to the front porch. I only remember opening the aluminum screen door to let myself in. It squeaked and rattled. To my left stood two tall police officers dressed in blue. They were leaning against a plain white wall in the living room. I felt like I was standing still, yet my body was moving because I passed in front of them and over to a brown tweed La-Z-Boy chair, where I sat down. I sat maybe four feet away from the officers.

I felt out of my body, watching myself sit down. The police said nothing, and I sat in that chair feeling as if I was paralyzed, drugged, waiting for them to tell me something, as my mom told me they would. I was telling myself that I needed to be nice to the officers. I needed to smile and address them. I shouldn't let my emotions show, even though there was a lot of crazy happening around me.

I felt fear, confusion, and deep sadness. I felt numb.

My mother must have heard me come in. She walked toward me from the vicinity of her bedroom, but she didn't say anything; she wasn't crying either. She just looked dazed, like she'd been hypnotized. She wore a one-piece belted dress. I think it was the light brown one she often wore. She was in her bare feet, walking closer to me. For a moment she stopped and just looked at me. Her eyes seemed blank and distant. She didn't speak. Instead, she turned around and went back in the direction of her bedroom.

The house felt eerie; it was quiet and dark, except for the dim ceiling light that shone over the hallway. I could hear my twelve-year-old sister's muffled cries from the back bedroom. Rita and my mom were the only two in the house besides me and the police. I don't know where my brothers were; my sister Josie was married and lived close by.

I couldn't understand why the police weren't saying anything. They just stood there silent with blank faces. I watched them for a moment in this seemingly horrible dream I was having. I was still trying to sort things out in my mind. Why weren't the police telling me what was going on? Had my mom lied to me? I went into a back bedroom where I tried to comfort my youngest sister Rita, but I couldn't. She was lying face down on her bed, sobbing into a pillow. "Daddy died." She was inconsolable, and soon I was crying, too.

Back in the living room, the two young officers about my age, 26, maybe a little older, continued to look straight ahead. I felt anxious and nervous because I didn't know what to say to them. It seemed they were looking at something on the opposite wall from where they were standing. So, I looked straight ahead, too. I stared at the screen door for a few minutes, thinking that my dad would walk through at any moment. I stared at the picture window, but it was still dark outside. I couldn't see anything. It was as if I was looking through a solid concrete wall.

I didn't want to ask the police officers questions. I wanted them to tell me something I needed to know. Whatever the details, I needed to hear it from them. My dad had died, but I just wanted them to say something. Anything!

My mother came out of my sister's room, but this time she approached me and asked, "Is there anything you want to ask the police officers?"

"Aren't they supposed to tell us something? That's what you told me."

I was angry and confused. Upset that my dad had died and that my mother had told me to come home because the police officers wanted to talk to us. But they weren't talking. Nobody was.

I couldn't move, let alone ask questions of the officers, but I felt I should be polite, as stupid as it sounds to me now, because my entire life, I was told to be nice to people because that's what Jesus wants. I felt it was up to me to make the police officers feel at ease instead of the other way around.

My mother's words echoed in my head. "Is there anything you want to ask the police officers?" Of course, I had a dozen questions I wanted to know the answers to, but my thoughts and my words were jumbled. Inside my head, I demanded they tell me what I needed to hear, what we all needed to hear. *What happened? Where was he? What did he do? How did he do it? Who found him? Was he alone? Are you sure it was my dad? Where is he now?*

Finally, I asked aloud, "How did he die?"

"I'm very sorry. He shot himself," an officer said. His face was stoic. He had no expression, no emotion, and he spoke the words as if they'd been rehearsed.

I was furious. My dad had killed himself and with a gun that had been hanging on a wall in our family home.

I left my mother's house at daybreak. I ran fast, so fast it felt as if I were flying. My heart was racing, beating hard, pounding wildly while my mind felt like what I would imagine a combat zone to be. I tried to organize my terrifying thoughts as I ran to my house. My scattered thoughts ricocheted and hit hard within my brain as if in a head-on crash happening repeatedly. Was it true, or was I dreaming?

"Son of a bitch," I said inside my head as I hurried home. "Son of a bitch," I mumbled. "Son of a bitch, son of a bitch, son of a bitch," I repeated before I finally screamed the words out loud. I was swearing, it felt good to say the words, yet it felt bad because I knew it was wrong to say them. After all, I was supposed to be a Christian, and I didn't swear. The strict religiosity of my childhood had crippled me. Not only was I feeling crazy but now guilt-ridden for swearing.

I blew fast through my back door, pleading, crying out to God, "Please, please help!"

I was panting, trying to catch my breath, half crying, half out of my mind, still trying to determine if this was some horrible dream, knowing very well that deep down, it wasn't even a nightmare.

What had happened was something far worse. My dad was dead.

I was all alone in my house and in my thoughts. My hands shook while I reached for the phone hanging against our kitchen wall in an attempt to call my husband. He worked for General Motors. I desperately punched in numbers with my index finger, unintentionally hitting the wrong keys, then having to start the process all over again, and again.

Ray had to come home. I needed him.

After my dad's suicide, I was afraid people I knew would kill themselves. So, I tried to be especially nice to everyone, more than I ever had. I felt I had to be careful of what I said because my words might be what would set a person over the top or cause them to hurt themselves or someone else. This was exhausting for me, and it was more distorted thinking. Even so, I could not have that on my conscience.

I remember arguing with my husband not too long after my dad's death. Ray does not have or has he ever had suicidal tendencies. But when he walked out of the house, got into his truck, and left, I followed in my car just to make sure he wouldn't kill himself.

RED

Another June morning, the tenth anniversary of my dad's suicide. I pause for a moment, and I continue to paint my toes red. I'm remembering, and I'm overthinking again. Red is the color I painted before my dad's funeral.

After the funeral, my nails were flaking and peeling red paint for well over a month. I didn't do another pedicure or apply new polish that entire time. Back then, in my mind, the nail polish somehow symbolized holding onto my dad's memory for a while longer. His suicide was devastating.

I looked up the meaning of the color red one day. It is often associated with the word stop. Even though he had been abusive, there is a part of me that still loves him.

He was mentally sick. Whatever it was in his mind that caused him to hit others stopped for him the day he died, but sadly, the memories of his abuse in some still living has not.

When I was a little girl, from the age of eleven until I turned seventeen, my dad would occasionally tell me that I would grow up to be bitter. I'd be alone, quietly minding my own business, when he would walk over to me and say, "Judy, you're going to grow up to be a bitter woman." His words still confuse me. Had I reminded him of someone else that was bitter? Now, I wonder if he saw me in himself. *Maybe the part of himself he didn't like.* I guess I will never know.

TWO DAYS AFTER

I don't remember my mom showing emotion after my dad's suicide. I didn't see her cry after he died. That doesn't mean she didn't hurt. It only means I didn't see any emotional reaction from her. However, two days after his death, I remember being really distraught. I was crying hard. I was trying to talk to her. My dad had shot himself in the head! He'd killed himself!

I was pouring my pain out on my mother. Without a word, without expressing to me what she thought about my feelings or her feelings or anyone else's feelings for that matter, she slapped me hard across the face. I was upset over my dad's suicide; I was angry, and I felt humiliated. I was an adult, and my mother slapped me.

I immediately left my mom's house, slamming the aluminum storm door behind me as my sister Josie arrived. Josie was barely behind the gated fence before we met each other. Her eyes were red and puffy. She'd been crying about my dad, too. I don't remember talking to her. Instead, I slapped her in the face as my mother had hit me. My sister's eyebrows lifted, her jaw dropped slightly, then her eyes widened and filled up with tears. We didn't speak. She stood in place, but I kept walking forward. I wouldn't look back. I felt terrible. I don't know why I hurt her. I wish I could take it back.

I didn't understand why my mom hit me, but then I remembered a time years before, it was a time after she'd left my dad, and we found ourselves on our way up to stay with my grandparents. I was in the sixth grade.

I wasn't allowed to talk to my dad. We had been at my mom's parents for a couple of weeks before I told my mother that I wanted to call my dad, that I wanted to talk to him and talk to my Grandma Randall too (my dad's mom). My mother looked at me, lowered her voice, and said, "No. You're not calling them. I don't want you talking to them."

We were in my Grandma Gina's bathroom. I was twelve but still a child. I was sitting on the toilet with the lid down, and my mother was brushing my hair out. I think it must have been after she'd given me a perm because my hair had a lot of snarls in it, and the brushing hurt.

I was crying. "Why? Why can't I call?" I asked. My mom's nose flared.

"I don't care what you say. I'm going to call them." I insisted. By this time, I was crying harder, holding my breath in between sobs. My mother was still standing over me with a hairbrush in her hand. Her face was red, her lips tightened, and I watched her eyebrows raise then lower again. Without trying to calm me down or reason with me, my mother slapped me hard across the face with her hand.

"You will do what I tell you," she said. Years later, John said he'd walked in on my mother slapping me over and over again across the face. My brother said it was disturbing.

THE FUNERAL

I showered, did my make-up, and put on a clean dress. I was getting ready for my dad's funeral; I went to my mom's house to wait several hours until we would all be ready to go to the funeral home together. Ray was working that day. His shift would be over in time for him to go, but I didn't want to be alone while waiting for him, so I went to my parents' house.

After walking through the door, my mom told me I smelled like B.O. I was twenty-six. She made me feel dirty and disgusting. I was so embarrassed.

I went home, washed my dress, showered, and put deodorant on again. I went back to her house once more. When I entered her home, my mother approached me. Without saying a word, she sniffed and shook her head no. I went home, showered, and rewashed the dress. It was so degrading. Not only was I dealing with the loss of my dad, but I was so disgraced at the moment that all I wanted to do was run away and hide forever, but I bristled.

How could I ever feel good about myself after this kind of abuse?

I did not realize it back then, but it wasn't about me, because who could smell bad after washing an already clean dress twice and taking three showers in a matter of two hours? I had always been self-conscious of my personal hygiene. I took care of myself. My mom was being nasty. It was about what was going on with her and not me. I tried to please, but if I could go back, I would never do it again. Although I had apologized to Josie, I believe this was my mother's way of punishing me for slapping my sister. I loved my mother, but she had serious issues too. She had traits of a narcissist. Sometimes it seemed to me that she was either unwilling or she refused to recognize the feelings of others unless it served her purpose. Even though she had lost her husband, it did not give her permission to be so cruel.

On the day my mom received my dad's personal effects, I watched her pull his reading glasses from a large manilla envelope. Without looking at them first, she handed the glasses to me. They were spattered with my dad's blood and brains. I took them from her. I was holding them in my hands, while at the same time I thought, *What am I doing?* I immediately handed the glasses back to her. I felt sick.

I think she'd already seen the glasses to pass them over to me so fast without looking at them first, and if this was the case, wouldn't a person wash the glasses off before handing them to their daughter or anyone? Why hadn't she just thrown them away? It was disturbing that she would do this.

My Grandma Randall called to ask my mom about the coroner's report that day. I listened in silence while my mom read the medical report to her mother-in-law over the phone. How terribly sad this must have been for my grandmother to hear such tragic death specifics about her son.

WADDLE HOME

When my mom got upset, she'd bring up, among other things, repeatedly, the fact that Grandma and Grandpa Randall never went to my parents' wedding.

"Why?" I asked. My mom didn't answer me.

The last time my mother said this to me was after my dad's suicide. It made me feel sad for her because I didn't want her to have this additional hurt. I decided to find out why for myself.

I called my aunt. "Hi Aunt Karen, how are you?" Before I waited for her answer, I said, "My mother is upset today. She told me Grandma and Grandpa Randall didn't attend my parent's wedding. This still hurts her. Why didn't they attend?" My aunt paused.

She laughed, at least that's what it sounded like to me, before she said, "They didn't come to our wedding either."

"Why?" I asked her.

"They just didn't," she said.

After the phone call with my aunt, I still didn't understand why my grandparents hadn't gone to any of their children's weddings, but I walked over to my mom's house.

"Mom, Aunt Karen told me grandma and grandpa didn't go to any of the weddings either. Yours wasn't the only one." I thought this was good to know. I'd always heard it was just my parents' wedding that had been avoided.

My mother nodded her head yes, admitting to me that this was true.

That was it. She spoke no audible words; she just gave me a nod, and I could tell she was still quite upset.

That's when I asked her about a particular incident that happened to me while I was growing up. Bad idea on my part. "Mom, do you remember when dad told me I'd probably sleep with a Black man?" My mother glared at me; she didn't reply or try to explain. She ignored me, but within seconds she told me how terrible her life had been.

"When I was young, my parents took my brothers to the races and left me home with relatives." My mother didn't want to talk about what hurt or concerned me.

My mother and I were standing outside on her front porch talking about her in-laws not coming to her wedding and her bad childhood. It was a cool summer night, yet it was warm enough for the neighbors to open their windows. For a while, our conversation seemed peaceful, but her voice was growing louder.

One of the things that troubled me about my mom was that her vocal expressions grew louder when she was upset with my dad or angry at any of us.

To me, it was as if she wanted the entire world to hear our private conversations. During these times, when her voice would grow louder, I would go around to all the open windows inside the house, and I would close them. But now, we were outside on the porch. There were no windows for me to close. I think I'd made her angry because I was beginning to feel those old pangs of shame rise within me, so I turned to walk away. That's when my mother called out after me even louder, "Waddle home, Judy."

APOLOGIZING

Recently, I thought back to my childhood once more, wondering if I'd ever unknowingly hurt my siblings. I call each of them because I want to say I'm sorry if I have. I've apologized to them in the past for known offenses on my part, and I feel the need to do it again.

Did I push my brother, Trace, down the basement stairs? We might have been twelve and thirteen at the time. I don't remember it the way Trace said it happened, but he swore I pushed him, and he laughed. He told my husband about the incident before we were married. Ray was amused while he repeated Trace's story back to me.

Sometimes, it seemed like we fought a lot—Trace and me. I do remember both of us being at the top of the stairs and me pushing, but it wasn't a hard push. I remember Trace going down the steps, but to me, it was as if he was exaggerating. He was standing on both of his feet the entire time going down the steps. I thought he was faking.

Trace and my younger brothers liked to go garbage-picking through the neighborhood on trash day. I hated when they did this. My family already had the reputation of being poor, so garbage-picking added to my humiliation. Trace knew it bothered me. If I said or did something he didn't like, he would threaten to yell out the front door as loud as he could, "Judy Randall garbage picks!" He did do this, and it was terribly embarrassing for me.

When my parents left me in charge of watching my younger siblings, Trace would do everything he knew he wasn't supposed to do, and we would argue about it. Sibling rivalry.

My dad told me to write what Trace and the other kids did wrong, and he would take care of it when he got home. So, I would write down what Trace did.

Dear Dad, Trace ate crackers, smashed them all up on the living room floor and wouldn't clean up his mess. Trace opened the front door and wouldn't close it, so now we have a million flies in the house. Dad, you said we all had to stay home, but Trace told Josie she could go to her friend's house. Dad, Trace yelled out the front door, Judy Randall garbage picks. Dad, this is my new list because Trace tore up my original list.

Maybe it bothered my brother that my parents left me in charge instead of him. I don't know.

Trace wrote his own list, which was a list of what he said I did wrong. I hadn't done anything he said. *Judy smashed crackers all over the living room. Judy wouldn't let me eat. Judy spit at me. Judy said shit. Judy took a belt and beat me with it. Judy went to the bathroom, and she didn't flush the toilet.*

When my dad looked at both written lists, he probably saw how petty they were and how they contradicted each other. So, he didn't do anything.

(Maybe I did push my brother down the stairs.)

I talked to Trace the other day. "Trace, did I really push you down the steps? I thought you were faking."

"No, you pushed me down the stairs." Trace laughs.

"I'm sorry."

"I'm sorry too. We did get into a lot of dumb arguments," Trace said.

I believe watching my parent's physical fights had played into our sibling relationship. It's all very sad.

I called Garrett, and we apologized to each other too. "Garrett, if I have ever hurt you, I'm sorry. Please forgive me."

"I'm sorry I hurt you," my brother says. To be honest, I don't ever remember him hurting me. We forgive each other anyway.

Part Two

I was in my sophomore year of college when I met Ray at an end-of-the-year party the college sponsored. Food, bands, and kegs of beer were set up behind the dorms. It was a bittersweet affair since I realized it would probably be the last time some of my friends from the dorm and I would ever see each other again, and it was. Like in high school, we all grow up and go our separate ways.

An acquaintance of mine introduced me to a group of fifteen people sitting around on the ground drinking beer and talking.

After being introduced, they all made an effort to turn around and say hello to me. All except for one guy. Ray sat unmoved while his back leaned into a tree trunk. He was facing in the opposite direction of his friends. He didn't turn around to look at me or speak. I only saw his hand go up, and then back down again. It was as if he were oblivious to what was going on around him.

This guy, for some reason, had my attention. I wondered why he hadn't tried to say hi as his friends had, but I moved on. The rest of the evening, I was happy spending time with my friends from the dorm.

"I heard you and Shelly are getting married?" I said to Ron, a Concrete Tech student. He was twenty, my age. I'd met him two years ago, our first day at the dorm. Shelly was a new student who arrived at school the following year.

"Are you going to Ferris State next fall?" I asked Angie. She was an R.A. studying to be a teacher. Ferris State University is in Big Rapids, Michigan. The university offered among other curriculums a Teachers Education program as well as a Criminal Justice program in my area of study at the time. Still, I was thinking about changing my major to get a teaching degree like my mother, her mother, and grandmother before me.

For old time's sake, a group of us walked across the road before dark to what is referred to as The Island, a wildlife sanctuary. Some of us had spent a lot of time there, especially on the weekends, crossing a small footbridge over the water to wooded walking trails and enjoying nature. Once again, we crossed the bridge together, hiked for a bit around the Thunder Bay River, then stopped to watch several Mallard Ducks and their babies swim by. We ate grilled hamburgers and drank mugs of cold beer from a keg while watching a local rock band play several sets.

Toward the end of the party, when everyone was starting to disperse and go their separate ways, Ray came up to me and introduced himself properly. He was smiling at me. He has the cutest dimples when he smiles. He has always reminded me of a young Robert Redford. I think I've seen every movie Robert Redford has ever made.

Ray is 5'11" and still has that slender but strong build he had when I first met him. When we stood in the dorm's lighted entrance, I noticed the natural highlights in his sandy blond hair shimmer. He smelled amazing. His scent was warm and comforting. The faded denim blue shirt he wore complimented his eyes. They were a beautiful shade of deep blue, and when they met mine, he asked me for my phone number. Then, it was happily ever after for us, for a while anyway. I stayed in the college town where Ray lived for two months that summer. I wanted to be close to him. I was falling in love.

I worked as a hostess at the local Big Boy restaurant in town. I was also thinking of going to Ferris State in the fall. I'd been accepted into the Teachers Education Program. I just had to get the financial aid documents filled out and sent in. My parents didn't want me knowing their financial business, so they would be the ones, namely my mother, who would have to help me with that.

Ray worked part time at a local gas station. He also delivered bulk newspapers to nearby towns at night so they could be delivered the following day. We both filed applications in other places for the chance of better jobs, but in a small town, it can take a while.

Being with Ray made me feel like I was starting over in my life. It was another new beginning for me after junior college.

I had dreams of wanting to live a life that was free from drama. I felt there was hope for our future together, although we told each other repeatedly during our late-night phone chats we didn't want to get married. Both of us growing up, enduring our parents' toxic relationships was the main reason we felt this way.

Living in this small college town where no one knew me other than a few locals I'd had classes with was a breath of fresh air. I was beginning to discover who I was, and what I liked. But by the end of July, I knew I had to go home. I wasn't making enough money for groceries or to pay the rent on a room I'd rented from a classmate who went home for the summer. I think it was twenty-five dollars a week. I had decisions to make about school too. Nothing like the last minute, but making decisions last minute was what I'd done my entire life. I couldn't make up my mind because I was afraid of making the wrong choices.

It was hard for me to leave Ray, but I couldn't make it on my own and he was struggling with his own financial problems at the time as well.

I decided I wanted to go back to school. "Mom, will you fill out the financial aid papers for me so I can go back to school?" I said. My mother was in the living room sitting in a brown tweed, lazy boy chair. It was early August and hot outside. The windows were open, but the curtains were drawn, so the room was dark, and it felt hot.

"I'm tired, Judy. I don't want to." There was a tone of disdain in my mother's voice. I looked at her. I breathed in a deep breath of air, then let it out.

"I'm tired too," I said. I was tired, and I felt defeated. I should have put up a fight. I gave in too quickly, but I didn't want to upset my mother because then my dad would get upset too.

I'd watched my siblings for my mother while she took classes to get not only her bachelor's degree but her master's degree as well. Yet, she was too tired to fill out a few papers for me. I would have done it myself, but again, she didn't want me to know my parents' finances. Doesn't a parent want the best for their children? I wanted the best for mine, and it didn't matter how tired I was. I wanted my boys to succeed. Didn't my mom want me to succeed? I find this a little difficult to comprehend now.

I WANTED EVERYTHING TO BE PERFECT

Ray and I were in our early twenties when we got married. I really loved this guy. I still do. He wasn't serious like I was. He was funny and mischievous, and he made me happy.

Sadly, the years took a toll on our relationship. Looking back, we were too young to get married, even though everyone else our age seemed to be getting married early at the time. I was twenty-two, and Ray was twenty-one.

At the beginning of our relationship, Ray and I had a new love. Exciting, amazing, and a brand-new, nothing-can-separate-us kind of love. Four years later we bought our first home, and four years after that, our babies were born. I loved being Ray's wife, and I loved being a mom. The greatest career I have ever had or will ever have was being a mother.

I really tried to be a good mom. I wanted everything to be perfect for my boys. I tried to break the mold, as my brother, John, suggested we needed to do years ago. I wanted to keep the experiences of my unhealthy childhood out of my new home and away from my sons. I can honestly say that I really tried, even though I did make mistakes.

I pretty much held it together until I found out my husband's job was relocating. That's when I seemed to lose my patience easily with Ray and my sons. I didn't like that about myself. The thought of moving to another state made me feel like everything in my life was out of control. I didn't feel safe. I felt scared, and because I was afraid, it scared my children. Ray and I argued in front of them, something I never wanted to do.

NEW GRANDMA

Before my sisters and a sister-in-law were ready to deliver their babies, my mom bought them all pretty, new robes to wear at the hospital and then at home. She didn't give me one. It hurt my feelings, but I didn't want to seem like I was the squeaky wheel, so I refused to ask her why.

I stood with my mother gazing and admiring my newborn nephew Matthew through the nursery window in the hospital. My mom was a new grandma. Matthew was her first grandchild, a blond, blue eyed, beautiful baby boy. This was a happy and exciting time for all of us, especially since my dad's death the year before. Matthew's birth was glorious sunshine after a deadly hurricane had swept through our lives.

While we stood together in front of the nursery window, I remember thinking how happy my mom was. She wore a colorful red, white, and yellow dress with heels. She'd lost weight and her small frame hovered over the nursery window. She'd get quiet, look over at me and smile, then look back at Matthew in his transparent plastic bassinet.

He was wrapped up tight with a blue and white receiving blanket.

"What a beautiful baby. Isn't he beautiful?"

I would smile back at her. "Yes, he is beautiful."

She did this several times, and each time, she would say the same thing to me, "What a beautiful baby. Isn't he beautiful?"

I would smile and answer, "Yes, he is beautiful." We were so happy, we both had tears in our eyes.

Several days after my baby boys were born, my mother came to visit for the first time with her boyfriend Lou's daughter-in-law. This was the first time I'd ever met Louanne. At the time my mother and I only lived a few miles apart from each other.

We walked together down the same hospital corridor that led to the nursery. Once again, we stood together in front of the same big glass window, like we had years ago with baby Matthew, only this time we were looking in on my little twins. I was waiting for her to say something about my babies, but she didn't. There was no conversation between us; there was only silence. Finally, I turned my eyes away from my own little blond, blue-eyed babies to observe my mother. "Aren't they beautiful?"

While I waited for my mother's reply, I couldn't help but notice that she'd hesitated. She looked over at me while her eyes narrowed and her lips pursed. She gave me a restrained nod. That was the only response I got from her. I wanted to cry but I wouldn't give her the satisfaction. I waited until she and Luanne left my hospital room before I drew the heavy, drab gray curtain around my bed. I didn't want to disturb my roommate. I brought a pillow to my face. I sobbed into the firm foam padding, while releasing breathy muffled sounds of hurt, pain, and defeat. My mother didn't seem to care about me, or my babies.

Unlike my mother had with me, I was determined to treat my children with love, respect, and acceptance.

I made sure my boys had nice clothes to wear and decent food to eat. I encouraged them to make new friends, to play, and to have fun. I reassured them over and over again that they were good, that they were loved, that they were wanted, and most of all that they were beautiful people inside and out. I encouraged their interests and their life goals. Throughout their lives I reassured them that God loved them and that he had great plans for them.

DRAMA

Ray and I have been through a lot together. We moved to the suburbs of Detroit, dragging our feet away from the cute little northern town Ray had grown up in, but the big city is where the jobs were. Living close to my parents and family drama was tough. Sometimes it seemed like we had visitors all the time. On Friday nights after work, we'd order a pizza, turn the lights off, lock all the doors, then crawl into bed with our pizza and watch TV. We were hiding; we needed our space.

My mother and Rita didn't get along after my dad's suicide. Rita came to stay at our house for a while. I felt like my mom was picking on my sister. My mom would humiliate Rita in front of her cousins and family members, tearing Rita down, accusing her of being defiant. They would all laugh at my sister. My mother wasn't protecting Rita like I thought she should, especially after Dad had died. Rita needed to feel safe. *She needed that!*

Some mornings before work, my mom would call as early as five a.m. yelling at me because she couldn't find her car keys. Rita nor I had been to my mom's house for days, and why would we take her keys?

My mother's new boyfriend, Dan, was an abusive man. My siblings and I tried to warn her about him, but Mom felt we didn't like him because he wasn't our dad. There were terrible stories I'd heard about this man firsthand from some of his acquaintances.

I worked for the Michigan Employment Security Commission, where we filed claims for people laid off from their jobs. If the claimants were eligible for unemployment, we'd issue checks to them. I was working the counter one day, a time when many automotive companies were laying off workers. I was helping a man file a claim. He wore gold-rimmed glasses, blue jeans, and a beige short sleeve work shirt. I studied the information on his application. He worked for General Motors, the same plant where my mom's boyfriend worked. It was a long shot because there were thousands of employees working at this plant, but I asked him anyway.

I said, "Do you know Dan Reese?"

The man had a black ink pen in his hand at the time. He was getting ready to sign his claim form to get an unemployment check, but he let go of the pen. I watched it roll away on to the floor. The man stood back away from the counter, and he focused his eyes on me, then paused as if trying to collect his thoughts.

He pointed his index finger at me, "Yes, and you stay away from him. He's bad." The man's voice seemed harsh; he was warning me.

I told my mother about this, but she wouldn't listen. My mom eventually moved into Dan's apartment with him. Dan lived in an area known for a lot of crime, especially after dark. Ray had worked a late overtime shift one night. He didn't get home until after one o'clock in the morning. Minutes after my husband walked through our back door, my mother called.

"Judy!" My mom sounded like she'd been crying.

"Mom, are you alright? Are you okay? What's the matter?" I was scared.

"Dan beat me up. Can Ray come to get me?" My mom was being victimized again. I felt crazy. My mother had just gotten beat up by a man we'd told her to stay away from, and we'd told her why she should stay away from him. Instead of considering her children's advice, her children who truly cared for her and loved her, she'd get snarky with us and laugh. Now, she'd gone as far as moving in with him. A known abuser's home. I wanted my mother to be safe, but I didn't want my husband going to a bad area of town to face an abusive man who was much bigger than he was. The man was over six feet tall, and he weighed close to 300 pounds. Dan had just abused my mother. I didn't want him hurting or, worse, killing my husband. Under these circumstances, it was quite possible that it could happen. My mother needed to call the police. I was panicking; I felt my knees go weak.

"Mom, no, Ray can't come there. Dan might hurt him." My mother hung the phone up on me. I didn't have her new address to call the police. I felt terrible because what kind of daughter does that to her mother?

The following day my mom moved back into her home; she didn't talk to me for quite some time. A year later, she apologized to me. As I have mentioned, apologies from my mother were rare.

MEETING RAY'S FAMILY

As I have also mentioned, I seemed to meet the same people in life. Different faces but similar personalities. As I got older, I started to notice that the people I encountered were in many ways like my parents.

I met Ray's mom along with other members of his family at his sister Lucy's wedding. The wedding took place outdoors in a park. I remember it being a beautiful setting. Music was playing, and barbecue chicken was on the grill. It was a cool overcast autumn day. The trees hadn't started to change colors yet, but it wouldn't be long before they would turn pretty orange, red, and gold.

A brisk biting wind kicked up; the breeze made me shiver. Ray gave me his jean jacket to wear. It wasn't a big deal for him to offer his jacket, but to me, it was everything. The jacket was warm and smelled like him: clean, fresh, and masculine. I felt loved, and protected, an amazing feeling to have.

Ray introduced me to his mother. Debra offered each of us a bottle of beer. The three of us stood together while Ray and his mom chit-chatted about pretty much everything: friends, family members, events going on in their lives, all names of people I did not recognize, and I listened. Ray's parents were divorced, and at the time, his mother was living in Indiana.

Debra was 5 '2", my height. She was in her forties; her hair was platinum blonde and cut short around her face. She wore big gold hoop earrings. I remember I liked them.

I was excited to be with Ray. It had been almost three weeks since I'd last seen him. I'd moved back home to work and save money, so I could get my own place. It was September, we'd only known each other for four months, but I was falling in love with him. And I was happy that he thought our relationship was serious enough to introduce me to his family that day.

Debra handed me a brown longneck bottle. "Thank you." I said, smiling at her. I felt shy. I took a swig, but the beer was warm, and it tasted bitter to me. I was still cold, so I leaned into the warmth of Ray's body while I held on to the bottle. I felt his arms wrap me in closer to him while I continued to listen to the conversation.

Ray's mom seemed nice enough, but I felt like she was sizing me up. I suddenly felt self-conscious. I was wearing a pretty, two-piece green pantsuit that complimented my eyes. My brown hair had a few blonde highlights and was styled in a long shag cut with bangs. I weighed maybe a hundred pounds at the time. Music continued to play in the background. People were chatting and laughing together. I brought the bottle up to my mouth and sipped on the beer. I still didn't like the taste, and me holding on to the bottle for so long had made the beer feel even warmer.

"You know Ray; there's a job waiting for you in Indiana," Debra said.

I was crushed. I felt tears well up in my eyes. Ray wasn't having much luck finding a decent job, but I didn't want him to go farther away from me. Throughout all our conversations, he'd never mentioned wanting to look for work out of state. At the time, it was bad enough that we were four and a half hours away from each other.

Ray finished his beer and handed his mother the empty bottle. Debra took it from him, then set it down on the ground next to a red and white cooler. I watched her lift the lid off the cooler with pretty, manicured nails. She dug down into the box to retrieve another beer for him.

Ray took the beer from Debra and then walked away for a moment. There I was, standing alone with his mother. I didn't know what to say, so I stayed quiet, smiling at her while searching with my eyes for Ray, waiting for him to return. I took another small sip from the bottle; when I felt like I couldn't drink more of the beer, I handed Debra my partially emptied bottle. She took it from me, lifted it in front of my face, shook it, then made a disapproving facial gesture.

"You're going to waste a good beer?" she said, then turned and walked away.

I couldn't believe how rude she'd been. I asked myself, "Did this really happen?" Had I done something wrong? Was this for real? I laugh now. I was good at reading people's emotions and my surroundings. I could tell she didn't care for me, but for some crazy reason, I wanted her to like me. I loved her son. I was relieved when minutes later, Ray was back standing by my side.

Because my mother and her mother-in-law did not like each other, I promised myself since I was a young girl that I would make sure I had a good relationship with my future husband's mother.

Through the years, I found myself trying to please people. There were times when I felt I couldn't do enough for them. I thought if everyone else was happy, then I would be happy. Oh wow, was I ever wrong. "Let me get your coffee for you." Then I'd jump up and get it. "I'll go to the store for you." *Even though, while I'm gone, I will be leaving my children and husband to fend for themselves.* Or, "Here, let me pull your chair out for you." "That's okay. I'll sit in the back seat. You sit up front with my husband." Or, "I'll wash your car for you." *(Even though you're perfectly capable of washing it yourself.)*

I was exhausted, but I'd sometimes put others' needs first before my family and my own needs. What was wrong with me? I soon realized that nothing about me was changing. I was still trying too hard to be nice. I wanted people to like me. I wanted them to accept me.

I have listened while family members talked about their sons, daughters, their children's spouses, nieces, nephews, sisters, or anyone else. Sometimes, their criticism of others became vicious over something as simple as the way another person wore their hair. "Did you see what she was wearing?" "She's so bossy, but if he's crazy enough to put up with it." "She only makes frozen meals for her family." "He's a dreamer if he thinks he can make money doing hair. He just doesn't like to work." "I wish he'd shave that hideous beard of his." "I don't know what he sees in her; she has a houseful of birds." "I just absolutely hate her make-up." "They discipline their children too much." "Their children need to be disciplined more." "You'd think she'd do something about her small breasts." "They aren't having sex, but who could blame him."

It seemed as though they talked about and found fault with everyone, especially when they were drinking and engaging with others. Sometimes the person they spoke of was sitting with them. They seemed good at being insincere and self-righteous. Their behavior made me feel bad for their target. I knew what that was like.

Glasses were filled while the ice cubes in our drinks crackled and fizzed. Oldies music played in the background along with laughter and conversation. For some odd reason, at those times, while family and visitors sat at the bar or around the kitchen table gossiping, I would pull my chair in extra close. I would listen intently to what they all had to say. I took mental notes. I didn't comment; I listened. In the back of my mind, I thought, *How terrible it would be for them to talk about me this way.*

Listening in was my way of making sure that I would not ever be like the person being talked about at the time. I continued trying to please because I didn't want anyone to say terrible things about me.

ARE YOU GOING TO MARRY ME?

Rays' mom and stepdad Bob took us out to a steakhouse for dinner after we had been together for well over a year. Bob was nursing his scotch and water when he looked over at Ray and asked him, while I sat within earshot, "So are you going to marry this girl, or not?" Bob directed his eyes toward Ray. Showing no teeth, the sides of the man's mouth curved up.

Bob was out of line, and his question caught Ray and me off guard. I was in love with Ray, he loved me; of course, we would get married, but we weren't ready. I was working a clerical job for an architectural firm at the time, while Ray had two upcoming interviews for electrical apprenticeships. We didn't have enough money for a wedding, let alone a nice place to live. My parents had eloped. I didn't want that for me.

Ray paused before he answered, "Probably not."

His words stung; even though I knew he was being sarcastic, I was hurt. I felt disrespected. I remember thinking, *This is news to me. I had no idea that this is how you felt.*

I remember having a long pause of silence while my eyes welled up with tears. I not only looked at Ray for his reaction, but I looked over at his mother, only to see what I perceived to be an amused grin on her face. I went into the bathroom and sobbed. I cried so hard that I felt like I wouldn't ever stop crying.

I glanced in the mirror, wiping my eyes with a coarse brown paper towel. My eyes were red and swollen. I was too embarrassed to go back to the table, but I felt I didn't have a choice. To reach the exit, I had to pass the table where we were eating. They would have seen me leave. I didn't want to make a scene by walking out or causing Ray to feel more uncomfortable than he already did, never mind how I felt. I know now I should have left.

Twenty minutes later, I sat at the table again, but I was still very upset. I looked over at Ray's mom.

To me, her face seemed expressionless and her demeanor icy. There was little conversation after I sat down, none of it addressed to me. Afterward, when we were alone, I let Ray know how his offensive words had made me feel.

"I wish you would've told Bob that it was none of his business."

"I'm sorry Judy. I know; I should've said something." Ray said.

There have been many times that I have allowed family members to treat me like this. Through the years, I became angrier at myself for allowing them to get away with their abusive behavior, but I wouldn't say anything. I was allowing it because I didn't have boundaries. To be honest, I didn't wholly understand what boundaries even were or that I was even entitled to have them. There were no boundaries in my childhood home. If I tried to stand up for myself back then, I was knocked down verbally or physically.

BRIDESMAIDS' DRESSES

Ray and I were married on a rainy September evening, a candle-light service at St. Paul's Lutheran Church, the church Ray grew up in. I hadn't been to the church I'd grown up in for some time. Getting married in my family church would never be an option. I didn't want or need more judgement cast down on me, a back slider, a sinner who had strayed.

The decorations were simple but pretty. White pew bows lined the aisle. Two flower arrangements sat on either side of the candelabra, pink and white roses, white carnations, and baby's breath. The flowers matched my bouquet. My dress was simple: white lace with cap sleeves and a thin pink ribbon wrapped around my waist.

My mother sewed the bridesmaids' dresses. The ensemble was so pretty. Pastel yellow chiffon dresses. Sleeveless floor length gowns that flowed. Each having a natural waistline adorned with a thin yellow ribbon and a matching cape that draped and fell over the girls' shoulders.

I asked my sisters, Josie and Rita, to stand up for me. I also asked Ray's sister Lucy to be a bridesmaid. I didn't want her feelings to be hurt, so I asked her to stand up even though my intuition told me differently.

I didn't know Lucy, other than exchanging a few words with her when I was with Ray. She was tall and slender with beautiful skin, and I thought she was pretty. To me she also seemed overly confident in herself and bossy. In a way, I admired how sure of herself she was. I was shy and afraid to speak up. I could have used a little of her attitude and self-confidence in my own life. I also noticed that Lucy had a way of manipulating others around her, especially her family. Whether they disagreed with her or not, they'd laugh off her antics, and she'd usually end up getting her way.

I always did things like this—tried to be nice so that I wouldn't hurt others' feelings. My problem: it was my own feelings that were getting in the way. I was so naïve. If I didn't know Lucy and she didn't know me, why would her feelings be hurt? This was so messed up.

At the last minute, I was trying to decide whether to have the girls wear the capes over the dresses or not. I thought both ways looked nice, but I sensed someone not wanting to wear theirs.

Before the wedding, when we were all dressed, and the girls were in their wraps, I stood back and smiled at them. They all looked so lovely.

"Do you want to wear the capes?" I said. I was trying to be nice but cringing at my words.

Josie and Rita quit smiling; for a moment, the twinkle in their eyes had disappeared. Lucy stood silent; her face was blank. My sisters looked at me like I was speaking a foreign language.

I wish I'd kept my mouth shut. My mother had worked long, hard hours making the dresses. I risked my mom's feelings being hurt by the girls not wearing them. Why had I even asked? What was the matter with me? I was worried about everyone, trying to please.

Before either of my sisters could answer—and I know they would've answered yes—Lucy applied bright orange lipstick to her lips, lifted the front of the cape, and blotted her mouth with it. Her emotionless face had come to life. There was a sparkle in her eyes, and the corners of her mouth lifted into a smile. She'd decided for all of us. Josie, Rita, and I gasped. I couldn't believe what Lucy had done and on purpose. My sisters reluctantly took their pretty yellow capes off. I was disappointed too. I had no words. I bristled.

A BIRTHDAY SURPRISE

Ray's sister Lucy called us one time early on in our marriage. She wanted to get her dad some new work boots for his birthday. She asked us to donate money toward this gift. Ray and I were happy to contribute, so we sent our share of the money.

A month or so later, while we were visiting family, Lucy's husband said to Ray, "You missed a great surprise birthday party for your dad." I'd been standing next to Ray at the time. Both of our faces dropped. *What surprise party?* I thought.

We weren't told about a birthday party for his dad, nor were we invited.

"Why didn't you tell me?" Ray asked his sister.

"I didn't invite you because I didn't think you'd come," she said.

Ray's feelings were hurt, and I hurt for him. Of course, we would have attended his dad's party.

GUESTS

Lucy lived in northern Michigan but had some business to attend to in Detroit, so rather than drive home, she asked if she, her son, and a girlfriend I hadn't met could spend the night at our house. I worked days at the unemployment office filing claims for the State of Michigan.

It was late, and I was in bed when I heard the back door open hard and reverberate. The wood door was old, and sometimes after it rained, it would swell and stick tight against the door jam. Footsteps, rustling bodies, and low voices entered our home.

I had left the back door unlocked because Lucy said they would be late. I set blankets and pillows out before I went to bed so they could camp out in the living room. We offered our spare room to them, but Lucy said no, they would be leaving early the following morning. After I heard them come in, I remembered that I should tell them where the towels were. I also wanted to let them know to help themselves to whatever they needed, including what was in the refrigerator, in case they were hungry.

I got out of bed, put a robe on, walked down the hallway, and entered the living room to let them know where everything was. They thanked me, and we said goodnight.

As I turned around to return to my bedroom, I heard Lucy and her friend laugh. Her son, who was ten or eleven at the time, asked his mother why they were laughing, and I overheard her say, "Because we don't like Aunt Judy." I don't know if she meant for me to hear her, but I did. I still didn't talk much to Lucy other than when I was with Ray, so I can't think of a reason why she felt this way about me.

GIFTS

Debra has done nice things for all of us. After Ray and I were married, and throughout the years, she would give me beautiful gifts: pretty towels, crystal stemware, and expensive china among other treasures. I thought she must love me and accept me to spend so much money.

Debra would do or say things to me that would make my heart melt, and other times, she could be really cold. My mother did this too. I have learned this is a form of manipulation. Sometimes when Debra visited, she'd prepare a delicious meal like steak or grilled salmon. Sometimes she'd take us all out to dinner. She gave me, my husband, and our children what I perceived to be carefully thought-out Christmas gifts, and she'd send money for our birthdays. I was not used to having such lovely gifts in my life. I was so appreciative. However, I soon started to feel that the gifts came with a price. It seemed I was getting insults in exchange. Through the years, I have endured personal innuendos and subtle hints about things she didn't like. For example, she's given me clothes for my birthday and Christmas that were too small. She has been bold enough to suggest that I could do something about my breasts.

During a family visit, I went into her kitchen smiled and asked her, "Is there anything I can help you with."

She gave me a stern look, and without saying a word, she purposely drew her eyes down to the crotch of the jeans I was wearing. From time to time, she'd mention that she didn't like my hair but used subtle words or stories about other women's hair she didn't like to make her point. Once when we were all together and amid visitors, she'd told them that she didn't like how my seven-year-old sons had behaved when she'd watched them for me years earlier. I had no idea. If she said anything at all that wasn't very nice, I would pretend her words and actions hadn't bothered me, while at the same time wondering if I had misunderstood her. I should have said something like, "I'm sorry, I don't understand what you mean by that?" But I kept quiet.

I wish I'd said something because by not standing up for myself or asking for clarification, I let her ill words and behavior fester through the years.

On Christmas one year, when our sons were small, we spent the holiday with Ray's mom at her home in Indiana. Ray's sister, Lucy, her soon-to-be husband Richard, and some of Ray's stepfather's relatives were also visiting.

We were all sitting around the dinner table conversing with each other, excited about the holiday, when unexpectedly, Bob, who was very drunk, looked at me and said, "Judy, you are nice like our friend Sally in Colorado, but you, like Sally aren't pretty." This outburst had nothing to do with the previous conversation at the table. Then Bob looked over at Ray's mother and sister. His eyes sparkled when he said, "But Debra, you and Lucy are beautiful."

I remember smiling, even though Bob was being terribly rude. I was fighting back my tears.

I had been told my entire life that I wasn't pretty, so why would I let this bother me? But his words hurt, and no one said anything. I didn't stand up for myself, nor did my husband stand up for me. Ray and I are both adult children of alcoholics. Not standing up for ourselves is another universal trait.

As usual, I didn't want to make a scene. I didn't want to come on as being too sensitive either. It was Christmas. I didn't want to re-live another drama-ridden Christmas as I had in my childhood, so I bristled.

But I should've said something. We should have packed up our things and left to go home.

It still angers me to think I put up with such impolite, nasty behavior and for so long. Not only from my parents but Ray's family too.

THE MESSENGER

When our boys got older, Ray's mother came to our home for Christmas, unlike when they were younger when we would go to her home. At these times, I felt she'd made Christmas special for the boys and Ray. Because my family was happy, I was happy, so it was special for me too. It was rare for us to have out-of-town visitors since our families lived out of state.

One Christmas, when she was planning to visit, I received an interesting phone call. I was cleaning, and trying to get last-minute Christmas things done before Debra's arrival when Lucy called.

"Hi Judy, how is Ray? How are the boys?"

"They're good. How are you?" I paused, wondering what Lucy wanted. She didn't call that often, and when she did call, it was because she usually had a message from her mother. For example, "Ray, Mom is worried. She hasn't heard from you. It upsets her when you don't call." Or the time years ago, when we connected to the internet via the telephone rather than Wi-Fi, Lucy would call: "Why are you always online? Mom can't call you."

I had a strong feeling I was going to find out the real reason for Lucy's call that day and in a matter of minutes.

I was expecting Debra to arrive later that afternoon. She had recently moved to Atlanta, Georgia, about a four-and-a-half-hour drive to our home. I assumed she was already on her way when Lucy called.

"What are you doing for Christmas?" I asked Lucy.

"We're staying home. Richard has to work," she said before adding, "I just got through talking to Mom. She doesn't like just sitting around your house when she comes to visit." I remember thinking, *Are we boring?* A part of me felt embarrassed. I'd actually thought Debra enjoyed our company when she came to visit. We'd enjoyed hers.

"Mom wants to get out and do things," Lucy said.

We did find fun things to see and do that Christmas and every holiday after when Ray's mom visited. We saw the beautiful holiday decorations at the Opryland Hotel in Nashville. We went to the movies, and at night we drove around neighboring towns to look at Christmas lights. We went shopping, out to eat, and to Christmas Eve services at church. I made sure we stayed busy.

One year at Christmas, Ray's mother arrived with her luggage and cleaning supplies, window cleaner and bleach wipes that I felt she wanted me to see. I felt like she was telling me that our house was not clean enough. Okay, in her defense, she was sharing a bathroom, but I have cleaning supplies; I didn't feel she needed to bring hers. I felt a little self-conscious anyway because of a comment she'd made regarding someone else's home.

"Mary's daughter is constantly cleaning. Her house is so clean it squeaks."

"Mom, can we have pizza tonight?" Nick asked me.

"Sure" I said.

Having pizza would make things a little easier for me, I thought. Ray was working that night, so he wasn't home. Debra sat at the table, visiting with all of us.

"Hey Grandma, I flew to New York today," Daniel said. The boys had flight simulators on their computers.

"You did?" Debra said, smiling at him.

While she was chatting with the boys. I pulled a pizza from the freezer, tore the wrapper off and placed it in the oven. Ray's mom sometimes told a story to get a point across. That pizza going into the oven prompted a story.

She said, "So and so's wife never cooks. She goes to the grocery store, buys frozen meals, and serves that to her family every night. I think it's terrible to serve your husband and children frozen dinners."

I didn't know how to respond, so I didn't.

"She doesn't work, so it's no excuse." Debra added.

We continued to find things to do outside our home when Debra visited at Christmas. Then one day, Lucy called again. "Mom's tired of running. She doesn't want to go anywhere. She just wants to stay in for Christmas."

Debra came to our home for a few more Christmases and then moved to Corpus Christie. She lives close to Lucy and Richard now and spends her holidays with them.

BOOBS, NAILS, AND THUMBS

One time Ray's mom, Debra, was talking to him on the phone. She mentioned that a friend's wife was out of the hospital and doing great. I asked Ray what was wrong. He said he hadn't asked. The next time I talked to Debra, I said, "I heard that so and so was in the hospital. I hope she's all right. What happened?"

She told me that this woman had a breast enlargement, and then she added, "There is something you can do about your breasts too."

"What?" This was so rude. I was thrown off guard by her comment. I had no words then, but I laugh now.

I don't have an issue with my small breasts, and to be honest, neither does my husband.

Ray also doesn't mind that I was born with short thumbs. The scientific name for this condition is brachydactyly D. My thumbs are disproportionately short and wide, with an accompanying wider nail bed. There are quite a few of us in the world who have thumbs like these, and there are different ideas on what the causes are. From what I have read, it's an inherited condition, and only one parent must have the gene to pass it on. It doesn't matter where or how I got my thumbs—I have them. I'm thankful for what I have; some people are born without hands.

One of the times I had artificial nails put on, I happened to lose a nail that was on one of my thumbs. My mom found it, and she laughed. She said, "I thought it was someone's toenail."

I am laughing now, but at the time, I was too embarrassed to confess it was mine.

While growing up, I never paid that much attention to my thumbs. I could see they looked different from my friends, but I didn't think about them that much. Once when I was in another room, I overheard my brother telling my mom that there was something wrong with Judy's hands. I was twelve.

Some kids teased and called me Thumbelina, but it really didn't bother me. I had too many other things to worry about. Like cleaning the house, ensuring my siblings were safe and my parents weren't fighting.

After we moved to Tennessee, a woman I'd recently met mentioned that her sister had thumbs like mine. She told me she was missing a chromosome. That was the first time I had ever heard that, but I still didn't let the reality of my different thumbs worry me. I think the idea of me having a missing chromosome was more concerning.

After Ray's stepdad died, his mom came to visit for a few days. As usual, Ray was working. Debra was mourning the loss of her husband; she had a lot on her mind. I genuinely cared for Debra, and I felt bad that she was hurting. Although it was a pleasant conversation, I can't remember what we were talking about that day, but I had to leave the room for a few minutes. When I returned, Debra was angry about the way my hands looked. I couldn't understand why she was so upset with me.

"What's wrong with your hands?" She blurted. Her jaw was tense, and her eyebrows furrowed. She seemed disgusted with me. I could tell by the tone in her voice. Again, I had no words. What could I possibly say to her? We had never talked about my thumbs—not ever in all the years I had known her.

I didn't have a choice in the matter of what my hands would look like in this lifetime. I was born this way. I was sad my thumbs had upset her, but my feelings were hurt, too.

Debra has always had her nails done, and they always looked pretty. I didn't get my nails done that often, but even when I did, I wouldn't put my hands out in front of her, and as I am writing this, I realize I do the same thing with other people. I guess it is a self-conscious habit not to put my hands—and short thumbs—on display.

Sometimes, when Debra and I would talk, she'd laugh and say something about the way I kept my hands hidden from her. She would ask, "Why don't you put your hands out in front of you?" At the same time, she would extend her own hands out front, then click the tips of her nails on the table.

I didn't want my children to experience the discord I had seen between my mom and Grandma Randall. So, I put up with taunts and insults. I wouldn't respond to Debra's rude behavior.

I wanted to speak up, but I didn't want there to be conflict or hurt feelings either. I kept quiet. I had a voice, but I was also afraid to use it. Besides those old tapes from childhood were still playing inside my head. "The squeaky wheel gets the grease doesn't it, Judy?" "You're passive aggressive." "You're not good; you're bad."

But enough is enough; I am taking my power back—the power I gave away unknowingly, the power that was stolen from me since I was a little girl.

I should have never questioned my perception. Not listening to my intuition or speaking up when I needed to have caused a lot of anger and confusion for me.

Part Three

I was so happy when I found out I was pregnant. I was twenty-nine, and I vowed not only to myself but the entire universe that I would be the best mother ever and nothing at all like my parents. I held off having babies early in my marriage, mostly out of fear. My parents could barely make ends meet. I didn't want my children to experience not having enough, let alone face the dysfunction that I felt my siblings and I had endured. I had attributed the fact that my parents not having much money as part of the cause for the physical and emotional abuse in our home.

My dad was a janitor in the local schools. My mom was a substitute teacher, and, in the summer, she took college courses. She was working on getting her master's degree. Relatives told me my parents had too many kids, and my parents reminded me repeatedly that we didn't have much money.

I wanted my children to have a good, healthy home. I wanted them to be provided for in the best viable way.

My brother John wanted the same thing for his children. I know all my siblings wanted this for their families as well.

"We have to break the mold," John said during one of our phone conversations.

I love that! My brother was right. When you are raised without boundaries, when you become aware of the wrong, it must stop! So, you break the mold.

The sad thing is that for a lot of families, the abuse goes on generation after generation because it is what they know and what they feel most comfortable with. I think when we're born, our brains, like computers, are blank until files get added to them. More and more, I began to realize that I was not born bad. I had learned dysfunctional behaviors because of my environment. I had downloaded a lot of corrupt files, and it was time for me to delete them.

It was difficult for me to understand why terrible things happened the way they had—why some people, no matter how hard they tried, felt they couldn't change their lives or situations. Why are some drawn to the very personality-disordered people they have tried so hard to escape?

People use shame and guilt to manipulate, especially the ones I loved and those I thought loved me. I am learning more about narcissistic personality disorders and how they affect relationships. I was also beginning to sense that there were not only alcoholics but narcissists in my family circle of non-trust.

THE CARVING

My husband's brother-in-law Richard, for all the years I have known him, has been very charming. He has opened doors for all the ladies, including me. He likes to dance, cook, and make and serve cocktails at our get-togethers, no matter whose home is hosting. Richard is a dance instructor, and he worked for a popular Christian bookstore that has since closed its doors. He has led us in prayer at every meal, always ending with a loud, authoritative, "Amen."

In general, he seemed to be a great guy. We loved him.

He once gave Ray an intricate wood carving that he had created. The entire carving looked like obscure letters and symbols, characters I didn't recognize.

Ray liked his gift, but from the first time I saw it, I got strange vibes.

Ray hung the multifaceted carving on the wall in our family room for everyone to see. The more I looked at this piece of art, the stranger it made me feel.

One day I couldn't take the strong feelings any longer, so I hid the carving under our stairway. If I didn't have to look at it, I wouldn't think about it.

A year later, while I had forgotten, Ray noticed his gift was missing, and he asked me where it was. I reluctantly went back under the staircase to retrieve it. I then placed it back where Ray had initially hung it on the wall, but it began to bother me again. The immense feelings I got from it felt dark and eerie.

I asked Lucy, Ray's sister, and Richard's wife, what the symbols and peculiar letters he had carved meant. She told me she didn't know but thought it was Mayan. "Richard had a long time to work on the carving," she said. Later, I asked Richard what the Mayan letters and symbols meant. He told me they weren't Mayan but random symbols he'd carved.

This piece of art continued to bother me. The increasing sensations of doom I got from it became hauntingly stronger each day. One afternoon, I couldn't take the persistent, disturbing ambiance

I got from the carving any longer, so I took the ornate artifact out to the burn barrel. I burned it, and then told Ray what I had done.

Several years later, I was playing around and searching Google. I looked up my name, which led me to search for other names. I proceeded to show Ray what I was doing. To give him an example, I cuddled up next to him with my laptop in front of me, and we looked up one of the nicest, most innocent people I could think of.

We couldn't believe the past Richard had. He'd been in prison, and at one time, he was on death row for his role in two robberies that left one man dead and another paralyzed. It was difficult for us to believe that this was the same person we'd known for almost twenty years. We were both hurt. I cried hard.

Ray called his brother to ask if he knew about this, and his brother told him yes. I think what hurt the most was learning the information the way we had—by accident in a random internet search.

Richard's past was probably why I picked up on the strange feelings from the intricate carving. Lucy was right. Richard did have a long time to work on the art.

Later, Ray's mother called and reprimanded me. She was upset we'd found out about Richard's history.

"You made Richard cry," she scolded. She was angry at me for telling my sons, but I didn't want them to find out about Richard the way Ray and I had. Our sons loved him, too.

Ray had every right to ask his brother about what we'd discovered as well. After all, it is a public record. I feel that it was wrong for Ray's mother to criticize me. But I was happy to read that Richard had made amends with his victim.

LOOKING BACK

Through the years, some of Ray's family members had been insolent. Then they started getting braver. Instead of waiting for Ray to leave the room to verbally attack me, they would spew their spiteful remarks, however sweetly, in front of him. Ray did nothing to stand up for me, let alone stand up for himself with them. This was hurtful too, for both of us.

When I tried to talk to him about things that concerned me, he would become defensive because I was upset. From there our differences could escalate. I didn't want the stress it caused between us, so I eventually gave in to him as I had with everyone else my entire life. I didn't want more drama in my home than there already was. I kept my mouth shut and let more anger build up within me.

How had it come to this, from being in love to so much disappointment, so much ugly? I know why now. We'd unknowingly invited his family's dysfunction and mine to come into our relationship.

Ray could trust me, but I couldn't trust him, as I have mentioned before, I had a tough time trusting anyone anyway.

I wanted to be loved and cherished. I wanted my husband to protect and stand up for me, but there were times he didn't.

Two people raised in different homes with recognized dysfunctional behaviors, then coming together, trying to make a marriage work is arduous. Our intent is to make our relationship excel, but now with counseling, boundaries, and respect for one another.

I know it's possible. Even with all the dysfunction around me, one couple stood out from the rest. When I was a teenager, I babysat for Mrs. Bennett, a neighbor lady who built her husband up with praise and admiration. While in conversation, married women laughed at their husbands in jest, but she would only say nice things about hers. I never heard her say a negative thing about her husband. I remember thinking this was the kind of wife I wanted to be someday. I loved Mrs. Bennett. She was tiny; she wore her brunette hair short. She took care of herself, and she always had the latest style of clothes. She had three little boys I absolutely loved. The oldest, Jimmy, had dark brown hair and brown eyes. He was quiet and kept to himself, but he was funny. Sometimes he'd get his dog Teddy to chase me around their house, and we'd all laugh. His brother Ronnie was two years younger. He was blond and blue-eyed. He was the talkative one. Some nights when he couldn't sleep, I'd let Ronnie stay up late, and I'd listen to him talk about baseball, his family, and friends. The youngest, Sean, was two, a toddler. He looked a lot like his older brother Jimmy.

Mrs. Bennett was kind and patient with me. Sometimes, I would walk to her house unannounced to visit. Even if she was busy, she'd always take time for me. I felt wanted and accepted.

On a warm summer night after nine, she came to visit me. This was unusual; she'd never done this before. She wanted to talk to me, not my parents, and she let me know that.

"Judy, can you talk privately?" she said quietly. Her expression was one of concern. My siblings were inside the house at the time. We went out into the backyard to talk, but my parents were in our above-ground pool, so we went back inside the house. Several times she tried to tell me what she wanted to say, but we kept getting interrupted. My parents got out of the pool, and they were now inside, chasing each other through the house in their wet bathing suits and in front of us. I was fourteen so I felt embarrassed. My parents didn't seem to care that Mrs. Bennett, an adult, was there because they didn't stop chasing each other even after saying a quick hello to her while running through the house. Mrs. Bennett never did get to talk to me, but I have a strong feeling it had to do with my dad recently hitting me. If she did want to talk, I think she must have changed her mind because she'd never mentioned it again.

I could have left Ray. There were times I felt I had a million reasons to leave, and I am sure he felt he had just as many intentions for wanting to leave me too.

MOTHERHOOD

One afternoon, while my twin sons were at school in their first-grade class, I turned on a radio program. The topic had to do with whether your children are depressed. I was killing time before school let out and before it was time to pick the boys up, so I listened. The qualified guest on the show—I do not remember her name or title—pointed out that your children are depressed if they draw in dark colors.

At pickup, the boys jumped into the car with exploding laughter and jubilation. They were so happy to be done with school that afternoon, excited to tell me about their day, and proud to share the pictures they had colored.

I hugged them, laughed with them, and then I swear I heard dirges being played inside my head when I saw their school projects. They had both drawn pictures in black and brown crayon. I smiled while I examined their work and exclaimed to each one how proud I was.

"What beautiful pictures!" I was pretending. The art of bristle. I didn't want them to see the fear in my eyes.

After we got home from school and my sons were outside playing with friends, I called my mother. My mom had taught school through the years. She had earned her master's degree in education. I explained to her what I'd learned from the expert on the radio show. I shared my fears regarding the hand-drawn pictures portrayed in dark colors that my sons had created in their class, and I told her how concerned I was that they were depressed.

While I disclosed my feelings to her, in the back of my mind, I was so sure that I had caused my son's depression.

Suddenly, my mother broke out laughing. "They're not depressed," she said. "There were probably more children than crayons, Judy." My mother continued, "They drew pretty pictures in school today. Now hand them some black and brown crayons. Let them color." She told me my sons were being creative, and I should disregard what the expert had said.

I relaxed and let go of my concern. My mom was right, and I did worry a lot.

RELOCATING

I grew up in Dearborn Heights, Michigan. It was my home for pretty much my entire life. I considered myself a city girl. I liked living in a neighborhood close to shopping malls and the convenience of pizza delivery.

After I got married and after the births of our twin baby boys, my family continued to live in the city until my husband's job relocated to Tennessee.

Ray moved ahead of us to start working in Spring Hill. I stayed behind with our sons. We intended to sell our home before joining him—a practical decision.

It seemed so much easier for my husband to relocate than it was for our children and me. He and several friends who had also worked at the GM plant in Ypsilanti, Michigan, moved to Tennessee simultaneously. They carpooled, went to car shows, went on camping trips, and attended several Detroit Lions games together. I didn't know his coworkers well, but there was a camaraderie among the guys.

Although Ray's work hours had been drastically cut, and we could barely make ends meet then, I kicked and screamed like a spoiled brat at the thought of moving away from extended family, our home, and the life I had known for thirty-eight years. I had friends and neighbors I'd grown up with. I knew the best stores to shop in. We had family doctors and dentists that we had gone to for years. I knew the best places for doughnuts on Sunday mornings, a bakery with the best Italian bread in the world, and a Chinese restaurant with my favorite Cantonese cuisine. Now, I was going into uncharted territory. This terrified me.

I should have been thrilled that Ray had a job to go to.

We soon learned that building a house in Tennessee was our only option because Spring Hill and the surrounding areas were mainly farm fields. There was not enough housing for the heavy population relocating to the area.

One evening while still living in Michigan, I walked to our local pharmacy, Mel's Drug Store. For years, I had loved going to Mel's and looking through the display of magazines that covered a wide variety of topics. I was going to miss Mel's, too. Usually, I would look through the pages of *Better Homes and Gardens, Family Circle,* and a few fashion magazines, but this time, I was looking for home builder publications. I flipped through the pages of *Countrypolitan Home Plans,* an issue filled with plans for Queen Anne architecture presented by Larry W. Garnett & Associates. The magazine had my attention.

I prayed for help finding house plans that would work for my precious family. My prayer was answered, but the answer didn't come easily.

It had been a challenge to accept that we were moving. . . And that we were moving to a state where I had never in a billion years dreamed of living.

At first, I thought it would be a breeze for Ray and me to live apart, but after only a week, it became difficult for me. I missed him too much. By the time school let out in June, six months later, we still had not sold our home, but my brother, John, helped me load up a rental truck, and the boys and I headed for Tennessee anyway.

I didn't tell Ray what I was doing. I just did it. I showed up in Tennessee. I could tell he wasn't happy I'd moved without us selling the house first; that was our original plan. I didn't want to hear the word, "No," from Ray. I felt like I had disappointed him for not waiting until the house was sold, but I was afraid to be alone without him. He'd moved to a state almost six hundred miles away from me. I worried he might meet someone new and leave me. I was weak. The thought of what my parents would say to me after we were maried came to mind: "You better behave or Ray's going to leave you."

There was little housing available to rent or purchase for all the people relocating to Middle Tennessee to work at the new Saturn plant. Many families bought property and built homes, but it was a process, and it took longer than expected to build. For us, it took almost two years before our home was completed and we could move in.

Most people needed a place for their families to live while they waited for their homes to be constructed.

Ray was renting a three-bedroom apartment with two co-workers. One of them moved out because he'd bought a house, and his family was now there to join him. My sons moved into his old room. We had our own rooms and our own bathrooms.

I'd found a house to rent in Franklin after moving to Tennessee. Franklin was a quaint small town in the next county that had been recommended to us as an exceptional place to live and raise a family. Ray didn't want to leave his co-worker to take care of the entire monthly payment alone until he could find another renter. He'd signed an agreement. So, we continued to stay in the apartment. Eventually, Ray's co-worker moved out when his house was completed. He was very nice and patient with us, although I know this was difficult for him and his family. I apologized for not being more considerate of them. I should have been stronger and stayed in Michigan until we sold our house. However, the sale took two years. What I really should have done was move into the Franklin house with my sons, but again, I gave in too quickly. My decision to stay at the apartment made me angry, and as usual, I held more anger inside.

Ray wanted to live in the country. He'd grown up in a small northern Michigan town. He was tired of living on the outskirts of Metropolitan Detroit. "I don't want to live where I can hear the wail of a siren every five minutes. I don't want to live ten feet away from the next-door neighbor's house either. I want my boys to grow up knowing nature as I did." These were all valid points. I agreed with Ray.

"Okay," I said, "but if we live in the country, I get to have what I want." I let Ray have his way, and I got my house. A reasonable tradeoff, but I did have my moments of remorse.

I wanted to live in the city—not in a rural county. The city of Franklin in Williamson County was recommended to us before we moved. It was a desirable location for families because of the wonderful school system. There was a variety of industries, as well, but we ended up buying property in the county I did not want to live in at the time.

Sometimes I felt like I didn't fight to live in the city. I gave in too easily. Against my wants and needs for our sons and me, I backed down, only to please Ray. I have always wanted to please not just Ray but everyone. Gradually, giving in to other people was breaking me. I was angry, but I continued to shove the anger deep down.

Growing up in one culture and moving and adjusting to another was difficult.

We've had our challenges, yet, throughout those sad and turbulent times, we stayed together. Ray was not physically abusive like my dad had been to me. Still, sometimes his insensitive words made me feel not only angry but also more insecure than I already was, and I have to admit I was insensitive toward him at times too.

Some women felt the impolite need to flirt with my husband, never mind that the ogling went on in front of me. Ray liked the attention. I didn't like that he was playing into their flirtatious games. I wanted him to let these women know that I was his wife. There were ways he could have shown them he wasn't interested, like slipping his arm around me, pulling me in closer to him, or planting a big, long kiss on my mouth in front of them, but that didn't happen. We'd argue about that.

After living in Tennessee for a while, I discovered why some locals were angry with outsiders—those of us who had moved to their town. We had taken the jobs that were promised to them.

I'd heard they'd been told they would be getting jobs at the new Saturn plant in Spring Hill. Around the same time, some families had their properties confiscated (Eminent Domain) because of

---

[4]Aldrich, Marta W. The Seattle Times, $83 Million Later Unfinished Dam Being Dismantled. October 10, 1999

a dam project that has since been stopped due to a rare mussel. When the dam project was scrapped, families were unable to get their properties back. Instead, most of their land has remained with the Tennessee Valley Authority, the largest government owned power company in the United States.[4]

I don't blame people for being angry. There were a lot of unspoken conflicts. I feel like politicians lied to them and took from them. It wasn't right.

I have lived in Middle Tennessee for almost thirty years now; it is my home. Even though I had a difficult time acclimating, which was mainly due to my fear of change, I have come to love the people, this state, and beauty of the land.

Moving to Tennessee was not an enjoyable experience for me. For example, one day, I took my sons to the library in town. We picked out some books and went to the front desk to check them out. I smiled. "Hello," I said to the librarian, an older woman with wire-rimmed glasses. I handed her our books, but her only reply was to dramatically slam a book down on the counter while glaring at us. For some reason, her behavior hurt my feelings.

I don't know; maybe she was thinking, *All these northerners moving here to take jobs at the new auto plant.*

At the time, I didn't understand her animosity.

Sometimes when I went to the local stores or mall, I got derogatory facial expressions and even rude comments from some of the town residents. This troubled me; it was hurtful.

I naively wore a Michigan ball cap into a small restaurant one day. I didn't know anyone in the quaint diner.

"Can I help you?" A pretty, young server asked me.

I smiled. "Yes, I'll have a root beer float, please." While I waited, I observed how polite she was to her patrons. She spoke pleasantries and placed their food and drink gently in front of them. When my drink was ready, she slammed the glass down on the counter in front of her before she gave it a hefty shove toward me. I watched my root beer float sail past me. Then if that wasn't enough, she threw the spoon at me. I know it's a funny scenario, but my eyes welled up with tears. In a small way, I was beginning to see what discrimination felt like.

The spouses of those relocating to Spring Hill, me included, didn't know anyone. It was also tricky getting our children and ourselves acclimated to an area that did not want us. I went back to the apartment one night and told Ray about a rude encounter I had at the store, and he asked me, "What did you say to them?" as if I had incited the confrontation.

I told him, "I didn't say anything."

I'd been shopping and minding my own business. When I went to cash out, a woman with a big white bow in her hair said, "You're not from here, are you?" I smiled, thinking this was a nice opening for conversation, but before I could answer her, another woman standing close by said, "No, she's not, but you know where she's from." Meaning I was a Yankee. I felt like outsiders like me didn't belong here, because we were taking jobs that had been promised to the residents of Middle Tennessee.

Deep down, I knew it wasn't me who caused the incident. But again, I gave in too easily. Giving in and claiming some responsibility for the friction avoided an argument with my husband. We had fought a lot since moving to Tennessee.

I met women who lived in the same apartment complex as we did. Although I didn't have a close friendship, their children and my boys went to the same school and played together.

"I probably should have stayed home until we sold our house," I said one day while a group of us were talking.

One of the women shared with me, "My husband told me there was no way I was staying behind to sell our home. He said we were moving to Tennessee together as a couple and as a family."

What this woman said that day had added to my insecurity. "I want our own place." "I want to live in Franklin." "I don't want to build anymore." "Why would you want me to stay in Michigan to sell our house first? So and so told me her husband said they were a couple and a family. Her husband said there was no way they wouldn't be together." "He loves his wife. Are you sure you love me? Are you sure you want me?" "Oh, by the way, the librarian slammed books in our faces today."

Ray defended himself, and I defended myself. We escalated; sometimes, our disagreements made us impatient with our boys, which caused them to act up. Our ill behavior was wrong. I regret we weren't the adult caretakers we should have been for our sons. Relocating was difficult for them, too, especially when their parents weren't happy or weren't behaving like adults.

SOMETHING MY MOTHER TOLD ME

Some nights when I cannot sleep, I go into the second-floor laundry room of our home. I draw the lace curtains back, and I open a small window that looks out over our property. I feel the fresh air stream inside, and I breathe it in.

Overall, it's dark outside until I look up far above the treetops and until my eyes meet the sky. On a clear night, I can see a vast array of tiny lights shining under the heavens. Every time I do this, it reminds me of something my mother once told me when I was a little girl. She said that after she was married, she sometimes felt lonely. She had moved from her home in rural Michigan to the city, the suburbs of Detroit with her new husband, when she was only nineteen. When she looked up at the stars, she told me she wasn't as sad because the stars reminded her of her home and growing up in northern Michigan.

The universe makes me feel small, yet I feel protected. God protects me. I especially feel his presence on nights like this. Our lives can get pretty crazy at times, and although I don't understand completely why God allows outrageous things to happen, I believe he has always been with me, especially through times of abuse, and that there is a definitive purpose for my life.

OUT OF CONTROL

After moving to Tennessee, I started to yell at my husband and sons for no reason. We'd had some unhappy experiences. I felt out of control.

We were expecting company one evening. The boys stayed home with Ray while I went into town. A twenty-minute drive is one way to get groceries for dinner.

On my drive home, I started going over things I felt still needed to be done before our guests arrived. I remember thinking, *I have to put a fresh tablecloth on before I set the table. I hope the tablecloth comes out of the dryer wrinkle-free, or I'll have to iron it. I don't have time to iron.*

When I left home, Ray was watching a NASCAR race on TV, and the boys were playing with their Nintendo Game Boys. *I hope*

Ray vacuumed and the boys dusted. The boys will need to pick up their rooms before company arrives. I hope they did a decent job dusting and making their beds. I hope they didn't let the dog in on my clean kitchen floor. I have to make the salad, and I still have to wipe down the bathrooms.

I started to feel more anxious, like everything was spiraling out of control. The minute I walked through the door, I started to yell. "Ray, did you vacuum? Did the boys clean their rooms?" I hated that I was like this.

I would go to bed at night, promising myself that I wouldn't yell the next day, but the following day, I would do the same thing. I have no excuse. How I behaved was wrong.

One Sunday at church, the pastor gave a sermon I will never forget. He said he hated his mother. I couldn't believe he admitted that he hated his mother and in front of the entire congregation. He told us his mom used to yell and scream over nothing. I felt ashamed. He was describing me. This is what I had been doing— screaming at my family because I was feeling out of control, and I was reacting out of fear. I came to find out the pastor's mother's father was an alcoholic.

After that day, I tried to be conscious of my moods and behavior. Whenever I started to feel out of control, like I was going to yell, I tried hard not to react, even if it meant going to my room and isolating myself. With practice, my bad conduct had turned around. I tried to stay calm and then asked myself what I was feeling. *Am I sad, overwhelmed; am I afraid; am I tired?* None of the feelings was an excuse for me to yell. To be honest, most of the time, I didn't even know what I was shouting about.

Eventually, I started to see that there was a reason I had been behaving this way. As strange as it may sound, I felt relief—relief to know that I wasn't born bad as I thought but that I had learned this behavior. My dad, like the pastor's grandfather, was an alcoholic, too.

About a year later, one of my sons said, "Mom, you don't yell like you used to." I was getting better. I was growing. My son's words had encouraged me.

Part Four

I was healing and coming into myself, one step at a time. But I would learn that a hurtful, chaotic childhood for me was nothing compared to the horrific pain of what was to happen next.

The following are notes from a journal I wrote while my son, Nicholas, was sick. Once again, my thoughts and journal entries are random selections. They are not in any particular order.

As I have mentioned, when times were good, I could never really be in the moment and thoroughly enjoy those times because deep down inside, I felt that something bad was about to happen. As it turns out, I was usually right. But it was also my cracked, dysfunctional way of thinking. I no longer believe this or think this way; it is so freeing for me.

When my son, Nick, was seventeen, he came home from class and told me he would be taking his first flying lesson the following Thursday. He also said that there wasn't anything I could do or say about it because he was paying for the lesson with his own money.

I remember standing back for a moment, just looking at him. I had no words. What could I say? I remember thinking how happy I was for him. I was proud of him.

The boys both had flight simulator games on their computers. They had played simulator games for years, but I never thought about them becoming pilots. I think this was the first time I realized that Nick was becoming a man, that both of my boys were becoming men. They were beginning to navigate their own lives.

AUGUST 16, 2004 – A DREAM

I dreamed all night of rabbit eggs, colorful Easter eggs, shooting out from the bottoms of my feet. Some of the eggs were broken, but they continued to fly through my feet, and they would not stop. After I awoke, I analyzed my dream. *I know why,* I thought. I had been up late the night before, researching leukemia on the internet. I came across the book, *You and Leukemia: A Day at a Time,* by Lynn S. Baker MD. It is a book primarily written for children but is a useful and easy to understand resource for all ages. The author used an analogy of fast multiplying rabbits to describe what leukemic blasts in the bone marrow are like.

AUGUST 2004 – BACK TO COLLEGE

Nicholas and Daniel were getting ready to start their sophomore year at Middle Tennessee State University. They were both on the Dean's List in their first year. I was so proud of them.

Two weeks before his diagnosis, Nick was in a good mood, laughing, and looking forward to starting school. I remember his exact words: "Mom, I'm not trying to hurt your feelings, but I can't wait to go back to school." He was so sweet. He didn't want to hurt my feelings. He and Daniel have always been considerate and caring of people.

I laughed and answered teasingly, "Nick, I'm not trying to hurt your feelings, but I can't wait either." I didn't mean it.

Once again, I was beginning to feel the pains of empty nest syndrome and dreading how quiet the house would be after such a fun-filled summer of travel together.

I was ecstatic for both of my sons, my only two. Twins. They were identical. At least that's what everyone told me when they were babies, but I could see a difference. As they grew older, even their voices sounded different to me.

Two little blond-haired baby boys with big, deep blue eyes and sweet, sweet smiles. Daniel was a little bigger weight-wise than Nick was, but not by much. Nick's face was slender, and as he got older, he grew taller than Daniel.

When they were about eight months old, we spent the night at a friend's house. We were sleeping on a pallet of blankets on the floor. Sometime in the middle of the night, one of the babies started to cry. I didn't want to disturb anyone, so I didn't turn the lights on. I picked the baby up not knowing whether it was Nicholas or Daniel. It was dark, I couldn't see, and even if I could, they were both wearing the same pajamas.

I held the baby close, rocking him in my arms until he got quiet. I remember thinking I don't know which baby this is. At the time, I felt anxious not knowing. I tried to calm myself, and suddenly, it came to me. I knew it was Daniel. I had picked up on his little spirit.

Our babies that my husband and I raised together had grown up fast. They were becoming men, delving into their own lives and personal relationships. So many possibilities surrounded them. So much potential for a good life was ahead of them.

Ray seemed happy that it would be just the two of us alone again. So many changes throughout the years had taken a toll on our relationship. We'd grown further apart. He wanted to work on our relationship. He wanted us to grow close again. I only remember looking at him and thinking, *Now what?* I was tired.

I felt there wasn't anything we had in common anymore except our sons and what revolved around them and their lives. Now, they were going back to school.

SUMMER 2004 – BEFORE THE DIAGNOSIS

The boys got out of school in May. We had company that night, and I stayed home to finish cleaning the house and prepare a meal while Ray went to Murfreesboro to help our sons move out of their dorm rooms for summer. I was so excited. My boys were coming home.

They were growing up. I loved the excitement and grown-up demeanor they now had and how Ray and I communicated in a much more adult way with our boys and they with us. I loved the funny stories they shared about school and all of the new things happening in their lives.

Nick was planning on becoming a trauma surgeon. He wanted to work in the ER. Daniel was in the aerospace program at school. He wanted to fly commercial and do missionary work.

I was so excited for that homecoming day. I wanted my boys to feel happy to be home from a year that was filled with not only good times, but also stressful times. I'd missed them. I hurried to make lemonade and bake a cake. I marinated chicken. We planned to grill out that night. I wanted everything to be perfect for them and our guests.

A large majority of families choose to homeschool in Tennessee. The friends we associated with homeschooled their children like us, under an umbrella school. Umbrella schools oversee the student's progress, making sure goverment requirements are met. I had homeschooled my sons since the fifth grade. Before their first year of college, I told them the test for all of us would be to see if homeschooling had paid off.

I am incredibly proud of my sons, not only for doing so well academically in school but because they love God, and they are moral.

Ray was planning a late-summer trip to Sturgis—a motorcycle

rally held annually in South Dakota. He was going to ride out with friends and then meet his brother, Greg, at the rally. He and Greg had been planning this trip to one of the largest motorcycle gatherings in the world for an entire year, and every time Ray talked about the event, I would get upset.

A week after the boys got home from school, we drove to Michigan for my nephew Eric's graduation, a nine-hour drive.

Nick and Daniel teasingly made me sit in the back seat while they drove; it was nice to be the passenger, to read a book and look out at the scenery on our trip.

I stayed with my brother John, and the boys stayed at their cousin Eric's. Eric is a year younger than the boys and has always been more of a brother to them than a cousin. While Nicholas and Daniel had blond hair, Eric's hair color was dark brown. He has big brown eyes, and a bit of Cherokee in his ancestry. I used to call the boys the Three Musketeers.

We went to Michigan early to help with Eric's graduation party.

The evening before graduation, I was getting ready to head back to my brother's house when Nick met me at the door. He wanted to go with me.

We got to John's house at about seven that night. Nick went upstairs to lie down while I stayed downstairs to visit with my brother and his family. A couple of hours later, I went upstairs to check on my son. I found him sleeping on the floor. I helped him get into bed, then went back downstairs. He slept all night, and he slept in until about noon the following day. I thought it was odd for him to be sleeping so much, but I ignored my intuition.

After Eric's graduation, we headed for New York. The boys and I had visited New York City several summers before while Ray was in Sturgis. We had so much fun in New York that we wanted Ray to experience it too. It was a traveling summer for all of us— Michigan, New York, and a soon-to-be trip to Chicago in August.

A week after returning home from New York, Nick woke up complaining about having an earache. I remember thinking, *Oh no, I'm not ready for this.* This thought has always struck me a little funny. I guess I knew what was going to happen, even though I didn't know. Sometimes, it's difficult for me to make sense of things until I look back on them later.

Nick had three viral infections while at school that year, and it was starting to bother me that he still wasn't feeling well. So, I suggested he go to the doctor.

The physician prescribed antibiotics, and he treated Nick for Swimmer's Ear.

In two weeks, we were going to meet John and his family in Chicago for a long weekend, a trip we had planned with them six months earlier.

But two weeks later, Nick still wasn't feeling well. Again, I noticed he had been sleeping a lot. Ray said he was probably gearing up to go back to school.

My brother and sister-in-law had planned a birthday party for their daughters at the American Girl Place. This would be our first time visiting Chicago.

Chicago, like Michigan, was a nine-hour drive from our home. Nick told me he wasn't up for the trip. He said he was tired and that he just wanted to stay home. Sadly, we left for Chicago without him. It was difficult for me to leave him, but Nick was a man and old enough to make his own decisions.

The following week, Ray was leaving on his trip to Sturgis, and two weeks after that, the boys would be going back to school. Summer was flying by fast.

Nick and Daniel had finished most of their school shopping, and they were bored. I suggested they rent a plane and go flying. That Tuesday was a beautiful day. You couldn't have asked for a better day to fly—sunny with few clouds and a mild breeze. The boys took my advice and went flying.

I was inside working on the computer when I heard a plane fly over the field near our home. I immediately ran outside; adrenaline surged throughout my body. I ran out of the house so fast I didn't have time to put my yellow flip-flops on. The screen door slammed behind me, and our black cat Vlady who was resting on the front porch, vaulted out of the way. "Vroom." The plane flew over the field. It was my boys. (I'm smiling at the memory of them in that little plane now.)

I remember thinking, *My babies, when did they grow up?* Now, at nineteen, both of them were pilots. They'd had their licenses since they were seventeen.

The plane soared, then turned away before it circled back. I was standing in our driveway looking up at them, waving frantically.

Nick was flying that day. The plane circled again before the boys flew about five hundred feet in the opposite direction.

I could see the plane, but I could no longer hear the engine; it had stalled. Nick was cranking the ignition, and I began praying, pleading, "God, please don't let them crash; please don't let them crash." Then I heard the engine start back up. I was relieved while I ran across the field, still waving up to my boys.

Do you know how scary that was for me? To see my sons in a plane overhead when the engine stalls out. The boys got home a few hours later. They were laughing. I asked them why the engine on that little Cessna had stalled out. They continued to laugh.

"It didn't stall out, Mom." They were teasing me. They wouldn't tell me what happened. I think it's because they didn't want their mama to worry. Later Daniel told me Nick was practicing stalls.

Little did we know that this would be the last time Nick would ever fly an airplane. In a few short days, our world was about to change forever.

Ray left Saturday to ride from Tennessee to South Dakota to his motorcycle rally in Sturgis. He was anxious and happy to go. I was seething inside. I honestly didn't know why I felt this way, but for some reason, I didn't want him to go. He went the year before, and I had no problem with that, but this year was different. Again, I didn't know why.

The boys and I talked about going to a museum in Nashville while Ray was away. The museum is about an hour's drive from our home. We tried to go on Monday, but something came up. Nick didn't feel like going on Tuesday. Wednesday was the day we were going to try again, but again, Nick wasn't feeling well, so we decided we would try for Thursday. Daniel really wanted to go to the museum, but he didn't want to go without Nick.

That night before I went to bed, I walked into Nick's room to say good night. He told me he wanted to go to the museum, but he wasn't feeling well. He said his chest was hurting, and his arms and legs ached. He said he was tired. I again suggested that he go back to his doctor. I told him to tell his doctor exactly how he was feeling and to be very honest about his symptoms.

AUGUST 2004 – DIAGNOSIS

On Thursday, the following morning, I woke up early to make an appointment for Nick. He went to see a doctor he and Daniel had been going to since they were eight.

Nicholas was nineteen when he was diagnosed with cancer. My son had leukemia. Why was this happening to my son? He had to have a lumbar puncture and spinal tap, so he hadn't eaten anything since the night before. Daniel and I didn't eat because if Nick couldn't eat, we weren't going to either.

Ray was still in Sturgis. I tried to call him, but he wasn't answering his phone. There we were, the three of us—Nicholas, Daniel, and me—to face this monster alone. I was so scared.

We were so frightened. Before the oncology staff left for lunch, they told me that the doctors would let us know Daniel's odds of getting leukemia since he was Nick's twin. So, there I was, alone, with the horrible fear of this unknown inside my head for several hours until the doctors returned. I still hadn't heard from Ray. I was terrified that both of my boys had this disease, as if only one of them having Leukemia wasn't horrible enough, before the doctors told us that Daniel's chances of getting it were very low.

I felt alone, but then what else was new? I had pretty much handled the bad alone my entire life anyway. I had to be brave for my sons, even though I wasn't being brave for me, and Ray wasn't with us. I tried hard not to show my scared, sad, angry emotions.

"You'll be alright, Nick. Everything's going to be alright," I said, wrapping my arms around him, trying to reassure my son.

"Daniel, Nick will be okay. I know he will. Don't worry, okay," I said, trying to smile, my eyes meeting his. Then I'd scream out silently inside my head, "Please, God. Please help."

If I was angry with Ray before he went to Sturgis, it was nothing like the anger I felt when I heard his voice. "Ray, why didn't you call me back? We're at the hospital, and the doctors say Nick has Leukemia. Ray, Nick has Leukemia!"

"I just got your call. The cell service is terrible here. It's so noisy, music is blaring, and everyone's screaming over each other to talk," Ray said.

"Judy, Nick's going to be okay. The diagnosis was probably all a mistake," he continued.

I wanted to believe my husband; I really did, but the tests returned positive for Leukemia.

I guess that was Ray's way of trying to comfort me. Maybe it was his own way of comforting himself too.

Nick was admitted to the hospital that night. It was almost nine o'clock, and we hadn't eaten all day, so I left the boys, hoping to find a restaurant close to the hospital, open and still serving food.

I got lost in the parking garage and drove around every floor level at least twice until I saw a family walking to their car. I stopped and asked them how to get out of there. I was upset about everything, especially Nick's diagnosis. They gave me directions and then drove away. I didn't think to follow them, so I got lost again, revisiting all the building's floor levels once more.

Several minutes later, I was sobbing, stressed, anxious, and driving in circles until I saw another family walking toward their car. I asked for their help and followed them. Finally, I was out of that ridiculous maze and was able to find food for my children, even if it was just hamburgers and fries. Not the healthiest to eat but my only option other than a vending machine.

It had been a long day. Nick was terribly sick, and my boys were hungry. I felt alone because Ray wasn't with us, and I felt stupid because I couldn't find my way out of a hospital parking structure. Everything felt out of control.

One morning in the weeks following, Ray took Nick to the hospital for his clinic appointment, and when he came home, he said that while he waited for Nick, a family was told their child had cancer.

"Judy, the doctors told a woman her son has cancer. She looked so scared. She started crying hard. I felt so bad for her."

I interrupted him. "I know exactly what that's like!"

When I look back, I see the subtle hints and thoughts I had before Nick's diagnosis. While in New York City that summer, we were sitting in the stands of Yankee Stadium watching the Yankees play. There was a little girl about seven sitting next to us. She had a feeding tube; her head was bald, and her face and body looked beyond swollen. I remember how badly I felt for the little girl and her mother, who sat beside her, tending to her needs.

While traveling back home from New York, we stopped at a restaurant. I went into the bathroom, where I saw a young girl who was maybe sixteen. Her hair was dark brown and curly. Thick tight curls that looked almost like a permanent but without the frizz covered her head.

We hadn't spoken until I stood over the sink to wash my hands. I heard her fussing in the mirror, but I didn't pay much attention until I saw her out of the corner of my eye, looking over at me.

When I turned to face her, she said, "I hate my hair."

"I think it looks pretty." I smiled.

"I had cancer. I lost all my hair, and the curls are what grew back. I hate it!" She continued to look in the mirror.

"I'm sorry you were sick, but I'm happy you are better now," I said, smiling again.

She continued to fuss with her hair while I left the room. I felt bad for her.

BLAMING ME

I believed for a long time that Nick's illness was my fault. I have moments where I still believe this.

After my babies were born, I went into the hospital nursery looking for them. I saw Daniel, but I didn't see Nicholas. He wasn't there. Daniel was in his bassinet, but Nicholas wasn't. I grew worried because the babies were not together. I couldn't find one of them. I didn't know where he was.

"Where is my baby?" I asked a nurse; she was a heavy-set woman with black framed glasses.

"He's under the Bili lights. Don't you know?" She said this to me sarcastically. I thought, *No, I didn't know where my baby was, that's why I asked you.* I felt guilty. I didn't know why. I just did. I was upset because they hadn't told me.

"Why?" I asked her.

"Your baby is a little jaundiced. It's perfectly normal for some babies to go under the lights," she said.

I wondered if my crazy caused Nicholas to get sick.

Maybe I didn't protect him enough. Maybe I didn't research the side effects of vaccines, medications, or ear infections. Was it something he ate or didn't eat? I think I have gone over everything in my memory, trying to figure out what made my son get this disease. Asking myself each time I thought of a potential cause, racking my brain over a past event—is this what caused the Leukemia?

The boys had a lot of ear infections when they were babies, and they were on antibiotics. Later, I read that antibiotics in the mid-eighties were causing ear infections in children.

Nick broke his arm when he was four. I left the boys with babysitters because I wanted to go out dancing with my husband and family that night. When I got home and checked on the boys, they were sleeping, but Nick's arm didn't look right. It was twisted out of shape. It was a bad break, and it would have never happened had I not been so selfish and gone out. He'd climbed up on our kitchen island and fell off.

I could not breastfeed the boys because of my thyroid disease. A breastfed baby is healthier. I knew that there had to be a reason why Nicholas got sick.

We all ate the same food; we lived in the same house, so why did only he get sick? Somehow, I just knew it had to be because of me.

Nick had been fighting three viral infections during his first year of college when he was eighteen. He had been treated for Swimmer's Ear that year as well. Ray was concerned; he worried that this combination of illnesses may have knocked our son's immune system down to an all-time low. We hadn't thought about this before.

One day, I asked one of Nick's oncologists what he thought had caused my son to get Leukemia. This very ill-mannered doctor made a hand gesture like he was injecting a shot into someone's arm. Yes, he did! I knew what he was implying. At least that's what it looked like to me.

AND SO, IT BEGINS

Three days after his diagnosis, Nick has an early appointment. Then he'll have surgery. A Medi Port will be inserted into his chest so he can start his first chemotherapy treatment.

This is a NIGHTMARE!

It's almost 5:30 a.m. We must leave home at 6:30 to get to the hospital by 7:30. I wish someone would wake us up from this horrible dream. We are not ready for this day, but somehow this day seems ready for us.

I'm angry. I'm angry at God, and I'm angry at the world. I am questioning. I'm still not trusting.

We are on time for Nick's first day of treatment, but as the day progresses, we accept reality. One of the first things we learn is that our perception of time and the hospital staff's perception of time are two different things.

Paperwork, meetings, doctor's orders, staff changes, and setbacks are the beginning of our new normal, and Nick's chemotherapy has been postponed until the following day.

When we got to the hospital, I was angry, also an emotion of fear. I held my feelings inside. I wouldn't let my emotions show; it would upset Nick.

The medical team had continuously said they would sit down with us to discuss the disease and Nick's prognosis thoroughly. We needed to understand and plan for the treatment protocol our son would have to endure. We would also be discussing his education. Would Nick be able to go back to school? He wanted to go back.

The medical team hadn't done this, at least not yet, and it seemed as if everything was "hurry up and wait." Everyone seemed to be going in slow motion. Everything, and I mean everything, seemed out of control. I was so frightened. We all were.

And I continued to pray, "Please, God, make this not true!"

Daniel is back at school. I miss him. He is getting none of our attention. He is on his own, and he has been on the back burner since Nick was diagnosed. I am feeling guilty about this too. He is having a tough time with his brother's diagnosis. I know Daniel; he's my son. The reality of our new normal is hard for him to accept like it is for all of us, but school helps keep his mind busy.

I'm home for the night. Ray is with Nick. Nick is in the hospital. He must stay there for the first month of his treatment protocol.

I make Nick's bed. I think back to the week before. Last Tuesday. Everything was so—here is that blasted word again—NORMAL! The boys were getting ready to go back to school. And now our world, our life, has changed overnight. Everything is so different.

YARNIA

Our property meets up to TWRA (Tennessee Wildlife Resource Agency) public land. In the summer of 2010, when Nick was feeling well between clinic and treatments, we'd hike down the shallow creek bed that started on our property to an even more extensive gathering of the waters. If we were to hike miles farther, we would eventually come to the Duck River. We enjoyed walking the land as weather permitted and Nick's health allowed until the fall of 2012.

We spent our time close to home. That's what Nick wanted. He didn't want to talk about the what-ifs of dying. He wanted to think about living, and we wanted that for him, too.

We all wore waders and carried our backpacks filled with cold drinks, snacks, sunscreen, bug spray, and walking sticks to stave off snakes or any other predators we might encounter; thankfully, we never ran into any.

Nick liked to hunt for arrowheads, and he found one. Daniel playfully claimed a little island on the creek bed. I suppose it once started out as a conglomeration of stones and debris that eventually stuck up high out of the water. We took our backpacks and explored. We had so much fun, and we made such beautiful memories.

On sweltering summer days, we would go down to the creek because it was much cooler there. I hardly remember the heat index on those sweltering hot mid-July days when we would go exploring. Nick called this place Yarnia, a sort of play on words—incorporating "Narnia" from the story *The Lion, the Witch, and the Wardrobe* by C. S. Lewis. In it, siblings are transported to the magical land of Narnia where they try to rid the place of the evil one.

The Y was from "yarn"—because we tied red yarn around a tree trunk to mark where to go in and out of the creek during thick summer vegetation growth. Maybe it wasn't so much the place, but the adventures of being together that made it special. Nick; Ray; Daniel; our daughter-in-law, Daniel's wife, Cassandra; and me. Those days together were the best.

In the last few years of Nick's life, we started camping. I wish we had done this when the boys were younger as Ray had wanted. It was I who didn't want to. The memories of camping in my childhood were awful. I didn't realize how much fun the sport could actually be and how close we would grow.

MIRACLES

I will never forget all the crazy emotions I felt when Nick was diagnosed. I remember driving home from the hospital to get some of his things: a chess game, some T-shirts, his brown slippers, and a book he'd been reading. I was in the car alone, I was screaming out loud, and I was crying hard.

This was a nightmare. I keep repeating that word, but this was really worse than a nightmare. It was unreal, and it was out of my hands. I felt helpless.

I crawled into bed with my clothes on. I didn't wash my face or brush my teeth.

No, I was going to have a heart-to-heart talk with God. How could he allow this? Why would he allow this? Why would he let an evil being such as satan live? (I refuse to capitalize the word satan.) Why didn't God destroy this evil entity rather than let him continue to cause all this pain and suffering in the world?

It was horrible for me to watch my son go through the painful side effects of his chemotherapy protocol and not be able to do anything about it.

Other children were suffering, and their families were hurting too. Why, God? I was so angry, and then I stopped. I said, "You know what? I'm counting on you for a miracle." And that is how I ended my conversation with him that night.

The following morning, I went downstairs to the kitchen. My sister, Rita, had come to Tennessee to help and to give us support. She was up early making coffee and doing the dishes. She told me she felt that there was going to be a miracle. It was good to hear uplifting words.

I grabbed a book for me, *Back to Eden* by Jethro Kloss—a classic on natural diet and wholistic health—and some things Nick had requested I bring back with me.

Miracle or not, Nick would still have to go through the chemotherapy protocol for this disease.

Some of the chemotherapy medications my son was taking caused sensitive reactions. Nick's senses seemed to be on high alert. He didn't want to hear any noise. He didn't want the TV on. The light in the room bothered him. Sometimes, even the sound of me turning the page of a book was excruciating for him.

Ray had spent the previous night at the hospital with Nick. When I walked into the room, both Ray and Nick had huge smiles on their faces.

"The doctor said I am in remission, Mom. Seven days and I am in remission, and I won't need any radiation."

Radiation? That was the first I'd heard about him possibly needing radiation therapy in his protocol, but his remission was good news. Then Ray said the doctor had described it as a miracle, without saying the word "miracle."

"It's rare for a patient to respond as quickly as you have, Nick," the doctor said.

I closed my eyes. "Thank you, Father," I whispered to God.

Later that afternoon while Nick was resting, I opened my book, *Back to Eden*. At the top of the page, I read, "Truly the day of miracles has not passed." This sentence had my attention. God had heard my prayer. I felt he was confirming it with Rita's uplifting words earlier that morning, the good news of Nick's remission, and now the author's quote. God was close, and he was talking to me.

The doctors told us that no one should touch Nick after the chemotherapy treatments started because the chemo could cause side effects for those who hugged or kissed him. While the doctors were explaining, I looked over at Nick to see the worry in his eyes. He looked scared and tired. I could tell that he was trying very hard to be strong. He was holding back his emotions. After the doctors left the room, I gave Nick a big hug, and I told him that I was not scared of any chemo drug, nor should he be afraid either.

LETTER TO FAMILY AND FRIENDS

September 16, 2004

Hello Everyone,

Thank you so much for your cards, letters, gifts, and prayers. This past month has been very emotional and exhausting for all of us, and especially for Nick. I cannot even begin to describe the crazy emotions we are enduring since Nick was diagnosed with ALL—Acute Lymphoblastic Leukemia.

This type of leukemia is seen in younger children under the age of 10. When ALL occurs after the age of 10, it is then a more high-risk leukemia. This type of cancer is when the bone marrow makes too many lymphocytes (a type of white blood cell). ALL is the most common type of cancer in children. Nick is being treated at a hospital in Nashville, Tennessee.

Last Tuesday, Nick had another bone marrow aspiration and spinal tap. His results were very good, and he is now in remission. However, he still must undergo many more months of intense chemo treatments so that the leukemia does not come back. They have seen it come back in others.

The first month of chemo for Nick was especially difficult. Beginning next Tuesday, he will get different medications, including a spinal tap every week for the next month. The doctors are in awe of how well he is doing, and he is what they refer to as a fast responder.

I know that it has been all the prayers sent out to him that have made his recovery happen fast. God is doing miracles, not only in Nick's life, but also in the lives of all of us who are praying for him. Please continue to pray. We are praying that he does not relapse because he will have to start the entire procedures all over again. We appreciate all the prayers. Praying for him is the most that we can do.

A week ago, we were on our way to the hospital for another treatment for Nick. He was very talkative that morning, so I just listened.

He told me that before he was diagnosed with leukemia, he asked God to work through him. Nick said he wants God to be glorified through this. He wants this disease to hurry and get over with so he can serve God.

Nick and Daniel are both honor students at MTSU. Nick's goal was to be a surgeon; now, it is to be an oncologist. Daniel is in the aerospace program, and he is now thinking of becoming a doctor so that when he does missions, not only will he, Nick, and their friend Travis, another pre-med student, be able to help with the medical aspect, but also fly to their mission destinations.

While Nick was undergoing his procedures the other day, a young woman was observing. She told me that she was doing this for school credit. She also told me that she had ALL just like Nick and that she was seeing the other side of the leukemia treatments she had received. She said she wants to be an oncologist, too.

Maybe someday soon, there will be a cure for cancer, and no child or adult will have to go through the pain and the hurt that this disease causes. It is not fair!

In the hospital, you see children sick, hurting, and undergoing painful treatments. Yet they still have smiles on their faces. Their attitudes seem positive. I admit that I was angry with God and questioned him a lot. I asked God for a miracle and then thanked him for that miracle. The following day, I went to the hospital with a book I had on herbs and vitamins. I opened a page and found, "Truly, the day of miracles has not passed."

I had some errands to run, so I spent the night at home, and when I returned to Nick's hospital room, I learned that the doctors told Nick and Ray in so many words that his recovery was miraculous. The doctors were impressed with his progress. For the entire day, everyone I talked to said they believed strongly—key word, strongly—that there was going to be a miracle. I know God was talking to me. He was comforting me. He was comforting us.

Please continue to pray for Nick. He likes receiving email.

I know that he would appreciate hearing from you. Thank you so much again. -Judy.

ONE DAY AT A TIME

September 21, 2004, was an exceptionally long, difficult day. Nick has been getting chemotherapy for one month now.

He went into the hospital at 9 a.m. for his clinic visit. We did not leave for home until 6 p.m. He was given several IVs before starting on a new chemo medication.

He will start the new med at home tonight, and take it by mouth. Nick has another med that he will give himself in his Medi Port starting tomorrow.

He had a spinal tap earlier today, so he has not had anything to eat since before midnight last night. Nick is now feeling nauseated. The doctors told us that these new medications can cause fevers and may bring his blood counts down lower which makes him more susceptible to infection.

One weekend, Ray and I visited his dad, Ed, in Ohio. Ed had never talked much to me. That afternoon, we sat at a white plastic table covered with a colorful vinyl tablecloth.

We were on his back porch waiting for Ray to return from running an errand. To break the silence between us, I shared with Ed how happy I was that Nick was in remission. Ed looked at me like he could not believe what I had just said.

He snickered and said, "The cancer will be back; it always comes back."

I felt a chill come over my body. I felt my soul deflate. I had so much hope. My father-in-law's words were defeating. I did not tell Ray what his dad had said to me for quite some time. I felt that if I repeated his dad's words, the cancer would come back.

Nicholas and Daniel—my only two children. I recall their first steps, both going in two different directions simultaneously. Back then, when they were just little guys, I will admit that there were times when I thought life was difficult, but it really wasn't. However, what we are dealing with now. . . Nothing could be more trying.

My boys are twenty. They are men. I know that it is important for them to fight their own battles, and now more than ever because my hands are tied.

I cannot take the chemotherapy and radiation for Nick. He has to do it. I can't stick my nose into my children's personal lives either because it is their business, and none of mine.

Sometimes, it feels as though I cannot ever say anything about anything. I have to keep quiet. But if I could take my sons pain from them, I would. You know I would.

I learn to keep my mouth shut even more, and this is difficult for me because all the time that I don't say anything, I am stuffing my hurt and pain and anger away without letting it go.

As the months and years progress, I am getting better at inaudible moments, screaming crazy inside my head. I must be strong for my children. I cannot show them how afraid or how vulnerable I am. But they are intuitive as well. I know they pick up on my emotions.

I wish it were me and not my child who has to endure the painful protocol—treatments that are not letting up, the after-effects that bring me to my knees while watching my son suffer. He throws up violently into the toilet or a cheap, yellow plastic tub; side effects from the chemo and radiation. When he cries out in pain, I know he hurts, but I can't make it go away, so I continue to scream inside.

When he was little, all it took was a kiss and a cookie to stop the sting. Now, I cry out silently, helplessly, holding back my tears, and I pray hard. I PRAY HARD! I smile outwardly, but I am really screaming!

I scream inside when the doctors are on rounds and come to talk to him, to us. One of the doctors has no bedside manner, and I want to tell him how cruel his words are, but I keep what I want to say shoved down deep.

In late October, Nick got pancreatitis from one of the chemo drugs. Doctors knew pancreatitis was a possible side effect since it had been reported in one percent of patients taking this particular chemo drug. Nick was one of the one percent. But they didn't tell us that until after Christmas.

For over a month, Nick's doctors said they didn't know what was wrong with him. Nick could not eat; he was in excruciating pain. He was put through all kinds of scans and tests to see what was wrong with him. He was suffering.

One evening, a doctor stood over Nick while he lay in bed with the same horrible pain—not just physical, but now mental anguish, too. The doctor's exact words: "We have done everything we can except slice him open, and we still don't know what's wrong." But you know what? I am thinking maybe this doctor knew Nick had pancreatitis all along.

Slice him open? I wanted to give the doctor a piece of my mind, but I couldn't. I didn't want to upset Nick more than he already was. So, I kept my mouth shut. I did file a report with patient affairs expecting more than a written apology, but in the end, that's all we got. I wanted the doctor to be reprimanded, but I don't think he ever was. He never apologized to us.

Nick had a second stem cell transplant on December 11, 2009. His first transplant was in 2006. In the first transplant, they used Daniel's stem cells. I had called and talked to a scientist from New York. She was written up in an article that I had read regarding stem cells. I explained to her that the doctors were going to use his identical twin's stem cells for Nick's transplant. She said, "Why are they going to do that? It won't work."

Did the doctors know it wouldn't work?

I told Nick about this, but his doctor and his team said the procedure would work.

The morning that he was to have his transplant, and while they were getting Daniel's stem cells ready to inject, I asked an assistant working with Nick's doctors if it were her child would she do this, and she said, "Yes, absolutely." Looking back, knowing what I do now, I sincerely doubt she would have accepted it for her child.

Nick's second transplant was a failure, too; we were told the transplant team didn't receive enough of the donor's stem cells. They infused the cells into Nick anyway knowing he needed more.

All Nick wanted to do was live!!!! Did the doctors know this wouldn't work either?

Even so, I continued to try and trust God for miracles. He was in control. I wasn't, and we were taking one day at a time, sometimes one minute at a time.

MORE JOURNAL ENTRIES

Nick wasn't feeling well, so I went to clinic with him. He didn't want me to take him, but I insisted. The doctors did a series of tests while we waited. At one point, Nick told me he felt like he was going to die. I tried to reassure him he was going to be alright, that he would be okay.

I turned down the lights so it was dark in the room. I asked a nurse for a blanket out of the warmer. I covered him with this and several more blankets because he was cold. I prayed silently for him while he tried to rest. He apologized numerous times because he felt so bad for me. He thought I was bored. I reassured him that I was not bored. I told him that I loved him and wanted to be with him. It made me feel sad that he worried about me. I wouldn't have had it any other way than to stay with my son.

I continued to pray for him while he rested. Sometimes when he was in the hospital, I would go to the chapel on the first floor to pray. This room was especially quiet while I knelt in front of a wooden pew or studied pictures portrayed in stained glass, beautiful pictures of doves and an angel standing guard over children. There always seemed to be a unique feeling of peace and love for me in this room.

Sometimes, I feel like I am so fake. I have to give my son hope. If I get upset, if I cry, if I show my feelings, then defeat will creep in. And there can be no defeat. No defeat! I refuse to succumb to the negative. I am determined, despite the statistics, that my son will live!

Hours and days go by during Nick's extended hospital stays. We never leave him alone. One of us—my husband or Daniel or a good friend of Nick's—stays with him. We stay by his side, offering support the best way we can.

Soon after Nick's diagnosis, I started printing out Bible verses that I placed on our refrigerator, in our cars, and in our bedrooms. I put them everywhere.

Uplifting scripture verses, God's promises were plastered all over the place. We were in a battle, and I was determined that we would not back down. We were going to fight. I had hope, but I was also bargaining.

I was going through the motions. I wanted to trust God, but honestly, I didn't trust anyone other than myself.

My entire life I remember getting on my knees to ask God for something, then as soon as I said amen, I would start thinking about all the ways for me to make my request happen.

However, when Nicholas got sick, no matter how hard I tried, I could not make him better. God had allowed me to depend on me for only so long, but now there was nothing I could do. And he didn't seem to be making a way for me to continue my behavior of depending on only myself and not him.

This was difficult for me to accept because, in my mind, I was a fighter, and if anyone was going to make something happen, it would be me; it had always been me.

I look out the window, and I cry while Nick sleeps because now he can't see me cry. It would make him feel sad.

I feel Jesus here in Nick's room. I believe He is in every room of every child in the children's hospital. He is with Nick, with me, with all of us in our own individual rooms, filled with fear, sickness, despair, and anger.

On a good day, a good day for him, is when he is able to get out of bed, walk to the window, and look out, but always attached to that awful IV tree. This mama knows that he screams out inside, too. This is a living nightmare for him, yet he is so strong.

We watch through the window in his room together. People are outside in front of the hospital. They are driving by, walking, or riding bikes, all of them doing so-called normal things.

I want Nick to do normal, too, but he physically can't. It upsets me. It makes me sad. I want Nick to have his normal life back. It hurts me to hear others complain about silly things, like broken fingernails or the weather, while my son is stuck in this room, in this disease, this prison of pain, dependent on others.

We are somewhere in the basement or a very cold, lower floor of the hospital. They measure Nick for the upcoming radiation therapy he will undergo. It terrifies me.

"Why? Does my son have to go through this? Why can't you make it stop? All you have to do is say the word, and he will be healed. Please do this! Please do this for him!" I plead with God.

I try to remember God's promises in my head, reciting Bible verses I have memorized, and I pray hard.

Nick is in another room. I am fighting back my tears. From where I sit, I can see him, but only a little. I can hear the radiologist explain to him what they will do for whole body radiation, and I listen intently while they tell him what he needs to do. And my son, the hero, continues to be brave.

I hate that sometimes no matter how hard I try, I can't make it better. I am screaming inside again, yet hating that sickening, fake, stupid smile of mine while I fight back insistent tears.

I'm trying to be brave. I desperately want to trust God for another miracle, but I am afraid God won't give me what I want. I want my son to be healthy, and I want my son to live. But I know that no matter what, God is the one in control, not me. His answer will be the definitive answer. He is showing me this more than ever. I also know that his way is not my way, even if I don't understand his way, and I will be honest, there are a lot of times I don't understand. I know God loves Nick, and I know he wants the best for him. But I also know that God will have his way however he chooses to heal my son, whether I like it or understand it. I just have to trust. All I can do, and the most I can do, is pray and hope that God answers the prayers I desperately want for my son. Again, I have to trust, but sometimes it's hard for me. I have a problem with surrendering my wanting to be in control.

MEMORABLE MOMENTS

Our family spent a lot of time together walking Florida beaches, hiking through parks and wooded areas, kayaking rivers, and metal detecting for treasure on private property we had permission to hunt. We looked for shells by the ocean, and we helped Nick carry heavy chert by the bucket load to the truck. Chert he'd found near a river so he could work on making arrowheads. He was getting very good at flint knapping.

We collected driftwood, river rock, and sea glass. Sometimes late at night, we would sit on the beach looking up at the stars listening to the ocean waves crashing to the shore and praising God for his mercies.

As the days of summer drew closer, I felt in my heart more and more that the time we would have together with our son Nicholas was getting shorter, and the moment we would have to say goodbye was drawing closer.

I held on to every precious moment we all had together, especially that summer. I wanted Nick's life to continue. I wanted him to get better and not hurt anymore. I wanted him to live like everyone else, to be free like the young adults his age, instead of being weighed down by this disease and the painful treatments that went along with it. There were so many emotions, especially when his counts were down and the doctors didn't have good news for him.

Through tears, we laughed and cheered each other on during those emotional times. I was determined that we were going to make happy memories together as we prayed, hoped, and trusted God.

During the quiet moments when days were growing shorter, I wanted to breathe my son in. I would study him, concentrate hard, and memorize a picture of him in my mind so that I would remember everything about my son. So I would never forget how he looked, his scent, his smile, and that I wouldn't forget his laugh. When he laughed, even throughout the most painful of times, it lifted all our spirits.

OCTOBER 2012 – DEAR NICHOLAS

I don't want to miss you. I don't want to have to hurt because you'll be gone, and I'll be left here. We will all be left alone to deal with a horrific pain that no one can ever make go away. We will hurt terribly.

I watch you more closely now. I study the way you laugh and talk, the way you sleep. I wonder if the meal we have together will be our last one or if there will be another summer like the past, when the long, hot days begin to shorten, and the cool autumn days begin to taunt us with the harsh promise of winter.

When we could see our breath in the chilly air, I somehow knew that this would be our last autumn with you. I think you knew it too.

I stared at you when you weren't watching, as if this would make you stay here with us forever. You said it was the best summer you've ever had. Mine too.

I miss you, yet you haven't left, but there is so much uncertainty now. You continue to be so brave. We've had so much hope, and so much faith for so many times, and yet the ups and downs of our hope is wearing thin, isn't it? Because we always seem to find ourselves back to square one, the monster returning and needing to be slain, again and again, only to take its toll on your body and now more and more on your mind. You are growing tired. You've told me so.

Every time that demon returned, we put our armor on, and we fought like crazy. We held our banners high, proclaiming that God would defeat this dragon for the last time and never let it return, but it has returned, and now there is another monster to slay. This one is a monster the doctors have never had to defeat, because they say you are unique, because no one has lived as long as you with what you have been through to see a monster like this.

The doctors are willing to try, although they say they don't know how to treat it or what the result will be. You are so brave, once again ready to do whatever it takes to defeat this evil, and all I want God to say is that you are healed so you won't have to go through any of this again.

They are poking at you, jabbing at you, doing spinal taps, lumbar punctures, echocardiograms, X-rays, blood tests, and I watch you. Again, I think you are good at being fake, too. You're so polite to everyone when I think you should scream and tell them all to back off! That's what I would like to tell them: "Leave my son alone!"

There is still hope, there is always hope, because I can't stop hoping, or I'm giving in to defeat. Crazy as it sounds, I feel like I will be letting you down by giving in to defeat. I can't do that. I can't let you down. I still have faith that God will come through for you, for us. He has to come through! We are praying, waiting for yet just one more miracle. There have been many miracles throughout this journey, but we are waiting for THE MIRACLE. "How much longer, Lord?"

You have gone through untold procedures and nasty side effects. And you have made it through when sadly, others did not. These were miracles, too.

It is 2012, and another October. Maybe a new treatment will be the key; maybe this will be the answer, maybe this is how God will heal you. We strive to hear God's direction for you.

We find ourselves wanting to hear God's audible voice. A voice that will tell us loud and clear what it is you should do. Should you seek more treatment, or should you stop it? I wonder, will trying to defeat this beast one more time finally work for you? I know you are wondering that, too. Will you be able to endure more? You have suffered so much already. Will this be the time you get better so that you can live? So that you can finally have a life and get to do the many things you have missed out on? I hope so.

"You have maybe six months," the doctor says.

For me, it is horrifying to hear his words. I am your mother. I cannot begin to imagine what this is doing to you. I am supposed to protect you. But I just sit here. I am by your side, quietly, listening. Again, I want to scream out, but I can't. I don't want to believe you are going to die.

And after this sad, devastating news, all you want to do is go to downtown Nashville and tell people about Jesus. So, we go to Nashville.

Nick really loved Jesus. He was bold when sharing God's word with others, and I am so proud of him for that. After being out of the hospital for a week in the summer of 2011, and as sick as he was, Nick passed out ice-cold water to the homeless and people who looked tired or thirsty. Along with the icy water and his kind words, he shared Jesus with them. He strived for the truth in God's word, and he genuinely cared about others, especially the children and young adults in the hospital who were dealing with cancer as well.

PRESENT

I have been painting. Changing.

The last time I painted the guest room was a decade ago. My daughter-in-law Cassandra picked out a pretty blue paint color. I think the name of it was Cornflower. It was the end of October 2012. His doctors had just told my 27-year-old son Nicholas that he had "maybe six months" to live. Thanksgiving was Nick's favorite holiday, so we were preparing for guests. I wanted to cover up the drab white that had been on the walls since the house was built nearly eighteen years before.

Even though we don't have family in Tennessee, we looked forward to a visit from my family in Michigan, especially this holiday year. I had less than a month to prepare. If this was going to be our last Thanksgiving with our son, I needed it to be the best.

Anyway, now, almost ten years later, I have decided to paint the room again. The room, like my life, needs transformation.

I have been painting for two days. When I do a project around the house, I concentrate on one task at a time; that way, the entire room isn't a disaster if and when I need to quit for the day. I wasn't always like this. I can remember tearing up an entire room in preparation for painting or removing old wallpaper before installing new.

Sometimes, messy paper, some of it wet, some dry along with sticky glue were stuck to the walls, not to mention the floor. Heaps of sodden dripping paper were everywhere while new rolls of wallcovering sat in the room too. My intentions were good because seeing new gave me the incentive to keep going, but the chaos in the room made me feel out of control, making me want to quit. The last time I worked like this was well over twenty years ago.

This morning I stumbled out of my bed and went into the guest room to observe what I had completed so far on my project. It is a beautiful morning. The sun is shining through five tall windows built into the round turret of our modern Queen Anne-style home. Three walls of muted flat sage green paint have now covered the blue.

I couldn't wait to see how the bedding would look in the room when my project is completed so I've already made the bed with pale green and cream striped sheets I purchased from The Company Store online. My plan is to finish the last wall and maybe the closet today. If I don't get the job done, I will try again tomorrow. I no longer berate myself for failing to keep up with random expectations I've made for myself.

I sit down on the new crisp percale sheets, and I take in the view so far. This room is on the second floor of our home. We are surrounded by trees, and from where I am on the bed, I can see out over the property. It's spring, and the new growth of vegetation is covered with various shades of green. I notice that the color of the room pops and flows with the world outside. I like it, I tell myself.

I lay my head down on a green floral pillow that compliments the stripes on the sheets. I look up to the ceiling then I glance around the room once again. I noticed an area I missed the day before. Under a windowsill surrounded by the new green paint is a splotch of the old blue. I make a mental note to fix this today as well. I think maybe I am ready for change.

I have struggled with change practically my entire life. To be honest, I am still not a fan of change. I never realized this until my husband Ray pointed this particular characteristic of mine out to me.

"Why do you fight change?" he asked me one afternoon while I was resisting something occurring in our lives I didn't like. I believe it was years ago when we were discussing our soon-to-be move from Michigan to Tennessee. I didn't want to go. I didn't want Ray to go.

I was good at defying events that were totally out of my control. It reminds me of when I'd put my hands on my hips to protest unwanted events as a little girl.

MARCH 2013 – ANOTHER SPRING

Farmers' fields surround our property. The colorless landscape seems to flow all around, as if someone took several dull crayons and began coloring outside the lines. Although it is raining, the birds still sing, and this morning, I wonder why they are not afraid like me; my son is terribly sick. I cannot enjoy anything good because the pattern in my life has been that after something good happens, something bad ensues.

Before the trees start to bud and the field grass turns green in the spring, the vegetation is the color of amber. The tall ornamental grasses I planted two years ago around our yard look like tall pillars of spindly bare golden twigs. According to the gardening magazines, a person should cut the grass back in the fall. That way, the new growth in spring won't have to fight quite so hard to flourish. My intentions were good; my intentions are always good, especially getting my gardening duties done before winter, but I did not follow through or cut back any of the vegetation. Now, I will have more work, or maybe I won't care.

This morning, barren trees stand out to me. The shades of black, gray, and brown cascade in different directions within my peripheral vision, and right now, they are set against a threatening, gray, stormy sky that looms in the background. I think I'm depressed.

Thunder begins to roar in the distance, threatening even more the impending rain. In my opinion, Tennessee has had enough rain for the year. The wind seems to have finally stopped, and right now, the world seems still and peaceful, but as usual, I wonder for how long. The clamor of thunder again deafens, and the flash of lightning accompanies it, almost hypnotic. For a few mesmerizing moments, my thoughts are transfixed on something other than my own reality.

I feel like there is so much pain in the world. So much. I'm hurting.

Nick does not want to talk about dying. He doesn't want to talk about it! So, we don't.

Then one evening, he wants to.

I listen to my son. I have to be brave for him. This is a moment that he feels strong enough to tell me. I sense my own fear when I look into his blue eyes, and when he looks back at me, and says, "Even though I don't want to die, Mom, if God wants me to go, this is the way I want my funeral . . . I don't want you to cry or to be sad, even though I know you will be."

What parent wants to think, let alone talk, about their child's funeral? That subject should never come up. Children should not die before their parents.

Three weeks before Nicholas passed, he was admitted to the hospital. They kept him comfortable, and they gave him oxygen. The oxygen was helping him to breathe and to feel better.

Every morning for a week, a doctor came in during rounds, pointed his finger into Nick's face, and literally told him he was going to die. One morning, this doctor entered the room and asked Nick how he felt with the oxygen.

"I'm feeling much better on the oxygen. It's helping me," Nick told him.

Then the doctor—the same doctor who I felt gave the intimidating hand gesture suggesting leukemia was caused by a vaccine, the same doctor who said they had done everything but slice him open—turned to his assistant on rounds, and said to her while he unplugged Nick's oxygen, "Write this down, that it was me who unplugged the oxygen, and not you."

The day before our son died, we were informed that his liver was failing. He didn't have much time. The doctor emphasized that he wanted to talk to Ray alone. I looked at my husband, our eyes tearing up, and I said to him, "I want to hear what he is going to say to you."

The doctor didn't like this. He got up in Ray's face—two inches more, and their noses would have been touching—and he said, "Are you going to let your wife tell you what to do?" Ray held his ground, and the conversation ended there.

I had suggested several times to Nick throughout his illness that we could find a different doctor, but Nick said no; he felt comfortable with the team he'd been with since the beginning of his treatments. Then one day, a few weeks before his death, he said, "I don't like him, Mom."

I have since learned this doctor is no longer affiliated with the hospital and hasn't been for years.

We never left Nick's side. We were with him all day and all night until the following morning after he'd left us. The medical staff brought him out of the medically induced coma the evening before his death. He was very groggy, but we managed to talk to him, and he talked to us. At times it wasn't easy to understand what he was saying, but we listened intently. Our son's entire body, his eyes, and skin were orange due to his failing liver. He'd been like this for several days, but this day, his last day, seemed worse. Just thinking about this day hurts; it really hurts!

Nicholas looked around at all of us, and he managed a smile. Then he asked Ray for some vanilla ice cream and my husband carefully fed small bites to him with a plastic spoon, but Nick ate very little. Ray held a small plastic cup of Sprite for him too, and he sipped it through a straw. After about an hour, Nick got sleepy, and his eyes closed. We held him and watched him breathe for several hours, we prayed, and we cried together.

"I love you, Nick; we're going to miss you," Ray said.

"I love you man," Daniel said.

"I love you, Nick," Cassandra whispered.

"Nicholas, this is your mama speaking. I love you."

On a beautiful April morning, Nicholas came into this world with his twin brother Daniel. God blessed me with two beautiful baby boys. Years later, on another April morning, I had to give one back.

Ray called his mother to tell her that Nick didn't have long to live. So, his mom, Lucy, and her husband Richard drove from Texas to our home. It's a fifteen-hour drive, too long of a trip to make without staying the night somewhere. Unfortunately, they arrived several hours after Nicholas passed. We were glad Ray's mom was here but sorry she missed seeing Nicholas before he left us.

Ray was sitting outside on our white distressed porch swing while I sat on the multicolored-brick porch steps several feet away from him. Lucy and her husband sat on chairs behind me. Ray asked me to sit with him. His hand tapped the empty space beside him, but I wanted to be where I was. I didn't want to move. I wanted to be still. I wanted the world to stop. I was looking out over the yard at tree buds opening to green leaves and flowers blooming. I was looking up into a blue sky filled with fluffy white clouds, wishing Nicholas was with us. I was thinking about how much my son had suffered, how it wasn't fair for him to die. I was thinking about funeral arrangements and how life would never be the same for any of us again. I was crying, mourning my son, missing him terribly, so I declined my husband's offer while I continued to sit quietly.

Then from behind me, I heard Lucy say to her husband in a low whisper, "It's because she's too fat."

I don't know if Lucy intended for me to hear her, but I heard. I didn't say anything. I just pretended that I hadn't heard her like I always have. I bristled.

Ray and I were mourning our son. His sister chose to spew those hurtful words on such an incredibly sad day.

It hurts to lose a loved one. I know how sad it feels to lose a parent; it's devastating for some. But to lose a child. . . I have no words to describe this overwhelming pain.

Not one member of Ray's family attended our son's funeral.

My family was there to support me, but no one in Ray's family showed up for him. Every member of his family had an excuse for why they couldn't be there.

There were so many emotions, so many things to think about planning and getting ready for the funeral. Disbelief: our son didn't really die, did he? This is just a bad dream, isn't it? Did we say everything we wanted to say to Nick? How will we live without our son? Why did this have to happen?

Finding ourselves in a funeral home choosing a casket for our child as if we'd been instantly transported from one location to the next. Which casket would be prettier, the silver or copper color? Picking out stationery, traditional or themed, and providing information for the local papers. What time do we want the visitation? When will we have the ceremony? Who will officiate? What music will be played? What pictures do we want? What clothes will he be laid to rest in? What clothes will we wear?

At the time, Ray accepted his parents and siblings' excuses, but afterward, when he felt somewhat rested enough to think about it, he became exceptionally sad. His own blood relation hadn't cared enough to be there for him.

SUMMER 2013 – AFTER

My husband and I had grown apart. Moving to Tennessee and building a house took a toll on our marriage. But Nick's death had taken an even bigger toll. I'm sad, angry, and I feel drained. Sometimes I feel as though I don't have the fight in me anymore, and it's true, I don't. But I can't quit. I won't let myself quit. I have to persevere. I've got to make myself keep moving.

Anything I once deemed important somehow isn't anymore. Cleaning the house, grocery shopping, paying bills; some days getting out of bed and getting dressed is too much for me, but I go with it. I give myself permission. It's easier than berating myself. I'm too tired for that.

Life's gut punches have taken a toll. So much has changed. Everything I once thought life would be or dreamed it would be is not even close to what I had imagined. Our lives have been altered, especially after the death of my son. I'm not good with change.

I find I am more distracted than I ever was. I can't concentrate, I can't think, I don't know who I am or who I'm supposed to be anymore because one of us is missing. I'm too tired to analyze or do research. All the years throughout Nick's illness, I scoured the internet, researching treatments, medications, and side effects.

I'm exhausted, and I'm feeling defeated. I'm not saying my remaining family members are not important. They are extremely important to me. But my worst fear has come true. My son died, and I couldn't stop it from happening.

Nick wanted to live. I was trusting God for Nick's healing, but what I wanted for my son was not what God had planned.

Death is so final, so absolute, and so out of my hands. I tried, I really tried to keep my son alive, but only God can heal. He did heal Nick, just not as I had hoped or what I imagined God's healing for my son would be.

The craziness, the flashbacks, the nightmares of Nick's treatments, and the last hours of his life. . .

I still don't understand. Why God? Why? Why my son? But then, why anyone's child?

FEATHERS

Psalm 91 was a chapter in the Bible that Nicholas particularly liked to read, and we often turned to this chapter when we were afraid, such as when Nick's blood counts were low or when he was sick or having a difficult time after any one procedure.

Through the years, the words in Psalm 91 spoke deeply to all of us. They were a strong reminder of God's protection, and they gave us continued strength as we read God's promises aloud together, especially verse four.

"He shall cover thee with his feathers, and under his wings shalt thou trust." Psalm 91:4 KJV

Once again, I see the image of a mother bird taking her young under her wing to protect them. God is the protective parent who nurtures and covers his children. The concept is that when we dwell in God, we find safety, warmth, and shelter under his wings. This gives comfort to the believer.

God makes his people aware that divine power is watching over them and protecting them.

In the autumn of 2012, I started to see feathers. I know it may sound ridiculous to some. I still don't understand it that much myself, but I got strong emotions from seeing the feathers.

Bird feathers, all varied sizes in length and shape. The colors of red, blue, brown, black, and orange. Really, there were so many assorted colors strewn over our yard, the driveway, or even in a public parking lot. They seemed to be everywhere I went. Normally, throughout my life, I would see maybe one at a time here or there, but not as many as I was seeing then.

To me, the feathers signified that there was going to be a sad up-and-coming trip for one of us. Nick would be taking a journey alone without any of us by his side. He was getting ready to leave. Whether we liked it or not, we were all getting ready to say goodbye.

God was preparing me.

One day, I had errands to run. I knew I was going to see feathers that day, too. I sat in my car, ready to leave the house, but I couldn't move. My eyes welled up with tears in protest. I remember thinking I didn't want to see another feather that day or ever again.

Hours before Nick passed, I stood with Ray, Daniel, and Cassandra around Nick's hospital bed. We were praying, singing, and talking to him before he went home to be with Jesus. I read Psalm 91 once more aloud (the last time I would read it to my son). I wanted him to hear me, so I stood close. As I read the familiar chapter like I had so many times before, something amazing happened. Psalm 91 began to take on another meaning altogether. I paused mid-sentence while reading the first verse: "He that dwelleth in the secret place of the Most High shall abide under the shadow of the Almighty." Psalm 91:1 KJV

Tears welled up in my eyes even more than they had been. God's protection was not only over Nick here on earth, but his protection would be over him in Heaven too. Nicholas was about to go from our arms into Jesus' arms very soon.

We had a Friday night visitation at the funeral home and a service for Nick. Family, friends, acquaintances, and nurses from the hospital attended. There were so many people attending that the line was out the door.

The following Tuesday was Nick's graveside ceremony, a morning filled with fluffy white clouds, blue skies, and sunshine. Ray, Daniel, Cassandra, a few close friends, and me stood together praying. We sang "Amazing Grace," and Ray read Psalm 91. I placed a bouquet of white roses on Nick's casket. Our friend Lyuda had a beautiful bouquet of mixed flowers she and her husband Victor brought. Lyuda placed her flowers next to mine.

We all gathered in an open field several feet from Nick's grave that day while six white doves representing angels ascended into the sky. The doves circled us overhead before one more white dove was released to join the others. This dove represented Nick's spirit that moments later joined the flock of angels. We all stood silent, looking up into the vast blue open sky watching the doves make their spiritual flight home together. The ceremony was so beautiful.

When the service ended, I turned to walk away. I didn't want to watch my son's casket being lowered into the ground. That's when I saw it, a beautiful, pure white feather lying on the grass in front of me. I placed this feather in Nick's Bible in the Book of Psalms, Chapter 91.

A SIGN

One week after my son passed, the day after his graveside ceremony, we had planned to sit by the ocean. Nick especially loved the ocean, so Ray, Daniel, Cassandra, and me went to Florida.

I took a long walk on a beach near Destin, Florida, after dark. My body and my mind were working hard, while my feet trudged through the cool, compacted sand. I was really upset. I was searching for a more deserted part of the beach where I could just be alone with my thoughts for a while.

I was thankful that the sound of the crashing waves drowned out the sobs of my raw pain screaming loud from somewhere deep within myself. The sounds were so foreign to me that I had to stop to see if the mournful noise I heard was truly coming from me. I have cried before, but this, this grief-stricken sound was different and something I had never experienced before.

I had to know where Nicholas was. I reasoned with myself: shouldn't a mother know where her child is.

I wanted a sign. *Should I ask God for a sign? Is it all right to ask God for a sign?*

The night sky was filled with clouds, but an opening seemed to appear in the center of them. One by one, shimmering stars began to peek through the parting clouds. The stars looked like bright flecks of white dancing against the dark blue backdrop. The universe now had my attention.

I felt insignificant compared to the vast heavens above me. I listened to the sound of breaking waves crashing against the shoreline from an ocean of water that extended way out beyond what I could see. For a moment, I closed my eyes and began talking to God. I wanted to know if Nick was all right. I wanted to know where my son was.

Was Nick there with God, or was my son just sleeping in the grave until Jesus comes back, as some religions believe, specifically the church I had grown up in? I can't grasp the idea of this belief, a belief that says my son pretty much doesn't exist anymore, that everything about him, not just his body but his soul, was in the grave, forgotten, waiting until Jesus returns. So, I asked God, my true Father.

While I continued to look up, an unending horizon, magnificent, began to present itself as if the curtains were being opened before a grand theatrical stage. Somehow, I knew that what I was about to see was intended for me only.

I saw a cloud that was shaped like a thumbs up. We were always giving each other a thumbs up, especially those times that Nick was feeling too sick to speak. We would ask him something like, "Are you alright?" If he was feeling well enough, he would give us a thumbs up.

While my eyes were still glued to the sky, I saw Nick's face. His eyes were looking back at mine. I knew then that he was more than all right and that, in no uncertain terms, he was with Jesus.

My eyes stayed transfixed, but my son's face soon faded as the clouds dispersed. While my eyes were welling up with tears, I began to feel more at peace, so thankful for a Father who not only loves deeply but comes down from where he reigns to comfort me, especially in my time of need. A week before Nick passed, he told me, "Mom, trust Jesus; God is the one to be glorified." Then he repeated it, "Trust Jesus, God is the one to be glorified."

FLASHBACKS

I opened my son's bedroom door, wanting to see him, to touch him, to hold him in my arms again, but I knew the reality. He wasn't in his room, and he won't ever be in his room again.

My mind went back to the day he left—the day he left us all behind. His home, his room, his things. I start to cry out. I wonder if he knew that day was the last time he would ever be home. I wonder if, through all his pain, he looked around at his surroundings and silently said goodbye.

Two weeks before Nick's death, I was standing at the bottom of the staircase, looking up at him, watching the paramedics bring him down on a lift chair. I winced. They were too rough. They weren't being careful enough.

"Please go slow, be gentle with him; he's hurting," I said, but they didn't seem to hear me, and all I could do was apologize to my son. "Nick, I'm so sorry, I'm so sorry."

As I entered his room, his scent was still here. It had been almost two months since he left, and his scent, although faint, was still here. I knew this would go away, too, one day soon. Too soon for me.

Everything in his room was the same as the day he left. I didn't want to disturb anything. I thought, *He was the last to touch his things.* He wouldn't let me clean his room or touch anything. Everything had its place, and that was where it stayed until he moved it, dusted it, gave it away, or threw it out. I caught myself saying aloud, "Nick, I'm touching your things." As if that would give him cause to come back home to us.

In his teen years, he never allowed me to do his laundry. He did his laundry because he was the only one who could do it right, in his opinion. I, his mother, who had done his laundry since the day he was born, couldn't do it right. I respected his wishes, and to be honest, he did do a much better job than I did.

There were two blue laundry baskets next to a beige wall in his room. They were both filled with clothing he had been sorting. Unfolded shirts: polo, flannel, gray, white, and a maroon T-shirt; sweaters, jeans, and socks were in one basket. The other basket was filled with dress clothes—shirts, slacks, and a faded-green Abercrombie jacket crumpled up and thrown in on top of everything else. I pulled his clothing toward me, and I breathed in his scent. I could smell the cologne he used. His scent, the one that wafted through the air when he was on his way in or out of the house to meet with friends or go to church.

I had been sitting in his room for ten minutes. I sat perfectly still, not moving, and yet I was exhausted. I was out of breath. I missed him terribly.

My son is never coming home.

I WISH I COULD GO BACK

It's hot August. It's been four months since Nick passed. I wish I could go back and hold my son. I try to remember how it felt to cradle him in my arms when he was a baby. How it felt to cuddle with him while reading stories before bed. To steal hugs from him whenever I could because as he grew older, he didn't want his mama embarrassing him in front of his friends. How I wish I could hold him just one more time and say, "I love you, Nicholas." The last time I held him was the early April morning he died in my arms.

In August last year, at this time, Nick was with us. He had been so excited about the possibility of us all camping together again this summer (2013), but sadly he isn't here to go.

Ray, Daniel, and I are going camping. We'll go to the same campground as 2012 when Nick was with us. This is an anniversary of sorts. Last summer, Nick baptized my husband—a beautiful memory of spiritual significance. A baptism in Lake Michigan surrounded by God, sand, and sky.

Everywhere I look, I think of my son. I miss so many things about him right now. I miss his eyes, beautiful sea foam green, and blue like the water. I miss his laughter. I miss his voice.

There were nights we'd stay up late waiting for Ray to get home from work, then we'd curl up in what we called our nests; each of us had our own favorite chair. We'd get comfortable, sometimes just talking into the wee hours of the morning. Some nights Nick would cook something for us to eat. We'd watch TV, and some nights, we'd read the Bible and pray together. I really miss those moments in time.

SO MUCH PAIN

August 2013, I find myself standing high on top of a sand dune. I am looking down at angry jagged waves crashing onto the Lake Michigan shoreline. Even though the sun shines, it is raining, too. The rain, combined with a cold northern breeze, feels like daggers of ice hitting hard against my face and my bare skin. It stings, but I don't care. I just stand still, silent, entranced, looking out over the water.

I don't seem to care much about anything anymore. One by one, the daggers delve into my body, but my eyes continue to scan the lake, glaring, scowling back at the water below me.

In the distance, I hear a child's laughter, and his screams of joy permeate the air. I turn for a moment to watch the small boy and his mom. They are holding hands while they run into the lake together. Then they jump back fast the moment the icy water hits their toes. They laugh. I wonder if this little boy's mother realizes how lucky she is to have him. I'm jealous.

I find my mind wandering nonstop, from one thought to the next like it usually does. My mind is rampant, I can't concentrate, and I want to cry out again. I want to hit something so hard it breaks, just like how my heart is breaking now. There are no words to describe my emotions. *I want my son back, but he's not coming back. I want this hurt to go away. The pain is unbearable. I just want it to stop. Why did Nick have to suffer? He died; he was cheated. We were all cheated. I'm tired. I'm angry. I want my Nicholas back!*

I want the world to hurt and cry with me, but the world does not understand. Besides, it wouldn't bring my son back to me anyway.

I know Nick is all right and in the arms of God. It's me, Ray, Daniel, and Cassandra. We're the ones left behind grieving. Grief is made up of moments of comfort and brief understandings and then times of being dashed to the sharp rocks on the shore. There's no straight, slanting-upward line out of grief. It's a jagged line of ups and downs—I'm okay, one minute, not the next.

I feel that desperate sound from deep within me start to emerge again. I fight hard to hold it back, but I can't. Before, I was good at holding everything inside, but not now. Now, I let it go.

A guttural cry so deep within myself emerges, and it scares me again. I still don't recognize this foreign sound. It's as if someone else was standing next to me. That's the one screaming out. Not me.

But I know I am the only one standing on this mountain of sand. I quiet myself for a moment. I let my breath out slowly, and this is when I notice that the lake's choreographic dance is playing my mood out precisely. The waves are emotionally charged with sadness, anger, and with such indescribable pain.

I cry out to God, begging him as if I were a two-year-old having a tantrum. "I can't do this! I don't want to do this! Please don't make me do this!" Tears heave from my eyes.

The world does not stop. Everyone seems to be moving on, everyone except for me.

Waves of grief crash on a million shorelines every day, but what no one understands is that a big part of my life ended on that sad April morning too. The day my son Nicholas left the earth.

2014

It has been one year, three months, and eleven days. I think about the past year, and how busy we have been making funeral arrangements, designing, and ordering Nick's headstone, writing thank-you notes, and closing his accounts.

They set Nick's granite stone a week ago at a grave site in the cemetery not too far away from where we live. Last year, I was tending a garden in the cemetery. I planted flowers beside a green metal stake inserted into the ground. The stake held a plastic sleeve. Enclosed was a small piece of paper with Nick's name printed on it.

A year ago, there in the garden, the reality of my son's death had not been cemented in stone. Now, this year in front of the stone, I will be tending his grave.

When I saw his name etched into the granite for the first time, I couldn't breathe. Seeing my son's name engraved on a stone marker in the cemetery made me fall to my knees. The realization: my son is gone, and he is never coming home.

ANOTHER CHRISTMAS

After I married, I was determined that crazy would not happen in my family. I can honestly say that in our home, there wasn't any fighting at Christmas, and if there was, I didn't know about it.

I worked hard to make Christmas joyful for everyone, and I loved doing it because it made me happy. I set the table with our best china, crystal, and cloth napkins. I prepared Cornish hens, turkey, and/or prime rib for our dinners with all the trimmings on Christmas Eve and Christmas Day. There were always a lot of presents under our tree too.

Opening the last gift under the tree seemed to be a let-down, so sometimes, I would have one more gift for everyone to open at dinner.

Then the worst thing that could ever transpire happened—my son, Nicholas, died.

My son Daniel and his wife Cassandra worked overseas for a while before they settled out of state where they have started their own Christmas traditions. It was Ray and I together, yet we felt alone. We went from years of family Christmases where our home was filled with people we loved to only the two of us; and it all happened too fast. We didn't put up a tree for the first three years after Nick's death.

Outside our home, Christmas music played. The decorations and celebrations seemed to go on for everyone else but us. A person would not be able to tell that it was December in our home because when our son passed, Christmas died for us, too.

Gradually, I started to bring back some of our traditions. We didn't have a Christmas tree or a decoration in our home until 2017. That's the year I set up our family Christmas tree again.

At the time, I felt tired, sad, and a little depressed. I was tempted more than once to haul the tree back to the attic, but I pushed myself to set it up anyway. When I finished placing white lights over the 9' tree, I decorated it with polka dots, stripes, and solid red, white, and shiny silver ornaments of assorted sizes throughout the branches. When I was finished, I stood back admiring it for several minutes. The tree was pretty; it brought back lovely memories of our family spending Christmas together. Even though tears filled my eyes, I was in a much better mood, happy that I'd finished my project.

That year I baked sugar cookies shaped like Christmas trees. Ray helped me decorate them with sprinkles and green and white frosting. I bought a doormat depicting a scene of Christmas trees in green, white, and blue. I placed it at our front entrance. My theme that year was Christmas trees. We bought gifts for Daniel, Cassandra, and our grandson, but Ray and I didn't exchange gifts or set the table or make fancy meals. I think we sat in front of the TV eating pizza.

I began in 2019 to decorate the entire house as I used to when my family was home when we were all together.

When my sons lived at home, not only would we have a family tree, but we would decorate a small tabletop tree in their bedrooms. This year, I put up a tree in each of their old rooms, and I decorated with some of my sons' favorite ornaments from growing up.

I'm feeling sad because my boys won't be home. They haven't been home for Christmas for years now. Sometimes, I wish I would have had more babies, not to replace my sons, but I imagine that having more children would have brought more joy for all of us. Not just at Christmas but all year round rather than the silence and too much quiet that lurks around this big old empty house now. Children bring life to everything. Their innocent curiosity, laughter, and whimsical chatter is what helps fill a home with love. I miss my children.

Sometimes, the quiet is just too sad for me. At times, I find myself envying friends whose homes are filled with the voices of their children and grandchildren, especially at Christmas.

Christmas 2019, and our house will be void of family once again. Ray and I have started a new tradition. We have a prime rib dinner at J. Alexanders a few days before Christmas. On another evening, we see a movie, then order a cup of steaming hot coffee while sharing a huge piece of chocolate cake from PF Chang.

We will welcome friends in for dinner sometime before Christmas this year. We plan to attend a Christmas Eve service, and I will prepare Cornish hens for our Christmas dinner. We will call our son Daniel, our daughter-in-law Cassandra, and our little grandson to wish them a Merry Christmas. We will get tears in our eyes looking at Nick's pictures that hang on our wall because we are missing him terribly.

I long to go back in time, even for five minutes, so that I can experience all of us together once again. But all that we have are our memories.

The two of us will cuddle up together, counting our blessings—and missing the ones that are not with us, wondering what our new year together will be like. I prayed it would be a good year, and for us, it was, because our precious little granddaughter was born in 2020.

Part Five

Almost four years ago, while I flipped through YouTube channels, I found Kristine Godinez, LPC (Licensed Professional
Counselor). I started watching her videos faithfully. The more
I listened to her, the more I felt like she was describing me. She
was describing me and the people I have been surrounded by my
entire life. I read her book, *What's Wrong with Your Dad?* I have
to say, we've had a lot in common as far as our painful childhood
lives went.

I will admit there were times that it was hard for me to listen to
her because any particular subject she talked about could bring
back dark memories for me. I would take a break from it all,
and then when I felt ready, I would continue to watch her videos
because not only did I know that she knew what she was talking
about, but I also knew that for me to heal, I had to face my pain
head on. I could not run away from myself or continue to stuff
the pain deep down any longer. Watching her videos helped me
open my eyes even more.

As I go back in time, I have allowed myself to relive my painful
memories. As I write them down, I am acknowledging the con-
frontations, and then I am letting them go. I no longer want to
hang on to the past, and this, I realize, is freeing for me.

Anger is an emotion of fear. I can see now that this is true
because as I look back on my life, it seems that most of my
childhood, and a big part of my adult years, were spent living
in fear.

Although I have come a long way in my recovery, I am still
trying to forgive myself for what I felt I had to do to survive. I
was a people pleaser, I didn't have boundaries, I didn't speak up to
ask my abusers why they were hurting me, and I didn't reach out
to people that could've helped me. Instead, I lied. I bristled; that
is lying too. I wanted to be loved and accepted, so I continued to
take abuse (trauma bonding). This is what I knew.

I am beginning to see, as Kris Godinez teaches, and says in so
many words, that we are not born with shame and guilt, but that
these are learned emotions because shame and guilt are used by
others to control and to manipulate.

As I work through the anger and rejection I've felt for so long,
I can feel myself growing stronger. I am seeing more that the

self-hatred I've lived with is leaving me. I know now more than ever none of the crazy inflicted on me was ever my fault. To finally realize this is significant. My abusers had addiction issues and unaddressed traits of a narcissist. As I have mentioned before, I am learning how to recognize these disordered personalities, and I stand clear of them.

Throughout my adult life, I've had a recurring dream. In the dream I am still living with my parents in their home. No matter what I do, I cannot leave. I feel trapped and confined.

I had a new dream the other night. In this dream, I told my dad that I had found an apartment and I was moving out. The dream was symbolic for me. It was also a personal confirmation that I am getting better. I am healing. I am breaking free.

God is so personal. Out of all the people in the world suffering with their own pain and tragedies, he takes his time for me too. He brought back memories of my past but did not let me go there alone. He went with me. He only allowed as much as I could take at any one time and only when he knew I was ready. I felt he wanted me to process each tragic event fully before I was ready to move on to the next.

WAKING UP

A few years back, I read the book *Perfect Daughters, Adult Daughters of Alcoholics* by Robert J. Ackerman, PhD. This is a book that really helped me open my eyes. I began to see the familiar traits of an alcoholic. I also saw traits of myself in the theme as an adult daughter. It was a waking-up moment for me to know that there are reasons why I'm the way I am. Early on, I believed I was born bad, but of course this was never true. Robert Ackerman offers useful and statistical information, along with personal experiences from adult daughters who share their stories in his book. Realizing I wasn't alone was healing for me.

Robert J. Ackerman writes, "Thirty-one percent of adult daughters experienced physical abuse as children, 19 percent were victims of sexual abuse, and 38 percent witnessed spousal abuse in their families. These rates of abuse were three to four times higher than among women who were raised in nonalcoholic families. Daughters who experienced not only parental alcoholism but also abuse were affected more and differently than adult daughters of non-abusive alcoholics."[5]

After doing more research, and while looking back on my life, I can see more than ever some of the adult-daughter traits I have.

- I keep my word, and I am loyal. People can trust me.
- I've wanted approval from others but did not trust them enough to believe what they said to be true. I have a tough time trusting anyone.
- I feel an intense sense of responsibility for everyone.
- I was, and still can be, hypervigilant. Most times, I find myself on high alert.
- I am sensitive to my surroundings, worried about possible hidden dangers around me or those I love.
- I find myself playing "what if" games inside my head, making plans about what I will do if something horrendous happens.
- I can be impulsive at times.
- Sometimes, I find myself overreacting to situations that are out of my control.
- I criticize myself without having compassion. I am my own worst enemy.
- When I've needed to stand up for myself, I've backed down because it made me feel guilty to defend myself.
- I've had difficulty following a project through to the end.
- I never felt good enough. I have had issues with low self-esteem.
- I've had abandonment issues.
- Angry people scared me. When my parents or anyone raised their voices, I wanted to appease their rage. I never knew what would happen next in these chaotic situations. I did whatever I could to avoid conflict.
- I've stuffed my feelings inside because I felt I didn't matter anyway.
- I didn't let myself feel at all.

---

[5]Ackerman, Robert J. PhD. *Perfect Daughters, Adult daughters of Alcoholics* (Health Communications, ©1989 - 2002) p. 46.

I am not an alcoholic, nor do I abuse drugs, but my substance of choice was food. I remember rehashing things that upset me, crying while stuffing my face—not tasting or chewing the food, just swallowing.

I have finally faced the fact that my dad was an alcoholic, and my traits as an adult daughter are universal.

HEALING

In school, we pass the first grade to get to the second grade. I always told my sons that to get to C, they must go through A and B first, and in that order.

We have things to learn in this life before we can move on, whether we want to know them or not. At least, this is what I have observed. Most of us crawl before we walk. We walk before we learn to run.

If we go from A to C and skip B, we will eventually have to go back to B if we want to get better. If we don't go back, we will struggle.

If we were abused mentally and/or physically, we need to go back to that point in time when we were broken. Sometimes it is difficult to go back to those places of darkness, but this, I found out, is where I stopped growing. This will cause challenges that will resurface at some point in life. It's hard to go back. Believe me, I know.

We have painful events in our lives; we are broken in one way or another. There is something we need to learn before we move on to what happens next in our lives. If we don't do it in succession, we will not mature or grow as well—mentally and socially.

I started with A. I am reasonably sure that I didn't finish A. I missed B, and that caused me to struggle with C, D, E, and beyond.

A therapist once told me a story that went something like this: An architect designed a beautiful fifteen-story building. Everything was going along fine until the builder, while working on the tenth floor, realized an error had been made back on the fifth floor. This meant that not only the fifth floor, but the sixth, seventh, and all the way up to the tenth floor were wrong. He knew the mistakes were small now but had the potential to become much worse with time. He and the architect discussed skipping over the defective floors and hope for the best, or they could go back to the damaged floors and make it right. Either way would be difficult but going back and repairing before building higher would be the least painful.

There didn't seem to be time for me to go back to my broken past. The tragedies in my life were not only painful but complicated. I was trying to deal with my past, but there were more heartbreaks that continued to happen even before I could grasp the reality of the last tragedy. I did try, but I struggled with going back to all those obscure places where I had been broken.

As a child, I was growing physically but not as much mentally and socially. As an adult, it made me feel inadequate, and I could see that I was different from my adult peers. In a sense, I was set back. And this only added to my feelings of low self-esteem.

I had lots of damaged floors in need of repair, but instead of going back to restore them, I kept building up.

It has been difficult for me to go back to the places of my brokenness. Although, for me to heal, I had to go back to the damaged floors and the anguish I continued to build over for years. Memories were coming back to me, taking me to those places of defeat, only this time, instead of pushing them aside, I prayed hard, and I delved in. I tried to process every hurt. The repairs have been a lot of work. I know I will continue to work, but while looking back over my past, I am relieved to know there were valid reasons for my anger.

If you have identified with any of the stories in my life—whether physical and emotional abuse or loss and grief—remember, we have a voice. We can use our harrowing experiences to help others.

I don't understand why tragedy happens or why we encounter the people we do, but I do know we are not alone. I also know we don't have to remain frozen with fear. We can break the mold not only for ourselves but for future generations. It takes one to start change. If I can help one person in this life by sharing my story, then it just might be that I will have helped many. I hope so.

I probably should have posted a read with caution warning on the front cover because no one wants to think about uncomfortable subject matter, especially the loss of a child or stories of children being abused. There are so many sad, horrific stories happening all over the world every day, and I am quite sure substantially more stories have emerged not only during, but after the Covid pandemic as well. This is all so insane!

The abuse of a child is an evil atrocity that will go on generation after generation unless it is stopped. My hope is that together, we will stop it. I know the stories we share and bring to light will generate more awareness to this horrendous brutality that sadly still exists today.

As a child, I didn't see myself as a victim, but I was. There are many of us out there, and yet none of us want to ever be considered a casualty of victimhood. I saw myself as being despicable and a disappointment to those around me. The abuse that happened made me feel even more unworthy and afraid. The sadness and fear is what eventually turned to anger and my own self-hatred.

My story isn't only about the abused and unprotected child. My intent is to draw attention to the abuser as well. They, too, are broken people, but that doesn't give them or any of us the right to be soul killers. No one has the right to hurt another living being. We don't own our children. Our job as parents is to love, nurture, and guide them so that hopefully they will grow to be healthy, mentally stable adults.

I will never understand how a parent can cherish one child over another. I don't get it. We are unique individuals. There is something extraordinary to love in every one of us. We matter!

Even though I will never receive an apology from my parents, I forgive them. There is a process to forgiveness, traumatic memories are difficult to forget. Forgiveness doesn't mean allowing myself to be mistreated or going back to a familiar abusive environment either.

There are personalities in the world that feel they are never wrong, and they will never apologize. I remind myself forgiveness is more for me and my healing than for those that have hurt me.

I have survived, and when the crazy thoughts start pounding inside my head again, I remind myself that I'm safe, and I am okay.

I walk away from toxic, rude, and impolite people, those who have no respect for me or anyone else for that matter. I surround myself with those who make me feel loved and happy. Healthy relationships and boundaries are important.

I am stronger. I am me . . . and learning that I am enough. I am a Warrior.

There are so many ways to get through our adversities. I'd like to say I chose God to get me through mine, but it was the other way around. He chose me before I ever accepted him. I didn't trust anyone. I felt unloved, but he was persistent. He continues to show me how truly loved I am. He has become the loving Father I never had.

God is, "A father of the fatherless," Psalm 68:5 KJV

Looking back on my life where I especially felt abandoned and alone, I'm now able to see that God was covering me. *He covered me when no one else would.*

Crisis Hotline Phone Numbers and Websites

Childhelp® www.childhelp.org
Phone: 800.4.A. CHILD (800.422.4453)
People They Help: Child abuse victims, parents, concerned individuals.

Child Sexual Abuse
Darkness to Light https://www.d2l.org/
Phone: 866.FOR.LIGHT (866.367.5444)
People They Help: Children and adults needing local information or resources about sexual abuse.

Family Violence
National Domestic Violence Hotline https://www.thehotline.org/
Phone: (800). 799.SAFE (800.799.7233) TTY: (800).787.3224
Video Phone Only for Deaf Callers: (206).518.9361
People They Help: Children, parents, friends, offenders.

Help for Parents
National Parent & Youth Helpline® https://www.nationalparenthelpline.org/
Phone: 855.4APARENT (855.427.2736) (available 10 a.m. to 7 p.m., PST, weekdays)
People They Help: Parents and caregivers needing emotional support and links to resources.

National Human Trafficking Hotline https://humantraffickinghotline.org/en
Human Trafficking
Phone: 888.373.7888
People They Help: Victims of human trafficking and those reporting potential trafficking situations.

National Alliance on Mental Illness https://www.nami.org/Home
Mental Illness
Phone: (800). 950.NAMI (800.950.6264) (available 10 a.m. to 6 p.m., ET, weekdays)
People They Help: Individuals, families, professionals.

Child Find of America
Missing/Abducted Children https://childfindofamerica.org/
Phone: 800.I.AM.LOST (800 426-5678)
People They Help: Parents reporting lost or abducted children, including parental abductions.

Rape/Incest
Rape, Abuse, and Incest National Network (RAINN) https://www.rainn.org/
Phone: (800). 656.HOPE (800.656.4673)
People They Help: Rape and incest victims, media, policymakers, concerned individuals.

National Suicide Prevention Lifeline https://988lifeline.org/
Suicide Prevention
Phone: (800). 273.TALK (800.273.8255)
TTY: (800).799.4TTY (800.799.4889)
People They Help: Families concerned individuals.

National Runaway Switchboard https://www.1800runaway.org/
Youth in Trouble/Runaways

Phone: 800.RUNAWAY (800).786.2929)
People They Help: Runaway and homeless youth, families.

Adult Children of Alcoholics & Dysfunctional Families
World Service Organizations https://adultchildren.org/
(310).534.1815

SAMHSA Substance Abuse and Mental Health Services
Administration https://www.samhsa.gov/find-help/national-helpline
SAMHSA National Helpline 1.800.662.(HELP) 4357

NATIONAL ASSOCIATION FOR CHILDREN OF ADDICTION
https://nacoa.org/
The mission of NACoA is to eliminate the adverse impact of
alcohol and drug use on children and families.
Phone: (301).468.0985

AL-ANON
Helping friends and families of Alcoholics https://al-anon.org/
Phone (888). 4AL.ANON (1.888.425.2666)

NATIONAL ASSOCIATION OF ADULT SURVIVORS OF
CHILD ABUSE https://naasca.org
Child abuse trauma, prevention, intervention & recovery.

About the Author

Judy Kowalsky wants to live in a world that is free from child abuse. If she owned the world, it would be mandatory that every child be deeply loved and respected, because it is their God given right. Children would grow up into well-adjusted adults and generation after generation of these loved individuals would make the universe a much better place to live. She believes love is what should run the world, and that every one of us is beautifully created with our own irreplaceable qualities.

She's lived through physical and emotional abuse, along with other unique challenges like having whittled popsicle stick wood in her mouth, replacements for her missing teeth. She learned to survive, but many don't.

Judy is an advocate for child abuse awareness, she remains a steadfast voice for those who are often unheard. She enjoys writing and quality time with her grandbabies and her husband, Ray. Judy also finds joy in decorating and redecorating her modern Queen Anne Farmhouse in Middle Tennessee. When not engaged in household pursuits, she can often be found immersed in a good book, while curled up in her favorite comfy overstuffed chair.